S. V. Ryan

Claims of a Protestant Episcopal Bishop

To Apostolical Succession and valid Orders disproved

S. V. Ryan

Claims of a Protestant Episcopal Bishop
To Apostolical Succession and valid Orders disproved

ISBN/EAN: 9783337162443

Printed in Europe, USA, Canada, Australia, Japan

Cover: Foto ©ninafisch / pixelio.de

More available books at **www.hansebooks.com**

CLAIMS

OF A

PROTESTANT EPISCOPAL BISHOP

TO

APOSTOLICAL SUCCESSION AND VALID ORDERS DISPROVED:

WITH VARIOUS MISSTATEMENTS OF CATHOLIC FAITH

AND

NUMEROUS CHARGES AGAINST THE CHURCH

AND

HOLY SEE,

CORRECTED AND REFUTED.

BY

S. V. RYAN, BISHOP OF BUFFALO.

IN TWO PARTS.

BUFFALO:
CATHOLIC PUBLICATION COMPANY.
1880.

TO OUR REVERED METROPOLITAN AND FIRST
AMERICAN CARDINAL,
HIS EMINENCE JOHN CARDINAL McCLOSKEY,
ARCHBISHOP OF NEW YORK,
THIS LITTLE WORK IS MOST RESPECTFULLY
DEDICATED
BY THE AUTHOR.

CLAIMS

OF

A PROTESTANT EPISCOPAL BISHOP

TO

APOSTOLICAL SUCCESSION AND VALID ORDERS DISPROVED:

BY

S. V. RYAN, BISHOP OF BUFFALO.

PART I.

CONTENTS.

I.—Origin of our little Treatise. 1
II.—Apostolical Succession essential to the Christian Church—It is not found either in the Anglican Church, as-by-law established, or the Protestant Episcopal Church of America. 19
III.—Communion with the See of Peter the Test of Legitimate Succession. 26
IV.—Protestant Episcopal and Anglican Succession Repudiated. 40
V.—Was Matthew Parker Consecrated? . . . 49
VI.—The Lambeth Register. 73
VII.—Was Barlow ever Consecrated Bishop? . . 92
VIII.—Futile Attempts to bolster up or supply for Barlow's deficient or doubtful Consecration. . . 101
IX.—The Edwardine Ordinal not the same as the Roman Pontifical—Invalidity of Form of Consecration devised by Edward VI. 111
X.—The Insufficiency of the Edwardine Ordinal, Continued. 130
XI.—Discrepancies between the Roman Pontifical and the Ordinal of Edward, Continued. 146
XII.—Conclusion. 169

PREFACE.

IN the year 1874, a number of Catholic gentlemen of Buffalo requested me in writing, to deliver a lecture at my earliest convenience, in behalf of the numerous poor of the city, and at the same time suggested the subject of the lecture in these terms : " We take the liberty to suggest as your subject, a review of a sermon delivered on the 31st ultimo, at Erie, by Dr. Coxe, on the occasion of the consecration of a missionary bishop—and published in the " *Commercial Advertiser,*" of this city—a copy of which we herewith enclose—a sermon which, it appears to us, strangely mixes up Catholic truth, with gross abuse of the Catholic Church; sound, time-honored Catholic principles with the most unwarrantable assumption." Acceding to their request I wrote to the gentlemen: " I have read the sermon of Dr. A. Cleveland Coxe, to which you refer, and indeed I concur with you in characterizing it as a strange medley of truth and falsehood; of sound, solid arguments, eloquently and forcibly put, in favor of principles which must lead any man holding them, who is logical and consistent, into the fold of the Catholic Church, and evidences of an unaccountable hatred, and a spirit of spitefulness towards the only Church that really upholds and carries out these principles. His sermon I will take as the text of my lecture ; the time and place I leave to yourselves to designate." The lecture was delivered in St. Joseph's Cathedral, Feb. 22, 1874, and afterwards printed in pamphlet form by the "*Buffalo Catholic Publication Co.,*" and the "*Catholic World*" noticing it in the

May number of 1874, was kind enough to say: "In his temperate but severe criticism, Bishop Ryan has made an end of his (Dr. Coxe's) claims to possess episcopal character and mission, and has refuted him out of his own mouth. We trust that this able and valuable pamphlet will not be permitted to go into oblivion, as pamphlets are wont to do, but be carefully preserved and made use of by clergymen and others, who have to deal with Episcopalians searching after the true Church, of whom there are so many in these days." Some time afterwards there was published here in Buffalo a small *brochure* entitled: "*Catholics and Roman Catholics*, by an Old Catholic, being a review of the lecture lately delivered in Buffalo by Rt. Rev. Dr. Ryan, etc., etc., etc.," in the "Advertisement" of which we read:

"Though I here subjoin my name, as author of this review, two reasons have influenced me to withhold it from the title page. First, I desire to avoid all appearance of personal controversy, and second, I wish to make prominent my position as an Old Catholic, for my criticisms are based on ancient Catholicity." (A. Cleveland Coxe, Bishop of Western New York.) This review of our lecture, we in turn reviewed in a consecutive series of articles, contributed to "*The Catholic Union*," respecting the wished-for *incognito* of the Rt. Rev. Divine, addressing ourselves to "Old Catholic," and confining ourselves, as much as possible, to the chief point of the controversy, his claims to Apostolical succession. A promise made at that time to friends, who urged the matter on us, and to whose judgment and wishes we thought we should defer, having a little leisure on our hands, during the past winter, we determined to fulfil by giving to the public, in a revised and somewhat altered form, the substance of those articles. Our reviewer charged us with making a personal and unwarranted assault on him, and now we beg to say, that we spoke and wrote purely in the interest of truth, and in this publication we have endeavored to discard all personal allusions, changing words and phrases so as, whenever possible, to avoid giving cause of complaint on this score, and if our language is sometimes strong, or if it has at times the appearance of want of courtesy, I think all unbiased readers will acknowledge that the fault is not on our side. We love truth and must defend it. We know the doctrines of the Church, and must repel false and erroneous charges, we must resent having ourselves and our holy faith belied and travestied, apparently for the purpose of creating and confirming prejudice against the Catholic Church, and keeping honest and religious minds in ignorance and error regarding her. We really care little personally, as far as we ourselves are concerned, to be called an ignoramus, to whom the elements of history must be taught, but when we are told, or rather when our respected non-Catholic fellow-citizens are told, that we are authorized by our Church to resort to the tactics of lying, and even to violate the sanctity of an oath, whenever the good of the Church conflicts with keeping it, we confess to a feeling of resentment. We smile complacently, when it is intimated that our "ignorance is of that kind, which the Old Catholics of Germany assure us is common among otherwise accomplished men, who have received their education in Roman Catholic seminaries," but when our own saints and doctors are misquoted, when canons of early councils are falsified and distorted, when the early Fathers of the Church are cited to affirm the very reverse of their teachings, and all to obscure the truth and injure the true Church, can any one wonder that we feel occasionally a little indignant?

We have no personal quarrel with our neighbor and we have never mentioned him or his communion, in lecture or the press, except to refute some false charge made against ourselves or our Church, or repel some slanderous aspersion on what is dearer to us than life itself, our holy faith. He does us great wrong then, when he tells the public that "many Roman Catholics seemed to be restrained by no laws of courtesy," and that this "comes of the oath which is exacted of Roman Catholic prelates at their consecration." This oath, and especially, the term *persequar*, has been so often fully vindicated and explained, that I will only say, that in translating it as found in the Roman Pontifical, *I will persecute*, he does violence to sound philological interpretation, just as he violates consistency, when a little further on, in a passage which he approvingly cites from St. Vincent of Lerins, he translates the very same words in a quite different way. "It is necessary," says St. Vincent, quoted by Old Catholic, "for all Catholics who study to prove themselves *legitimate sons of Mother Church to stick fast to the holy faith of the holy fathers* and to abide in it; but to detest, abhor, pursue and *banish* all profane novelties of the profane." *Ut profanas vero profanorum novitates detestentur, horrescant, insectentur, persequantur.* (xxxiii. commonitor, II.) Yet, although what he rightly regards in St. Vincent, as righteous zeal for the holy faith of the fathers in pursuing and banishing profane novelties and errors against faith, he characterizes in us as an *intolerant vow*, and gives a rendering of the good old Latin verb to suit the sentiments he chooses to impute in either case, still we assure him that we do not wish to be discourteous to any one, much less to persecute or assault brethren and fellow-citizens, differing from us in religious faith. Though in all candor, we must confess that we have seen from him precious little of that "loving spirit of our own Church," of which he speaks, but have known him, in the language of the writer in the "*Catholic World,*" above referred to, as "A prelate, conspicuous for arrogance and reckless assertion, and for his vituperative and defamatory assaults on the Catholic Church," and though we have perhaps, in self-defence, been sometimes forced to call attention to those unlov-

PREFACE. vii

able features in the character of our Old Catholic reviewer, and point to evidence of grossly false statements regarding the Church and her teaching, it was always with reluctance that we used language that might appear to savor of personality, for in truth before God, we have no personal feeling against the gentleman. If then we now publish these articles in a more substantial form, it is because many whose judgment we respect have insisted on our doing so, affirming that they are calculated to do much good, especially with those who have some idea of Church authority, Church government, "a divine commission coming down from the Apostles," a divinely appointed ministry, with powers to perpetuate itself and thus bring down through the ages a succession of faithful witnesses to the Christian revelation, incorruptible guardians of the precious deposit of faith once committed to the saints. No one sincerely believing in a Church thus organized and thus to be perpetuated can, we think, read the following pages without being convinced, how utterly absurd it is to look for such a ministry, such a succession in the Anglican establishment, and if not there, then as the venerable Dr. Ives remarked, most assuredly not in the Protestant Episcopal Church of the United States.

I need hardly tell my readers, that in this work they will find very little of my own. I have even made it a point whenever possible to rest my statements and conclusions on the authority of others, and have not hesitated to quote freely and verbatim from Catholic authors. In this perhaps, I may have done some service to the Catholic student, by making accessible to him authorities which unfortunately in some cases, are either out of print or very rare. I need not name here again the authors from whom I have so unstintingly borrowed, as I mention them all in the course of the work. I fear that certain repetitions of subjects and arguments may savor somewhat of serial contributions where it is necessary to show in each article the general scope of the argument, and its bearing on the whole, yet if this does not detract from the force and conclusiveness of my arguments, I make little account of a defect of this kind in a work, which in a literary or artistic point of view, has, I fear, many more serious short-comings. The first part is entirely independent of the second, and constitutes a whole without it, and I was only induced to write the second part, when I found our reviewer by so many false references and misstatements of Catholic doctrine mystifying, misleading and prejudicing his readers against the Catholic Church and her claims as the true spouse and mystical body of Christ, coming down from the Apostles, absolutely one in faith, divine in her origin, imperishable in her structure, infallible in her teaching, identically the same in her sacraments, in her orders, in her government, "yesterday, to-day and the same forever." Yet, I think the dogmatic and historical points treated in the second part will be found interesting and instructive, and here, too, the only credit I take to myself is that of bringing within easy reach, some matters of profound interest and serious controversy, scattered over the wide range of Church history. Just here, I am reminded of one other point on which I have not touched, and which is made much of in the *advertisement* to Old Catholic's *brochure*, and often elsewhere.

I beg then my reader's forbearance, while I quote again : " Learned in what is Roman, they (accomplished men, who have received their education in Roman Catholic seminaries) are left mere children in all that is Catholic. Of the ancient Catholic constitutions they know nothing, because they are not even permitted to learn that such constitutions exist. The brilliant von Schulte, who was so long the favorite canonist of the Pope himself, has inflicted a deep wound upon the Papacy, by joining the 'Old Catholics ;' and he is reported to have said that he was honestly enslaved to the Vatican, till he woke up to the fact that the whole system he had been supporting is based upon the forged decretals and other spurious documents, which he had always been taught to accept as genuine. This discovery and the exposure of these facts, by Döllinger and his associates has lighted a spirit of Reformation in Germany, which is extending to other countries of Europe, and will not long be kept down in America." I have given this passage at so great length to show the pabulum on which "Old Catholic" babes are fed, and I need hardly attempt to analyze it. I feel confident, that if our episcopal prelate wrote to-day, he would not assume the title and role of an "Old Catholic," or base so many bright hopes on a movement that has, in the short space of a few years, proved a most miserable failure, second only perhaps to the later disgraceful collapse of the so-called "Independent American Catholic Church." Started under brightest auspices, a powerful German Empire to back it, an imperious imperial chancellor its foster father, the prestige of whose name, *Bismarck*, imparted to it, even at his birth, prominence, and *eclat*, what has ever it been? what has it ever done? what is it now? not a single bishop would touch the polluted thing begotten in sacrilege, disobedience and despotism, a few priests mostly of disreputable antecedents, and a handful of worldly, self-styled liberal laymen; from the beginning it languished; its life is now well-nigh extinct. Never since the beginning of the Church's history, even in the early days of the Nicene, Ephesian or Constantinopolitan councils, were there such unanimity in the episcopate, such loyalty in the clergy, such firmness, independence and genuine Catholic spirit in the laity, and this the "Old Catholic" movement has made evident and emphasized. What a fearful wound then, the brilliant von Schulte has inflicted on the Papacy by joining the "Old Catholics!" But who has told our enthusiastic convert to "Old Catholicism" that he was so long the favorite canonist of the Pope himself? If von Schulte ever said, "what he is reported to have said," in the above passage, we certainly pity him. Enslaved to the Vatican until he woke up to the fact that the whole system of the Papacy was based on forged decretals and other spurious documents! What are these other spurious documents? The forged decretals we know, every school-boy knows, or may know just what they are, their character and value. Our ecclesiastical students find all about their history, their origin, and their author in the text books put into their hands, and the unprofessional layman may obtain full and accurate information concerning this Isidorian collection of canons and decretals in *"Appleton's American Cyclopedia,"* under the titles "Canon Law" and "Decretals." To suppose then that the brilliant von Schulte was imposed on by the spurious Isidore Mercator or Peccator and thus enslaved to the Vatican, is simply ridiculous. Time was, when simple minds could easily be deceived by unauthentic or spurious documents, provided the doctrine taught and the laws promulgated were not strange or novel, provided no innovation was broached that conflicted with the well-known faith and traditions of the Church. People did not care, or were not able to closely scrutinize the foundations or authorities on which they were made to rest. But in our day, in this nineteenth century, there is no excuse for the brilliant von Schulte or any other churchman, who allows himself to be duped by a literary adventurer of the ninth century.

We can now go back of the decretals, search the original documents, and it is precisely the doing of this which has brought men of research and patristic learning, to believe in the Papacy and all the authoritative teaching of the holy Catholic Church. To say nothing of Newman and Manning and a host of other really learned and conscientious Anglicans. Dr. Ives in our own country, an eminently able and amiable prelate of the Protestant Episcopal Church, goes back in his research to the very foundation of the Papacy, and quotes from genuine original documents the testimony of the earliest Fathers in support of the same. —(*Trials of Mind, L. Silliman Ives, LL.D., Boston,* 1854.) Dr. James Kent Stone does the same in his "Invitation Heeded," and I will conclude this point, by quoting his pungent remarks regarding these forgeries:

"Another indication of the real antiquity of the Papal claim to supremacy is the frantic assertion, that the Papacy has attempted to antedate its assumptions by the use of forgeries. I can hardly help treating contemptuously this unscholarly talk about the pseudo-decretals, being weak enough to take satisfaction that I so far suspected its trivial character, as never to indulge in it myself. Let it suffice then to remark: 1. That the Isidorian collection of canons was certainly not made at Rome, wherever else it may have had its origin; and that it was not compiled in the interest of the Popes, but as Guizot says, 'to serve the bishops against the metropolitans and temporal sovereigns.' 2. That the materials used in its composition were not new, but old, being mostly taken from early Papal rescripts, and synodal decrees and the writings of the Fathers. In an uncritical age the counterfeits escaped detection and came into gradual use, as being in accordance with a long established and recognized system. In a word, the imposture grew out of the supremacy, not the supremacy out of the imposture. 3. That the pious fraud was exposed and reprobated centuries ago. All the world knows, or ought to know, that a Catholic would no more think of grounding the Papal supremacy on the compilation of Mercator, than would a Scotchman of vindicating his national literature by appealing to the Ossianic poems, or the good merchants of Bristol, of proving the ancient respectability of their city from the contents of 'Canyng's coffre.' The forged decretals may be matter for curious and learned investigation, but they are certainly ruled out of the debate between Catholics and Protestants, as has been often shown. If Protestants expect ever to capture the citadel of the Papacy, it is time for them to stop playing Chinese antics before an old mound, which was never used for military purposes, and which nobody dreams of defending."—("*The Invitation Heeded,*" Seventh edition, *N. Y., pp.* 270-271.) It is then, assuredly, not very creditable to a *brilliant* man to be so easily duped, and so long and shamefully enslaved to the Vatican. But what, may we ask, are those ancient Catholic constitutions of whose very existence we are not permitted to have any knowledge? Will not some kind friend, or zealous "Old Catholic" enlighten us, and tell us where we can get a glimpse at them? We promise to introduce the study of them into our excellent and flourishing seminary at Suspension Bridge, and it shall no longer be said that this *kind of ignorance is common among those educated at Roman Catholic Seminaries.* But pleasantry aside, we firmly believe that what is not known and taught about the Church of Christ and her constitutions in our Catholic seminaries is not worth knowing, and after the divine constitution of the Church embodied in the revealed Word of God, the Church of Christ has no constitutions, ancient or modern, but such as have been framed and indited by Popes in rescripts, bulls, decretals, etc., or found in canonical enactments and ecclesiastical laws formulated by the bishops of the Church in Diocesan synods, provincial, national, plenary or œcumenical councils, confirmed and approved by the supreme authority of the Sovereign Pontiffs, the Popes of Rome, Peter and his successors in the Holy See.

✢ STEPHEN VINCENT RYAN,
Bishop of Buffalo.

Buffalo, Feast of the Help of Christians, May 24*th, A. D.* 1880.

PREFACE TO SECOND EDITION.

IN publishing a second edition of our little work rebutting the claims to Apostolical Succession made by some of our friends of the Protestant Episcopal Church of America, I must tender my sincerest thanks to the Most Rev. Archbishops and Bishops and the Rev. Clergy throughout the country for the kind and flattering words in which they have been pleased to welcome its publication, and to the public in general for the favor with which it has been received. I did not think it necessary in the first edition to make special references to my authorities, because it looked to me too pretentious, and like affectation of learning and importance not warranted by my unpretending little treatise, composed so largely of extracts from the learned works of other authors. Some have, however, thought differently, and believing that it would take its place among the standard works on the subject of Anglican and Protestant Episcopal orders, they asked me to make it more complete and satisfactory by referring with more precision to the works and authors quoted. Acting on this suggestion I have gone over the whole matter again, correcting some faults, and typographical errors, and making as far as possible accurate references to the authorities on which I have drawn. On historical points I have consulted Dodd's Church History of England, by Rev. M. A. Tierney, F.S.A.; History of the Anglo-Saxon Church, and History of England, by John Lingard, D.D.; Six Historical Lectures, by Rev. J. Waterworth, M.A.; Alzog's Universal Church History (Pabisch and Byrne); Histoire Universelle de l'Eglise Catholique, par l'Abbé Rohrbacher

A

PREFACE TO SECOND EDITION.

I can hardly say how much I owe to the following learned works. "The Validity of Anglican Ordinations," by the V. Rev. Peter Richard Kenrick, D.D., V.G., now the venerable Archbishop of St. Louis, whose little work is a mine of accurate and reliable information, theological and historical; "The Question of Anglican Ordinations," by E. E. Estcourt, M.A., F.S.A., a work of conscientious, scholarly research, exhuming treasures of original documents, which throw new light on the question discussed; and "The Ordinal of King Edward VI.," by Dom Wilfrid Raynal, O.S.B., detailing its history, theology and liturgy. To these three works, and we may add for those of Ritualistic tendencies, "The Anglican Ministry," by Arthur Wollaston Hutton, M.A., we may confidently refer any one wishing to study thoroughly the subject we have so briefly treated in the following pages. We must not forget our obligations to the following works: "The Trials of a Mind in its Progress to Catholicism," by L. Silliman Ives, LL.D., late Bishop of the Protestant Episcopal Church in North Carolina; "The Invitation Heeded," by James Kent Stone, S.T.D., late President of Kenyon and Hobart Colleges; "My Clerical Friends," by the lamented Dr. Marshall. We confess to have also made free with the "Cursus completus Patrologiæ," by the Abbé Migne, "Œuvres complètes de Bossuet;" the works of Cardinal Wiseman, Card. Manning and Card. Newman, and Rt. Rev. John Milner, D.D., F.S.A.; "The Moral and Dogmatic Theology," and "Primacy of the Apostolic See," by Most Rev. Francis Patrick Kenrick, D.D.; "The Catholic Church and Christian State," by Dr. Joseph Hergenröther, Prof. of Canon Law and Church History at the University of Würzburg: and "The History of the Councils," by Dr. Charles Joseph Heféle, Prof. of Theol. in the University of Tubingen, now Bishop of Rothenburg. The reader will notice that my "Old Catholic" friend has also sent me back not only to study the Theology of

B

St. Liguori, and a dogmatic treatise by Prof. Hurter, of the University of Innsbruck, but to the "Roman Pontifical," "Lives of the Saints," by Rev. Dr. Alban Butler, and even the "Catechism of the Council of Trent." If, however, this forced study will help any of my readers, and particularly any of our separated brethren, to a juster and truer knowledge of some controverted points of Catholic doctrine, or dispel prejudice and erroneous impressions from the mind of even one individual, I shall be well recompensed for my labor. If I have succeeded in bringing within reach of some religious minds earnestly seeking after truth, a clear and accurate statement of certain wickedly distorted and falsified facts of history, and certain industriously obscured and discolored records of those sad and mournful reigns when the English Church and English nation were violently, and O! how wickedly, torn from Catholic unity; if by reference to authentic sources, and genuine, original documents it has been shown, when, how, and by whom this radical change in the religion of the English people was effected, and the mutilation and adulteration of the old liturgies and ordination services brought about; if the hollowness of the pretences to antiquity and claims to Apostolical succession, valid orders and a true priesthood on the part of the Anglican State Establishment, and the utter groundlessness of the charges against the doctrines and practices of the Catholic Church and Supreme Pontiff, have been made plain; may we not hope that, by the grace of God, persuasion will soon follow conviction in many thoughtful, truth-loving minds.

Surely pious and religious souls will not be deterred from embracing the truth because of the sacrifices, the social or domestic ostracism which conversion to the true Church, and faith of Christ often entail. "He that taketh not up his cross and followeth me is not worthy of me."—(*Matt. x.* 38.) "For the Spirit himself giveth testimony to our spirit, that we are the sons of God. And if sons heirs also; heirs indeed of God and joint heirs of Christ; yet so if we suffer with him, that we may also be glorified with him."—(*Rom. viii.* 16, 17.) "He that shall be ashamed of me and of my words, of him the Son of Man shall be ashamed when he shall come in his majesty and that of his Father and of the holy angels."—(*Luke ix.* 38.) S. V. R.

Buffalo, Feast of St. Joseph, A.D. 1881.

CLAIMS
OF
A PROTESTANT EPISCOPAL BISHOP
TO
APOSTOLICAL SUCCESSION AND VALID ORDERS DISPROVED.

I.

ORIGIN OF OUR LITTLE TREATISE.

IN the early part of the year 1874, at the request of a number of Catholic gentlemen of Buffalo, I delivered a lecture in our Cathedral in reply to a sermon preached by Dr. Coxe, at Erie, Pa., on occasion of the consecration of John Franklin Spaulding, D. D., and published in full in one of our city papers. The leading points of the "Sermon" and "Reply," may be gathered from the following extracts:

"If a corporation of men still exists on the earth, bearing that identical commission given by Christ to his Apostles after his resurrection, by historical transmission, their existence as such a corporation of witnesses is irrefragable proof of the fact that Christ rose. Now, nobody can deny that from the time of Pontius

Pilate until now a continuous line of men has been found in divers parts of the world, perpetuated by the laying on of hands of those who were before them."— (*The Corporate Witness. A Sermon by A. Cleveland Coxe, preached Dec.* 31st, 1873, *in St. Paul's Church, Erie, Pa.*) To this we replied:

"This is perfectly true; this is orthodox Catholic doctrine. It is plain from sacred Scripture, and known to every Catholic child instructed in the rudiments of Christian Doctrine that the risen Saviour organized a ministry, instituted a commission that was to be perpetuated to the end of time; but that Dr. Coxe, or the ministers and bishops of the Protestant Episcopal Church of the United States bear that identical Apostolical commission by historical transmission, the learned divine does not prove, or even attempt to prove; and whilst nobody can deny that from the time of Pontius Pilate until now a continuous line of men has been found perpetuated by the laying on of hands and the empowering of the Holy Ghost; that the line comes down continuous and unbroken from the Apostles to the Protestant Episcopal Bishop of Western New York, we, with the immense mass of Christians, beg most respectfully to question—nay, emphatically to deny. Apostolical succession, we aver, is one of the leading doctrines of the Christian Church; but we hold it to be a gratuitous assumption that the Protestant Episcopal communion is that Church, or can prove her identity with that Church by uninterrupted succession from the Apostles. It will not do to say: 'We are profoundly convinced of the reality of our Apostolic commission,' for *we* can, with equal positiveness and depth of conviction aver, you have not the slightest claim to it; you cannot prove your title. If you cannot prove it satisfactorily, incontrovertibly and beyond the shadow of reasonable doubt, is it not trifling with men, is it not a mocking of God, this pretended empowering under the ' same charter and same promises ' as 'the original Apostles?' And until we have this clear and incontestible and convincing proof, may we not rally the Protestant Episcopalian as he did his Methodist Episcopal brother, when John Wesley attempted to consecrate Coke a bishop:

'Our John on Coke his hands has laid,
But who laid hands on him?'

(*Bishop Ryan's Reply, delivered in St. Joseph's Cathedral, Buffalo, Feb. 22, 1874.*)

"The Apostolic ministry is sent forth geographically around the circumference of the globe, chronologically to the end of time. So far, and so long, 'ye shall be witnesses,' but who shall be witnesses? Ye, Apostles. Is there anything in Scripture more clear, then, than the perpetuity of the Apostolic office? Those whom our Lord thus addressed personally were not to bear their personal witness here in our part of the earth, yet, said the Master, 'ye shall be witnesses unto me, unto the uttermost part of the earth.' Again, they were not to survive the ordinary limit of human life, yet, he says, 'Lo! I am with you always, even to the end of the world.' Could any language be more explicit? We assert that the Apostolic order and office still exist. No ingenuity can make void this evidence that our Lord designed to perpetuate its corporate identity until his coming again."—(*The Corporate Witness.*) In our Reply we said:

" Here we again tread Catholic ground. With this

doctrine, this line of argument, and even this language, barring perhaps some peculiarity of style and phraseology, you, my Catholic friends, are familiar. You have often heard it before from this pulpit. Neither the doctrine nor the argument is new, and I quote it at such length only to exhibit the strange, and, to me, inexplicable phenomenon, so often displayed, especially among our estimable and cultivated Episcopal brethren, of a man holding principles and professing doctrines that must, if logically followed up, inevitably land him in the Catholic Church; yet, turning his back upon her, closing his eyes to the light of reason, his intellect to the plainest truths of revelation, the most evident declarations of sacred Scripture.

"Of course, the Apostolic order and office still exist; of course, our Lord designed to perpetuate its corporate identity till his coming again. His divine word is pledged for it; his veracity is at stake; his Godhead and divine mission guarantee it: ' As the Father sent me, I also send you;' 'Go teach all nations; I am with you all days till the end of time.' But neither Christ our Lord nor his revealed word declare that the Apostlic order and office exist in the Protestant Episcopal Church, or are transmitted by the mutilated, and oft modified form of consecration used in the Anglican or Protestant Episcopal ordination service. Nowhere in Scripture are we told that this corporate identity was designed to be perpetuated or reproduced in a communion that had no existence until some fifteen hundred years after the Apostolic age. Here again is a grave assumption, which we cannot take on credit; we demand proof; we find bare assertion; grand but unproven claims. But hold! yes, here is an attempt at proving legitimate descent from the Apostles, by way of illustration. In answer to the objection that 'the original Apostles were extraordinary in their gifts and functions and hence in the nature of things could have no successors,' the preacher very justly argues: 'The first President of this Republic had extraordinary functions and relations in his high office; it was his to plant, to lay foundations, to be the father of his country. In all these things he can have no successor. Such were his extraordinary and personal distinctions. Do we argue, therefore, that the American Presidents are not the successors of Washington?' The illustration is excellent, the argument unanswerable *in the mouth of a Catholic bishop*, holding his commission immediately from a Pontiff who traces his succession in unbroken line to the Apostles—a Catholic bishop, deriving his orders and his mission, his authority, right to rule and govern the Church over which the Holy Ghost hath placed him a bishop, from the legitimate successor of him to whom Christ committed the care of his whole flock, and who can furnish the clearest historical evidence of his legitimate descent. Abraham Lincoln or Ulysses S. Grant can claim to be successors of Washington. Could Jefferson Davis do the same, who rebelled against the old legitimate government and set up an establishment of his own? He declared that the powers at Washington had violated the constitution and broken the compact between the States, just the plea made by the reformers to justify their revolt against the authority of the See of Rome.

The argument, then, that is conclusive in the Catholic Church, from the fact that every Catholic layman knows that the pastor who ministers to him and teaches him has his orders and authority, by the laying on of hands and the grace of ordination, from a superior pastor or bishop of a diocese, who, in turn, is directly authorized and commissioned by the Pope, or the supreme pastor, the supreme head of Christ's Church on earth, who again comes down from Peter by one continuous unbroken chain, of which we can count every link from Pius to Peter,—is absolutely without force in a Church which has thrown off the authority of Rome, and cannot trace its lineage to the Apostles. This succession of chief pastors is the main, if not the only guarantee, as well of our Apostolical commission as of the Apostolicity of your faith and doctrine. It is to the chair of Peter and the regular succession of incumbents in that time-honored and divinely-guarded See, that the early fathers and saints and doctors, in every age, appealed, against unauthorized teachers and the innovations of heretics, and rebellious schismatics. Thus St. Augustine confounds the Donatists: 'Come to us, brethren (he writes), if you wish to be engrafted in the vine. We are afflicted at seeing you cut off from its trunk. Count over the bishops in the very See of Peter, and behold in that list of fathers how one succeeded to the other. This is the rock against which the proud gates of hell do not prevail.' Again he says: 'I am kept in this Church by the succession of prelates from St. Peter, to whom the Lord committed the care of his sheep, down to the present bishop.' (This was, remember, in the 5th century.) And St. Optatus, against the same heretics, enumerates all the Popes from St. Peter to the then reigning Pontiff, Siricius; 'with whom we and all the world,' he says,

ORIGIN OF OUR LITTLE TREATISE. 7

'are united in communion. Do you, now, Donatists, give the history of your episcopal ministry.' Tertullian, before, did the same, and challenged the heretics of his time to produce the origin of their Church, to display the succession of their bishops, so that the first of them may appear to have been ordained by an Apostolic man who persevered in their communion; and giving a list of the Pontiffs in the Roman see he says: 'Let the heretics feign anything like this.' St. Irenæus, illustrious bishop of Lyons, disciple of St. Polycarp, who was himself a disciple of St. John the Apostle, names all the Popes to St. Eleutherius, then living, and says, 'it would be tedious to enumerate the succession of bishops in the different churches; we refer you to that greatest, most ancient and universally known Church founded at Rome by St. Peter and St. Paul, and which has been preserved there through the succession of its bishops down to the present time.' St. Jerome knew no other sure way of settling the disputed rights of bishops, and writes to Pope Damasus in regard to the heated controversy between St. Meletius and Paulinus, rival claimants of the see of Antioch:

'I am joined in communion with your Holiness; that is, with the chair of Peter; upon that rock I know the Church is built. I do not know Vitalis; I do not communicate with Meletius; Paulinus is a stranger to me. Whoever is united to the chair of Peter, he is mine.'

So, also, St. Athanasius, whose illustrious name is dishonored by being coupled with the 'Reformers,' appeals to the Pope against the heretical intruders into his see of Alexandria, and the violence to which he was subjected by the imperial power, and is protected in his episcopal character, and his episcopal rights vindicated by Pope Julius I., who wrote thus in the year 342 to the Eastern bishops, who sustained by the power of the State, had driven Athanasius from his see:

'Know you not that the canonical rule was to recur first to our authority, and that the decisions must proceed from it? Such is the tradition that we have received from the blessed Apostle Peter, and I believe it to be so universally acknowledged, that I should not recall it here if these deplorable circumstances did not constrain me to proclaim it.'

I dwell so long on this point, although a little beside my purpose, because it shows us a Pope in 342 very similar to our own Pope in 1874, as to this claim and exercise of jurisdiction over the whole Church, East and West, and it shows us the great Athanasius appealing to the Pope against the Emperor's violence and his servile, heretical, courtly bishops to be anywhere but in the same boat with the *martyred* 'reformers,' who denied the authority of the Pope, acknowledged the spiritual supremacy of the king, and were by his authority intruded into the sees of lawful prelates."
—(*Bishop Ryan's Reply.*)

"Christ said we should have such witnesses that they should bear their testimony till the consummation of ages. We believe his promises, we accept them in their plain meaning. And as they are able to demonstrate that their commission is identical with that which was left upon the Mount of Olives, your bishops claim, however unworthy, to be the successors of the Apostles."—(*The Corporate Witness.*) We replied:

"Now here again we demur, and deny *in toto* the whole claim of the bishops of the Protestant Episcopal Church of America and the bishops of their mother

Church of England to Apostolical succession, or that the Apostolical commission has been preserved and transmitted in their communion, or sect, or church, as you may be pleased to call it, for the reasons which I will now give, as briefly and summarily as possible.

If the bishops of the American Protestant Episcopal Church have this apostolical succession, or this commission identical with that which Christ our Lord gave his Apostles, they derive it from the established Church of England, which they recognize as the mother Church; but if the Anglican bishops have no title to this claim, they cannot give it to others. There is an old axiom, *Nemo dat quod non habet*. Now, the Anglican Church has no part in the Apostolical commission, unless it can trace its orders and its mission regularly from the Apostles through the Catholic bishops. But this it can hardly consistently attempt to do, as it declared in one of its Homilies the Catholic Church to have been 'drowned in abominable idolatry, most detested of God and damnable to man, for the space of eight hundred years,' and in one of the thirty-nine articles 'that all the Apostolical sees erred in matters of faith.' Could Matthew Parker, the first Anglican bishop, whilst denying the authority of the Pope, and in open revolt against the Apostolical See, claim to hold his authority and his commission from the Church whose corruptions he denounced, and not one of whose bishops would impose hands on him? In the early Church, bishops appealed for their legitimacy, for their rights and power, for their Apostolical succession, to the Roman Pontiff; his see was styled eminently and emphatically *the Apostolical See;* he was the trunk to which all the branches should be united.

But the Church of England revolted against his authority, severed itself from his communion, renounced it on account of its 'idolatry,' and was denounced by it, in turn, as heretical.

It is a universally admitted principle of Church government, recognized here in our own country by the practice of every Church, and by decisions of the courts of justice, that a clergyman from whom authority is withdrawn according to the rules and laws of the Church to which he may have been attached, who is no longer recognized as a minister by his proper ecclesiastical superior, can no longer claim to act for that Church; his ministrations are not regarded, his ministerial functions are no longer lawful. (I wonder if Bishop Cheney is recognized as a legitimate bishop and successor of the Apostles by Bishop Coxe? We know not what action the Episcopal body may have taken in this matter, but we do know that he cannot be so recognized, unless at the cost of consistency, authority and unity.)

We also know from the history of the Christian Church in all ages, that when a bishop or a priest, or bishops and priests, revolted against the Church in which they were ordained and commissioned, they were by the very fact deprived of all authority to act in the name and by the authority of the Church; they were silenced or suspended, deprived of their faculties and deposed from their sees. This was the case with the early heretics, the Donatists, Eutychians, the Arians, and others, who had validly ordained bishops; but surely no orthodox Anglican or Episcopalian will aver that these heretical bishops were successors of the Apostles. Something more than valid ordination or the laying on of hands is necessary to perpetuate the Apostolical commission. On these principles, held and acted on by all religious denominations in the government of their respective societies, we maintain that Matthew Parker, first Anglican bishop, even if validly ordained by the laying on of hands, with due form of prayers and solemnities, and a lawful ordainer, could not transmit jurisdiction, or a share of Apostolical commission, or right to minister in the Church, because he himself did not possess it.

But we absolutely deny the validity of his consecration, and thus strike at the very root of all pretensions in the Anglican and Protestant Episcopal Church of America to Apostolical succession. We can only summarily state the grounds of our positive unconditional denial. It is very doubtful, and can never be proved that he was ever consecrated at all, or that there was anything more than the farce of the 'Nag's Head.' The Lambeth Register is probably a forgery. Even if it be genuine, and the consecration took place as asserted, at the hands of Barlow, an apostate monk, it is very doubtful that Barlow himself was ever consecrated, or ever anything more than a bishop elect. Even if Barlow was a regularly consecrated bishop, and went through the form of consecrating Parker, the form used, namely, that *devised*, as the act has it, by Edward, was notoriously insufficient and invalid, so that acts of Parliament were deemed necessary to supply defects, in this wise:

— 'And all persons that have been or shall be made, ordered or consecrated archbishops, bishops, priests, ministers of God's Word and sacraments, or deacons, after the form and order prescribed, be in very deed, and also by authority hereof, declared and enacted to be, and shall be archbishops, bishops, priests, ministers, and deacons, and rightly made, ordered, and consecrated.'

Thus there is some ground for styling them 'Parliament bishops,' as they were commonly styled; and at least it is evident that there was doubt as to the validity of the form devised by Edward, to which this statute of Elizabeth (1566) refers. In Harding's controversy with the Anglican Bishop Jewel, he asks: 'You bear yourself as the legitimate bishop of Salisbury, but how can you prove your vocation? Who hath laid hands on you; how, and by whom were you consecrated?' and, in reply to the declaration of the latter, that he was consecrated by Parker, Harding subjoins, 'How, I pray you, was your archbishop himself consecrated? Your metropolitan, who should give authority to all your consecrations, had himself no lawful consecration. There were, indeed, some lawful bishops in the kingdom, who either were not required to impose hands on you, or who, being required, refused to do so.' And again, rallying him on the statute of Parliament making valid, defective forms of consecration: 'If you will needs have your matters seem to depend of your Parliament, let us not be blamed, if we call it a Parliament religion, Parliament gospel, Parliament faith.'

Learned divines from the very beginning reproached the bishops of the establishment with invalidity of their orders. Sanders, regius professor of canon law at Oxford, in the time of Elizabeth, says: 'For being destitute of all lawful ordination, they were constrained to crave the assistance of the secular power, by authority whereof, if anything were done amiss and not according to the prescript of the law, or omitted and left undone in the former inauguration, it might be pardoned them, and that after they had enjoyed the episcopal office and chair many years without any episcopal consecration.' Bristow, another divine of the same period, who died in 1582, says: 'In England the King, yea the Queen, may give their letters patent to whom they will, and they thenceforward may bear themselves as bishops and may begin to ordain ministers.' And of Parker and others who had been Catholic priests, he says, 'they were deemed, without a new ordination, to be not only priests, but bishops and archbishops, either by virtue of the royal letters, or by a certain ridiculous consecration of those who had received no power to consecrate, except what the Queen had given them.' Whatever opinion we may form as to the question whether Parker was consecrated at Lambeth or not, and as to whether Barlow, his pretended consecrator, was a bishop or not—(these are matters of opinion to be determined by historical research,)—it is absolutely certain, that, on account of the form used, Anglican, and consequently Protestant Episcopal, orders are vitiated and invalidated; and hence, though the Church has acknowledged the validity of ordination in the Greek Church, and even the validity of the consecration of the Jansenist bishops of Holland, and, in fact, of all who preserved the regular ancient form, yet she never would recognize as bishops or priests, those ordained by the forms devised by Edward VI.; and Dr. Milner expresses the mind of the Catholic Church when he says, 'that the form used in the English Church previous to 1662 is just as proper for the ceremony of confirming, or laying hands on children, as it is for conferring the powers of the episcopacy.' The Church established by law seems to have felt this herself, for, in that year (1662), just one hundred and three years too late to save Anglican orders, convocation changed the form, evidently with the aim of supplying the defect pointed out by Catholic divines. Macaulay, in his history of England, affirms that, in 1661 Episcopal ordination was *for the first time* made an indispensable condition for Church preferment.' Lord Macaulay is, indeed, a brilliant essayist, but rather an unreliable historian, and his statements, unless corroborated by other testimony, we would hardly trust; yet we know from other sources that then, as now, the Church of England and its daughter in America might be said to hold anything and everything on this point of Apostolical succession, or the transmission of episcopal powers by the laying on of hands.

Let us see the opinions of some of the early reformers. Let us see how Cranmer himself, the model reformer, according to Dr. Coxe, viewed this matter. Cranmer says: 'In the New Testament he that is appointed to be a bishop or a priest needeth no consecration, by the Scripture, for election, or appointing thereto, is sufficient.' Again: 'Bishops and priests were no two things, but one office in the beginning of Christ's religion.' Again: 'A bishop may make a priest, by the Scripture, and so may princes, and governors, also, and that by the authority of God.' Burnet, in his history of the Reformation, tells us: 'Cranmer had, at this time, some particular opinions concerning ecclesiastical offices—that they were delivered from the king as other

ORIGIN OF OUR LITTLE TREATISE. 15

civil offices were, and that ordination was not indispensably necessary, and was only a ceremony that might be used or laid aside, and that authority was delivered to churchmen only by the king's commission.' In his address to Henry, in connection with the other mean, servile English bishops to whom the noble and venerable Fisher of Rochester was an illustrious exception, Cranmer said : 'All jurisdiction, civil and ecclesiastical, flowed from the king, and that they exercised it only at the king's courtesy.' Courayer, himself an apostate, the ablest defender of Anglican orders and Apostolical succession, says: 'Cranmer and Barlow, two of the prelates appointed to reform the public liturgy and form of ordination, were notoriously erroneous in the matter of orders, and it is but too apparent that the chief aim of these divines and prelates was to extinguish episcopacy.' The same author says of Barlow : — 'Among many errors which he was accused of spreading, he was charged with having maintained this proposition— that if the King's Grace, being the supreme head of the Church, did choose, denominate and elect any layman to be a bishop, he so chosen should be as good a bishop as he is, or the best in England.' I will conclude this point with the forcible words of Dr. Milner :

'The acknowledgment of a royal ecclesiastical supremacy in all spiritual and ecclesiastical things and causes, (oath of supremacy as when the question is who shall preach, baptize, etc., and who shall not, what is sound doctrine, and what is not) is decidedly a renunciation of Christ's commission given to his Apostles, and preserved by their successors in the Catholic Apostolic Church. Hence it clearly appears that there is and can be no Apostolical succession of ministry in the established Church more than in the other congregations or societies of Protestants. All their preaching and ministering in their several degrees is performed by mere human authority. On the other hand, not a sermon is preached, nor a child baptized, nor a penitent absolved, nor a priest ordained, nor a bishop consecrated throughout the whole extent of the Catholic Church, without the minister of such function being able to show his authority from Christ for what he does, in the commission of Christ to his Apostles— (All power in Heaven and earth is given to me: go ye, therefore, teach all nations, baptizing them, etc., —Matt. xxviii. 19)—and without being able to prove his claim to that commission of Christ by producing the table of his uninterrupted succession from the Apostles.'—(*End of Rel. Controversy, p.* 228, *N. Y.*)

You are then perfectly right, Dr. Coxe; the Apostolic ministry was to be perpetuated by transmission of the commission given by Christ to his Apostles; but it is and can be perpetuated only in the Catholic Church, and by the unbroken line of pontiffs in the only Apostolic See that has had such an uninterrupted succession, the See of Rome, and whosoever believes in the existence of such a historic transmission, must, if logical, acknowledge in Pius a successor of Peter, and in the Pope a primacy of jursidiction, supreme authority to guide and govern the universal Church, to commission and qualify witnesses, to the uttermost parts of the earth—must, in one word, become a Catholic. We thank, however, the outspoken bishop for this enunciation of an essential principle of Christian faith, for this recognition of an essential mark of the true

Church, this strong testimony to the divine character, constitution and organization of the Christian ministry, and in all earnestness and Christian charity, we ask him and our many estimable Episcopalian friends in Buffalo to investigate for themselves this interesting subject, without bias or prejudice—to examine the records of the Christian Church, and to prove to themselves their claims to come down from the Apostles; to trace their hierarchy to the Apostolic age, so that with undoubting certainty and absolute conviction of their reason they may consistently hold their communion, their Church, to be identical in ministry, in orders and mission, with the Apostolic Church.

Does truthful history warrant such a belief? On the contrary, does not history show to any unbiased reader, that the Church of England started with Henry VIII. making himself the head of the Church and source of all its authority and jurisdiction, modifying the Church discipline to meet this most unapostolical and unwarrantable pretension, and thus forcibly and miserably tearing away the English Church from the parent stock, forcing her into rebellion, cutting off all communication with the main trunk and seat and source of Apostolical jurisdiction, the only see in the whole of Christendom through which it is any way possible to trace Apostolical succession?"—*(Bishop Ryan's Reply to the Corporate Witness.)*

To this reply, Dr. Coxe published a rejoinder, "*Catholics and Roman Catholics, by an old Catholic*," which in turn was reviewed in a series of articles in the "*Catholic Union*," published in Buffalo. The substance of these articles we are now induced to republish in a more permanent form, in the hope that the discussion of the question of Apostolical succession may prove interesting and instructive, especially to our worthy and esteemed Episcopalian friends, who believe with Dr. Coxe that, " from the time of Pontius Pilate until now, a continuous line of men has been found perpetuated by the laying on of hands and the empowering of the Holy Ghost," and who, in good faith, and with unquestioning docility, accept the claims of their bishops to be successors of the Apostles, with " commissions identical with that left on the Mount of Olives." As this is no personal controversy, but one on which we enter solely in the interest of truth, and with a view of promoting the salvation of souls, we shall refrain as much as possible from personal allusions, and as we purpose to confine ourselves to the question of Apostolical succession, we will allow ourselves to be carried away by side issues, or to the discussion of other matters, only in as far as they may have a bearing on this question, or may be forced on us.

II.

APOSTOLICAL SUCCESSION ESSENTIAL TO THE CHRISTIAN CHURCH—IT IS NOT FOUND EITHER IN THE ANGLICAN CHURCH, AS-BY-LAW-ESTABLISHED, OR THE PROTESTANT EPISCOPAL CHURCH OF AMERICA.

WE deny then *in toto* that Apostolical succession has been preserved or transmitted in the Protestant Episcopal Church of America, or in the Anglican establishment. Let it, moreover, be borne in mind that there can be here no question as to Apostolical succession being an essential doctrine of the Christian Church. It is well demonstrated from Holy Writ, that our Lord founded "a corporate order of witnesses, who should be an extension of Himself, a prolonging of His personal mission," and nobody can deny that "from the time of Pontius Pilate until now, a continuous line of men has been found in divers parts of the world, perpetuated by the laying on of hands of those who were before them." It is evident from sacred Scripture, it is known to all who read their Bible, that the risen Saviour organized a ministry, a body of teachers, and sent them to teach all nations, promising to be with them to the end of ages, and hence their commission was to continue, they were to be perpetuated to the end of ages. Continuous and unbroken succession from the Apostles is, then, unquestionably, a fundamental doctrine, an essential note of the Christian Church. We are willing to allow that, "only in the perpetuated historic identity of the Apostolic commission can we find monumental evidence of the fact of the resurrection," and consequently of the truth of Christianity; and again: "the canon of Scripture itself depends on it; you cannot prove your Bible authentic without it." Only those who can satisfactorily and certainly trace the historic identity of their ministry with, and their legitimate descent from, the Apostles, can have any certainty of the reality of the resurrection, of the truth of Christianity, of the canonicity and authenticity of the sacred Scriptures. But this identity and Apostolic succession, confessedly essential to the true Church of Christ, the Episcopal Church cannot show, and therefore the Episcopal Church cannot prove herself the true Church of Christ. Nay, more, only in the Catholic Church, in communion with the See of Rome, *the* Apostolical See, can this identity be found and clearly demonstrated, and therefore all who hold this identity, this succession from the Apostles as a necessary characteristic, and distinctive mark of the Christian Church, must, if logical and consistent, go over to Rome, towards which their faces are plainly set. Woe betide them if they look back. Unfortunately, Lot's wife is not a solitary instance of the terrible judgment awaiting those who close their eyes to the light of truth, and harden their hearts to the inspirations of grace, who through undue attachment to the things of earth, or over-much affection to family and friends, love of lucre or pride of intellect, through want of moral courage to bear the poverty and humility of the cross, stifle the voice of conscience halt in their search for truth, and turn back when on the very point of escaping from the Babel of confusion. Many such in our experience we have met, monuments of the justice of God, beacons of warning to those who close their hearts to grace, their eyes to truth, real pillars of salt, their lives produce only dead sea fruit; notwithstanding outside deceitful appearances they are filled with ashes and wormwood.

As to the value to be attached to assertions like these: "The succession in the Church of England is more demonstrably canonical and regular, in all particulars, than any other succession in Christendom," or " It may be shown that nobody competent to form an opinion, and who has taken the pains to investigate the matter, has ever professed a doubt concerning Anglican succession;" our readers will be able to judge presently. Apostolical succession requires, as those making the above assertions admit, something more than valid ordination. We may admit not only the fact, but also the validity of a bishop's consecration, and yet deny him, even when validly consecrated, any participation in the divine commission given by Christ to His Apostles, any claim to Apostolical succession. Valid ordination is essential to, but insufficient for, legitimate succession. In the whole history of the Christian Church, there is nothing more evident than this, that when a bishop or priest, or bishops and priests, revolted against ecclesiastical authority, or contumaciously erred against faith, they were silenced, suspended, deprived of their faculties, deposed from their sees. The Church, which had commissioned them and given them authority, jurisdiction, a right to teach, and assigned them a mission in which to exercise their ministry, simply revoked their commission, recalled her grant of powers, and annulled all license to act for her, in her name, or by her authority. Thus she acted towards the validly ordained and rightly consecrated heretical Donatist, Eutychian and Arian bishops; and who among our orthodox Anglicans or Episcopalians will recognize such excommunicated, deposed and deprived heretical bishops as successors of the Apostles. She holds the same principles to-day; schismatical and heretical bishops such as the bishops of the Greek Church, the Jansenist bishops of Holland, and Reinkens, the itinerant "Old Catholic" bishop of Germany even if validly ordained, have no share in the Apostolical commission, have no jurisdiction, they are not sent, and "how shall they preach?" They are thus cut off from communion with the Church, broken off from the chain of Apostolical succession. Again, it is equally certain, and the history of the Church from the days of the Apostles bears witness, that bishops appealed in proof of their legitimacy, their right and authority to take and hold and govern their respective sees, to the See of Rome, the See of Peter, because from the very beginning of the Church the bishops of the whole Christian world acknowledged the primacy of the See of Peter, the universal jurisdiction and supreme authority of the successors of Peter, whom Christ Himself commissioned to feed and govern his whole flock. This primacy of jurisdiction was necessary to maintain in unity of faith, a Church destined to spread over and embrace the habitable globe, from ocean to ocean, and from pole to pole. This supreme authority vested in *the* Apostolic See, not by the canons, but by the Lord Jesus Himself in founding His Church, the bishops in every age admitted, and none perhaps more unequivocally than the great Bossuet, whom "Old Catholic" loves to quote. "All," says the eloquent bishop of Meaux, "are subject to the keys of Peter, kings and people, prelates and priests; we own it with joy, for we love unity, and glory in obedience."—(*De unitate ecclesiæ*.)

Communion with the See of Rome, recognition of spiritual supremacy, and primacy of jurisdiction in the See of Peter, were not only the test of orthodoxy, but the proof of legitimacy and the guaranty of Apostolic succession. Now, the Anglican bishops in the time of Henry VIII., Edward VI., and Elizabeth disowned all allegiance in spiritual matters to the Sovereign Pontiffs, revolted against Peter's authority, and renounced his spiritual supremacy, and thus was brought about that change in the religious system under which, says Rev. Mr. Waterworth, in his historical lectures on the Reformation, our forefathers during at least a thousand years lived and died.—(*Lecture* 1, *p.* 29, *et passim*, 1842, *Philad.*) It was Henry's lustful revenge and rapacity that removed the keystone of the arch, the principle of unity, by which under one head appointed by Jesus Christ, there was formed of all the nations and kingdoms of the earth, one Catholic or universal kingdom, believing in one Lord, one faith, one baptism, and one Church.

The historian, Dr. Heylin, in the preface to his "History of the Reformation," acknowledges "that Henry, finding the Pope the greatest obstacle to his desires, divested him by degrees of that supremacy, which had been challenged and enjoyed by his predecessors for some ages past, and finally extinguished his authority in the realm of England." The king's authority was substituted for the Pope's, the king's spiritual supremacy, and not the Pope's, was now invoked, and the king was declared to be the fountain of all jurisdiction, both temporal and spiritual. In the oath of supremacy exacted from all archbishops and bishops in the reign of Elizabeth, the prelates were obliged to swear that their right and mission to preach and to minister were derived from the civil power only, and before consecration the bishop elect was made to "acknowledge and confess that he holds his bishopric as well in *spirituals* as temporals from her alone, and the crown royal." Not from the Apostles, then, to whom it was said "go and teach all nations," etc., but from a vindictive, lustful king, a sickly boy, and a bad woman, do the Anglican bishops derive their commission and jurisdiction, and very correctly does Dr. Milner, whom no one acquainted with the man or his writings would call ignorant, argue that "the acknowledgment of royal ecclesiastical supremacy 'in all spiritual and ecclesiastical things or causes' is decidedly a renunciation of Christ's commission given to His Apostles, and preserved by their successors in the Catholic Apostolic Church.—(*End of Relig. Controversy, p.* 223, *N. Y.*) Hence it clearly appears that there is, and can be, no Apostolical succession of ministry in the established Church.

The line of Apostolical succession in the Church of England was then broken in the reign of Henry VIII., the breach widened under Edward VI., the rupture partially healed under Mary, was re-opened under Elizabeth, when the chain reaching from Augustine and through him from the Apostles (for he was sent and commissioned by Pope Gregory), down to Cardinal Pole, was ruthlessly and hopelessly severed by Parker's intrusion into the See of Canterbury. Parker held his commission, and acknowledged on oath that he held his commission and jurisdiction, his right and authority to preach, teach, and administer sacraments from the crown, from her majesty, and her majesty's pliant Parliament.

III.

COMMUNION WITH THE SEE OF PETER THE TEST OF LEGITIMATE SUCCESSION.

ARBITRARY and tyrannical rulers, aided by servile Parliaments, and an intimidated clergy, dissevered the Church of England from what was known throughout Christendom, East and West, as emphatically and pre-eminently *the* Apostolic See, the See of Rome, the only See to which it is possible to-day for the Christian Church to appeal, to prove with certainty her Apostolical origin, to attest the historic transmission of the Apostolic commission, to vouch for the corporate identity of her bishops with the original witnesses. To this Roman See, centre and source of unity, because vested with supreme authority and universal jurisdiction, and to the unbroken succession of Sovereign Pontiffs, in the same, the primitive Church, the early fathers, saints and doctors ever appealed against unauthorized teachers, innovating heretics, and rebellious schismatics. Whosoever were not united to the chair of Peter, were not regarded as successors of the Apostles; nay, by the fact of their not belonging to that leading succession, they were, as St. Irenæus tells us, to be suspected as heretics and schismatics. A bishop, then, even when rightly ordained or validly consecrated, if he apostatize from the faith, rebel against the recognized authority of the Church, and be cut off from her communion, cannot pretend to any share in the commission which comes down by historical transmission from the Apostles; hence, though Matthew Parker succeeded Warham and Pole in the See of Canterbury, even allowing that he were actually and validly consecrated, he would no more be a successor of the Apostles than Jeff. Davis was a successor of Washington. This Dr. Kenrick thus expresses : " As well might Cromwell be considered one of the Stuart kings of England, or Napoleon Bonaparte one of the Bourbon race, as Matthew Parker, even if validly ordained—be regarded as a link added to the chain of Catholic archbishops of Canterbury, reaching down from St. Augustine to Cardinal Pole, in whom that illustrious series of Pontiffs finally ceased."—(*Anglican Ordinations, p.* 27, *Philad.*, 1841.)

We moreover assert that full communion with the See of Rome was the test of orthodoxy and legitimacy, not only in the primitive Church, but was the test of the orthodoxy and legitimacy of the bishops of England, down to the time of Henry VIII. To the testimony already adduced from Rev. Mr. Waterworth, and Dr. Heylin, in his " History of the Reformation," we will only add the following : Dodd, in his " Church History of England," quotes a remarkable speech which some, says the historian, ascribe to Bishop Fisher. " Whoever the person was, he takes the liberty to say that the cause (the royal supremacy) was of the greatest consequence, that he could wish the king were capable of that power he aimed at ; that it was an attempt directly opposite to the practice of the English nation, in all former ages ; that it was depriving the ecclesiastical body of a spiritual head, much more necessary than in temporal affairs; that no spiritual jursidiction was ever looked upon as valid, without the approbation of the See of Rome ; that the See of Rome was the centre of unity, by whose authority heresy had always been suppressed, and princes reconciled by submitting to her decisions and arbitration; in fine, Rome was a kind of court of chancery to all nations that professed Christianity; and those that were divided from her, would be like branches cut off from the tree of life."—(*Dodd's Church Hist., v.* 1, *p.* 242.)

Please to mark well the words that the "*attempt of Henry was directly opposite to the practice of the English nation in all former ages ; that no spiritual jursidiction was looked upon as valid without approbation of the See of Rome, and that those divided from Rome would be like branches cut off from the tree of life.*"

This certainly does not tally with what the claimant of Anglican succession asserts on this subject : "*Henry's supremacy was based on ancient rights of the crown which he merely re-assumed ;*" and, "*gradually by unlawful encroachment the Papacy was formed in Western Europe, and so, gradually, its usurpation extended to England.*" And again : "Queen Mary, the bloody, created the Roman hierarchy by law, while Henry VIII. never did anything of the kind; but merely continued the Church as he found it," and "to suppose that Elizabeth established the Church of England in any sense other than that in which it was the law of the land under the Plantagenets and the Papacy, is a very ignorant mistake," etc., etc. We must remark that in refuting these assertions, made with all the recklessness, effrontery, and disregard to historic truth, usual with certain parties, we do little more than condense and summarize the facts of history touching this matter, admirably brought together by the learned Cardinal Wiseman, whom, no doubt, these gentlemen would write down an ignoramus, who has either never investigated the matter, or is incompetent to form an opinion.

Venerable Bede informs us that Pope Eleutherius sent over missionaries to the Britons, and converted them. And when the Pelagian heresy had infested the Island, Pope Celestine sent St. Germanus to correct and purify it. A Pope then, not a king, commissioned the missionaries and bishops of the early British Church. Again, that slaves might become sons, that Angli might be made Angeli, Pope St. Gregory sent Augustine from his monastery on the Cælian hill, who reconverted the Island under the Anglo-Saxons, and established the legitimate succession of the Episcopacy, which continued until the *encroachments* and *usurpations* of spiritual supremacy by Henry, and his worthy daughter Elizabeth. Is it with a design to mislead, that we are told, " When the Patriarch Gregory, Bishop of Rome," (though the same writer says, it was impossible for the Pope to assert even a patriarchal authority over England) sent Augustine to convert the Saxons, the missionary found there an existing British Church dating from the Apostolic times." He might as well have added from the Venerable Bede, to whom he refers, that it was, as we said above, a Pope of Rome who gave authority, mission and jurisdiction to the bishops of the British Church. Again we are told, " Augustine was consecrated first archbishop of Canterbury by Gallican bishops."

Dr. Newman even before his conversion says in one

of his essays, " Disingenuousness is a characteristic of heresy." It evidently is a marked feature of some controversialists. By the Pope's authority, Augustine, a priest and monk, with his monk companions, goes to evangelize the Saxons; by command of the same Pope Gregory, Augustine was consecrated a bishop by Virgilius, the primate of Arles, but Virgilius had no authority to send him to England, he could give him no jurisdiction over that island. Virgilius could only do what every validly ordained bishop can do to-day, confer the episcopal powers of order, but not of jurisdiction ; only the Pope could assign a mission, impart jurisdiction or authority to exercise those powers, within a given territory. To Virgilius himself the same Pope had granted the *pallium*, the badge of the archiepiscopal dignity, giving him authority over all the bishops of Gaul. " Because," says St. Gregory, " it is plain to all whence the holy faith came forth in the regions of Gaul; when your Fraternity asks afresh for the ancient custom of the *Apostolic* See, what does it, but as a good child recur to the bosom of its mother? And so we grant your Fraternity to represent us, in the churches which are in the kingdom of our most excellent son Childebert, according to ancient custom, which has God for its author."—(*L. V. Epis.* 53, *Op. S. Greg.*) But Gregory, not Virgilius, constituted Augustine archbishop of London, sending him the *pallium*, authorizing him to consecrate twelve suffragans.

The see was afterwards by the authority of the Pope transferred from London to Canterbury. By the direction of the Pope, the archbishop of York was to be subject to Augustine during his lifetime, and afterwards the two metropolitans were to be independent, and have precedence according to seniority of consecration. Afterwards Pope Honorius I. sends the pallium to the two archbishops with special powers to either, to name the other's successor, "*in virtue of the authority of the Holy See*, in consideration of the great distance which separates England from Rome."—(*See Wiseman's Essays, pp.* 184-5-6, *vol.* iii., *N.Y.*, 1873.)

Pope Adrian created the bishop of Lichfield a primate, subjecting to him many of the suffragans of Canterbury. Pope Leo III. rescinded his predecessor's decree, and restored to Canterbury its former suffragans. Long and heated were the contests for superiority, between Canterbury and York, and to the Pope the rival claimants appeal, to determine the disputed prerogatives, and their alternate triumphs were due to decisions of the Pope in favor of one or the other. St. Bernard tells us in his life of St. Malachi, archbishop of Armagh, that he (St. Malachi) undertook a journey to Rome to obtain the pallium for himself, and for a new archiepiscopal see, the erection whereof he desired to have confirmed by the Holy See. From all this it is plain that the Holy See did from the beginning order the hierarchy of the Church of England, transfer, divide, and otherwise vary the jurisdiction of metropolitans. Among other examples occurring, after Augustine and his immediate successors appointed in virtue of authority from the *Apostolic* See, Venerable Bede informs us that Wigard was sent to Rome by Egbert, king of Kent, and Oswi of Northumbria, to be consecrated by Pope Vitalianus, and the reason given by the two monarchs for wishing to have the archbishop consecrated at Rome was—"*Quia Romana esset Catholica et Apostolica ecclesia.*" Because the Roman was *the*

Catholic and *Apostolic Church*. Although the clergy complained and grew sometimes restive on account of papal provisions, whereby the court of Rome filled vacant benefices with strangers; until the time of Henry VIII., we never read of any denial of the Pope's authority to confirm archbishops, or of his jurisdiction over them; he had ever a legate in England who took precedence and passed judgment in their causes, and until the time of Henry VIII., the privileges and rights of the Holy See were never impugned or disputed, recent declarations to the contrary notwithstanding.

The conclusion so pertinent to our argument, which tne eminent and learned Cardinal Wiseman logically forces from the mouth of Anglicans fond of appealing to ancient canons and customs and privileges of patriarchal sees, is—" That the bishops now existing in England, even supposing the validity of their orders, were instituted and appointed, the Bishop of Rome not only not consentient, but repugnant thereto, and vehemently condemning the same as an infringement of his immemorial rights, secured to him by canons and customs *become ancient*, though they hold authority by law, have not, and never have had, since the Reformation, any ecclesiastical, hierarchical or Apostolical succession, authority or jurisdiction whatever, in matters religious or spiritual; that they are not the inheritors or successors of those who held the sees until that time; that, consequently, they are in the eyes of the Church Catholic, intruders, usurpers and illegitimate holders of the same."—(*Ibid, p.* 188.) The above will be a sufficient answer to the extravagant assertion, that the supremacy of Henry was nothing novel, but based on the ancient rights of the crown, and that the Church of England was never a Roman Catholic Church. Let us hear what the Church of England herself has to say on this point. In the year 1534 (26 *Henry VIII., c. 1.*) Parliament, under orders from a despotic king, declared that the Bishop of Rome had no jursidiction over the Church of England, and that the king was rightfully her supreme head. In the year 1536 the Church of England, in convocation at York, declared: " We think the king's highness, nor any temporal man may not be the head of the Church by the laws of God, * * * and we think by the law of the Church, general councils, interpretations of approved doctors, and consent of Christian people, *the Pope of Rome hath been taken for the head of the Church and Vicar of Christ, and so ought to be taken."—* (*Strype's Mem., quoted by Dr. Ives, p.* 93.) Again, in the first year of Elizabeth's reign both houses of convocation, and the two Universities, declared it to be the faith of the Church of England : " That the supreme power of feeding and governing the militant Church of Christ and confirming their brethren is given to Peter, the Apostle, and his lawful successors in the See Apostolic, as unto the vicars of Christ."—(*Waterworth Hist. Lect., p.* 308, *Dodd's Church Hist.,* App. *No.* XXXIX., *p.* 261.)

Our readers may perhaps like to hear what Henry himself says on this subject, in his defence of the Sacraments against Martin Luther : " Luther cannot deny but that all the faithful Christian Churches, at this day, do acknowledge and reverence the holy See of Rome as their mother and primate. * * * And if this acknowledgment is grounded neither on divine nor human right, how hath it taken so great and general root? how was it admitted so universally by all Christendom? how began it? how came it to be so great? yea, and the Greek Church also, though the empire was passed to that part, we shall find that she acknowledged the primacy of the same Roman Church. * * * Whereas Luther so impudently doth affirm that the Pope hath his primacy by no right, neither divine nor human, but only by force and tyranny, I do wonder how the mad fellow could hope to find his readers so simple, or blockish, as to believe that the Bishop of Rome, being a priest, unarmed, alone, without temporal force, or right, either divine or human (as he supposed), should be able to get authority over so many bishops his equals throughout so many different nations. * * * Or that so many people, cities, kingdoms, commonwealths, provinces and nations would be so prodigal of their own liberty, as to subject themselves to a foreign priest (as now so many ages they have done), or to give him such authority over themselves, if he had no right thereunto at all." (*Henry VIII., Def. Sac. contra Lutherum, Dodd's Ch. Hist. p.* 239.) Perhaps, too, it might be interesting to recall what Dr. Lingard says in regard to this assumption by Henry of spiritual supremacy. "Henry had now obtained the great object of his ambition. His supremacy in religious matters had been established by act of Parliament. * * * Still the extent of his ecclesiastical pretensions remained subject to doubt and dissension. That he intended to exclude the authority hitherto exercised by the Pontiffs, was sufficiently evident. * * * Henry himself did not clearly explain, perhaps he knew not how to explain, his own sentiments. If, on the one hand, he was willing to push his ecclesiastical prerogative to its utmost limits, on the other he was checked by the contrary tendency of those principles, which he had published and maintained in his treatise against Luther."—(*Hist. Eng. v. vi.*, p. 176, *Philad.*, 1827). But he did push this pretended prerogative of the crown to extreme limits, when he made Cromwell his vicar-general, allowed him precedence as such before all the lords spiritual and temporal not only made him sit in Parliament before the archbishop of Canterbury, but made him supersede that prelate in the presidency of the convocation. The degradation of the bishops was, however, not yet deep enough. It was resolved to extort from them a practical acknowledgement that they derived no authority from Christ, but were merely the occasional delegates of the crown. He suspended the powers of all the Ordinaries of the realm, and by making them petition for the restoration of the same, made them acknowledge the crown to be the real fountain of spiritual jurisdiction. When they submitted with abject servility, and petitioned for the restoration of their suspended powers, a commission was issued to each bishop separately, authorizing him during the king's pleasure, and as the king's deputy, to ordain, etc. The same assumption and arbitrary exercise of the prerogative of the crown, and spiritual supremacy were continued under Edward and Elizabeth, with this difference, that under Henry the bishops, brow-beaten, intimidated and demoralized, yielded, with the exception of the heroic bishop of Rochester, and thus in some sense appeared to lend the sanction of the Church to Henry's tyrannical usurpations, whereas under Elizabeth they atoned for their pusillanimity and cowardice, redeemed the honor of the episcopacy, and, with the solitary exception of Kitchen of Llandaff, spurned the oath of supremacy, and without even one exception they refused to be made the tools of the royal popess by conferring a fraudulent, illegitimate consecration on her appointees.

All this we have detailed so lengthily to show that in the Church of England (and the same may be shown of every Church in Christendom), from her earliest establishment, and especially since the introduction of Christianity among the Saxons by St. Augustine, down through every age, even to the time of Henry and Elizabeth, the supremacy of the Pope in things spiritual was acknowledged. The Pope exercised jurisdiction over the island, and the bishops, archbishops and primates, down to Parker's illegitimate intrusion by the civil power, held their commissions from the Apostolic See, and thus were linked on to the unbroken Apostolic chain, the legitimate succession of their bishops thus coming down from the Apostles.

How clearly and conclusively is this shown by Archbishop Heath of York, in the eloquent and forcible speech, which he delivered in the House of Lords, against the spiritual supremacy of the crown in the year 1559. His able speech may be found in full in "Dodd's Church History of England;" (*App. XXXV. p.* 247) from which we quote the following extracts:

" By relinquishing and forsaking the Church or See of Rome, we must forsake and fly, first, from all general councils; secondly, from all canonical and ecclesiastical laws of the Church of Christ; thirdly, from the judgment of all other Christian princes; fourthly, and lastly, we must forsake and fly from the holy unity of Christ's Church. * * * First, touching the general councils, I shall name unto you these four: the Nicene Council, the Constantinopolitan Council, the Ephesine, and the Chalcedon. * * * At the Nicene Council, the first of the four, the bishops did write their epistle to Sylvester, then Bishop of Rome, that their decrees then made, might be confirmed by his authority. At the council kept at Constantinople, all the bishops there were obedient to Damasus, then Bishop of Rome. * * * At the Ephesine Council, Nestorius, the heretic, was condemned by Celestine, the Bishop of Rome, he being chief judge there. At the Chalcedon Council, all the bishops there assembled, did write their humble submission unto Leo, then Bishop of Rome; wherein they did acknowledge him there, to be their chief head, six hundred and thirty bishops of them. Therefore to deny the See Apostolic and its authority, were to contemn and set at naught, the authority and decrees of these noble councils. * * * Fourthly, and lastly, we must (by forsaking the See of Rome) forsake and fly from the holy unity of Christ's Church, seeing that St. Cyprian, that holy martyr and great clerk, doth say that the unity of the Church of Christ doth depend upon Peter's authority, and his successors'. * * * And by this our forsaking and flying from the unity of the Church of Rome, this inconveniency, among many, must consequently follow: that either we must grant the Church of Rome to be the true Church of God, or else a malignant Church. If you answer that it is a true Church of God, where Jesus Christ is truly taught and his sacraments rightly administered, how can we disburthen ourselves of our forsaking and flying from that Church, which we do acknowledge to be of God? If you answer that the Church of Rome is not of God, but a malignant Church, then it will follow that we, the inhabitants of this realm, have not as yet received any benefit of Christ; seeing we have received no gospel, or other doctrine, nor no other sacraments, but what was sent to us from the Church of Rome,— first, in King Lucius, his days, at whose humble epistle, the holy martyr Eleutherius, then Bishop of Rome, did send into this realm two holy monks, Fugatius and Damianus, by whose doctrine and preaching we were first brought to the knowledge of the faith of Jesus Christ, of his holy gospel and his most holy sacraments; then, secondly, holy St. Gregory, being Bishop of Rome, did send into this realm two other holy monks, St. Augustine, called the Apostle of England, and Meletius, to preach the self-same faith planted here, in this realm in the days of King Lucius; thirdly, and last of all, Paul III., (*Julius III. is doubtless meant*) being Bishop of Rome, did send hither the Lord Cardinal Pole, his grace (by birth a nobleman of this land), his legate to restore us unto the same faith, which the martyr, St. Eleutherius, and St. Gregory, had planted here many years before. If, therefore, the Church of Rome be not of God, but a false and malignant Church, then have we been deceived all this while; seeing the gospel, the doctrine, the faith and the sacraments must be of the same nature as that Church is from whence it and they came."

This disposes of the ludicrous assertion, made with so much apparent self-complacency and assurance, that: "The first archbishop of Canterbury was consecrated at Arles, in France (597) and thus introduced the Ephesine succession from St. John, through Irenæus and Photinus." This assertion is moreover too childish for any one who pretends to know anything about primitive Christianity. Must we teach again the first elements of Christian Doctrine, the first principles of Church organization, and government? must we repeat the plain distinction between orders and mission? must we go about proving what has already been acknowledged, what the Episcopal Church teaches and acts upon, viz.: that something more than a valid consecration is necessary to confer jurisdiction, a share in the commission and apostolate instituted by Christ to evangelize the nations and convert the world? Arles could consecrate, only Rome could send Augustine with Apostolic authority to England, to preach the faith and transmit Apostolic succession to the English hierarchy.

IV.

PROTESTANT EPISCOPAL AND ANGLICAN SUCCESSION REPUDIATED.

WE cannot, perhaps, offer anything on the subject of the pretended legitimacy, jurisdiction, and consequently Apostolic succession of the Protestant Episcopal prelates of the United States, more conclusive and clear than the earnest words of the lamented and estimable Dr. Ives, late bishop of the Protestant Episcopal Church in North Carolina: " The real character of the Episcopal authority and mission of the Protestant Episcopal Church in America must depend upon the character of the source from which they are derived.

" So that any defect which the Mother Church of England may have inherited from the system of Elizabeth, seemed to me clearly entailed upon the daughter in the United States.

" Now then, I entreat my old friends to allow me to call to their minds that view of the mission and jurisdiction of the English Church, as established by Elizabeth, which destroyed my confidence in her claim to my submission. I asked myself—not as a Catholic, not as a controversialist—but as one deeply anxious to know the *will of God*, and to know, if possible, that that will would sustain me in my *Protestant position*— I asked myself, who sent Archbishop Parker? 'For how can he preach except he be sent?' Who put the

Gospel into his hand? told him what it contained? what was the *depositum* of faith and sacraments and worship of the 'one, holy, Catholic Church' committed to him, and commissioned him to teach that faith, dispense those sacraments, and conduct that worship, and, when death should come to terminate his Apostolic work, to hand on that '*depositum*' to the successors of the Apostles yet to arise? I made this appeal to my conscience again and again. 'Who thus sent the first archbishop of Elizabeth, gave him his *mission* to act in *this* or *that* way for God?'

" When Elizabeth ascended the throne, I saw two powers only, who even claimed the right of spiritual jurisdiction of England, and thence the right of giving *mission* to exercise 'the office of a bishop in the Church of God!' the Pope and the queen! The Pope sustained in his authority by the *whole Church* in England; the queen sustained by her *Parliament only*. *The Church*, therefore, in England, could not have commissioned and sent this archbishop. *She* was utterly against him. Against him in her faith, her sacraments, her worship, her judgment, her authority! she stood forth, with the successor of St. Peter at her head, professing the Catholic faith, dispensing the Catholic sacraments, and enforcing the Catholic ritual, and requiring all who went out under her authority to defend this faith, guard these sacraments, and observe this ritual! The archbishop of Elizabeth appears, in defiance of the successor of St. Peter, professedly bearing another faith, other sacraments, and commissioned under another ritual! Who *sent* him? Whence derived he the authority to execute the office of a bishop in the mystical body of Christ—the one, holy, and Apostolic

Church. Really, I could discern no authority earlier than the queen and Parliament of England! And, therefore, that *my own* commission to act for Christ had its origin in *man!*"—(*Trials of Mind, pp.* 156–7.)

Convinced by such conclusive and unanswerable arguments, drawn from a profound and conscientious study of the whole question in all its aspects and bearings, with the pages of Church history lying open before them, and the doctrine and canons and usages of the early Christian Church thoroughly sifted and scrutinized, many of the purest, most gifted and scholarly minds in the Anglican establishment in England, and the Episcopal Church in America have not only doubted the Anglican succession, but finding it to be a myth, have laid down their lucrative livings, to enter the Catholic Church as simple laymen, and received orders in the Church from bishops possessing Apostolic succession, or else, like Dr. Ives, have lived and died in the ranks of the laity, in the midst of the world, shining out as bright exemplars of heroic Christian virtue. Such in England are the Mannings, the Newmans, the Wilberforces, the Fabers, the Allies, and many others; those in our own country we will forbear to mention; they are too well known, men whose massive intellectual build, comprehensive, cultivated minds, logical acumen, vast and varied learning overshadow and completely dwarf, in our opinion, at least, those who have the hardihood to assert *that no one competent to form an opinion, and who has taken the pains to investigate the matter, has ever professed a doubt concerning the Anglican succession,* and *that it is more demonstrably canonical and regular in all particulars than any other succession in Christendom.*

No one has doubted the Anglican succession!! The whole Catholic Church doubts it, or rather positively denies it, the Greek Church disowns it, the Protestant world ridicules the pretension, the whole of Christendom outside the Anglican and American Episcopal Church denies and rejects the unwarrantable claim. Yet outside of that comparatively small communion there must be some thoughtful men, *competent to form an opinion.* Nay, on this point, as well as every other fundamental Christian tenet, there is division, even in the little body of the Anglican Church herself, and I am sure I need not reiterate that in the Protestant Episcopal Church in America, many not only doubt it, but scout the very notion. An Anglican bishop, not many years ago, preaching on a solemn public occasion in St. Paul's Cathedral, London, denied it in strongest language, and the only reprimand he received was, that he was not asked to print his sermon! Where were the Apostolic witnesses of the faith? were they all sleeping sentinels on the watch towers of Sion? no one to give the alarm? no one to protest? If Apostolical succession can be thus publicly denied by a bishop of the Church of England, are we not justified in placing credence in what a learned English writer, a convert to the Catholic faith, author—among other genial productions—of " My Clerical Friends," (which we would advise our Episcopal readers to peruse thoughtfully) says : " The mass of our countrymen have so little esteem for the doctrines of the Christian priesthood and the Apostolical succession that they can hardly be persuaded to treat them seriously." The same thoughtful writer, who certainly has thoroughly studied and dispassionately investigated the matter, though perhaps some would declare him incompetent to form an opinion, again says: "The modern English assertors of Apostolical succession know that the men who formed the Church of England and composed both its ritual and its theology, detested the very doctrines which *they* have learned to approve, and would have destroyed even that semblance of a hierarchy which they have preserved, if the Tudor sovereigns would have suffered them to do so." Nay, even Hooker, so often quoted as authority, did actually teach that, *it was quite possible to do without bishops;* that *there may be sometimes very just and sufficient reason to allow ordination made without a bishop*, when, forsooth, *the exigence of necessity doth constrain to leave the usual ways of the Church*, or *when the Church must needs have some ordained, and neither hath, nor can have a bishop to ordain*. The terse and well-informed English writer above referred to says of Hooker, "No one knew better than he that the first link in the Anglican hierarchy was forged, not by an Apostle or Patriarch, but by the masculine hand of Elizabeth Tudor, and therefore too prudent to expose the new hierarchy to a strain which it could not bear, he thought it good policy to say, 'We are not simply without exception to urge a lineal descent from the Apostles by continued succession of bishops in every effectual ordination.' In life he had denied the Apostolical succession whenever the 'exigence of neccessity' made it superfluous, in death he uttered a still more energetic protest against it, without any necessity at all, by sending for, not an Anglican minister, but Saravia, who had never received or pretended to receive Episcopal ordination."—(*My Clerical Friends, p.* 25, *N. Y.* 1873.) Not only then Cranmer and Barlow, but even the favorite Hooker ("wise in his generation and rightly styled by posterity, the *judicious* Hooker") thought lightly of Apostolical succession in the Anglican Church, which, nevertheless, we are told was never doubted by any one capable of forming an opinion, and rests on the same evidence as the Scripture itself. But the reason given as an apology for the low views of these Reformers concerning the episcopate is too amusing: " How could they have known better while they were under the Papacy. Popes had taught them that bishops were only presbyters, in order to magnify themselves as the only and universal bishops." This we pronounce a positive and unqualified falsehood, but granting that, "such was the common teaching of school divines before the Reformation," how does it help the Anglican's case?

Anglicans themselves admit that a church in schism forfeits all right to the lawful exercise of hierarchical powers or jurisdiction; that bishops of a schismatical communion could not lawfully, though they might validly, exercise ecclesiastical functions; could not be admitted to a voice in a general council, or communicate with other bishops, until they retract their errors or schismatical principles, and then when returning to the unity of the Church, they should be formally recognized by ecclesiastical authority and reinstated in their sees, or removed to others, or else remain suspended. Anglicans themselves admit that Apostolical succession cannot exist outside the true Church of God, and St. Augustine most positively declares that even those who maintained the integrity of faith, but fell from unity, were outside the pale of the Church. "You are with us," he says, "in baptism, in the creed, in the other sacraments of the Lord, but in the spirit of unity, in the bond of peace—in fine in the Catholic Church itself—you are not with us."—(*Ad Vincent Rogat. Ep. xciii. ch. XLVIII., Wiseman's Essays, p.* 202.) But like the Donatists and early heretics, Anglicans and Episcopalians justify their separation from the Church, their breach of unity, by urging the corruptions of the Church, the usurpations of the papacy. " England, in rejecting a usurping papacy fell back on her ancient Catholic rights, and began to renew and to regain, as her old law, all her primitive relations with all the Apostolic Sees." But they forget that one of the pleas for setting up a new establishment was that " all the Apostolic Sees had erred in faith." " England," we are told, " is not in communion with Pius IX., for his new dogma rends him from communion with all his own predecessors and with all antiquity." But at her very setting out in life, the Church of England had solemnly declared that for upwards of eight hundred years the whole Church was sunk in damnable idolatry.

We may paraphrase the answer given to a similar charge of the Donatists by the early doctors, thus: Either the Church was so corrupted as to be no longer the Church of Christ, or it was not; if it was, then the promises of Christ had failed, and His Church had ceased, the gates of hell had prevailed, He was no longer with His Church, the Spirit of Truth, the Holy Ghost, no longer dwelt with her; there is then no succession, no historical transmission of powers from the Apostles. But if the Church was still the Church of Christ, if Christ's promises did not fail, and if His plighted word was made good, that He should be with those, whom He sent, to the end of ages, then those who went out from her on pretence that she had erred and had become corrupt, and that the corruptions of the Church rendered it impossible for them to remain in communion with her, simply condemn themselves, and render their claim to succession from the Apostles preposterous in the extreme. If their charge of apostacy and idolatry be true, how are they going to make connection with the pure primitive Church? how overleap that fearful chasm of upwards of eight hundred years of abominable corruptions, idolatry, heresy and crime? how stretch the chain of succession across that foul and reeking abyss? Why Pius IX. has by one new error "rent his communion with all antiquity, and Bishop Ryan, by the errors of his Church since the Vatican Council, or even since the Council of Trent, has lost all right to the name of Catholic, all claims to Apostolical succession, how then could the Anglican Church, after eight hundred years of such dreadful crimes and errors in even every Apostolic See, have been able to recover and transmit legitimate descent down to the reformers?

This, says our spicy English writer, is "as if a man should contend proudly for a pedigree derived through countless generations of felons. What? call the whole Catholic priesthood the spawn of Antichrist, and then attempt to prove that your orders are manifestly divine because you can trace them to that source; revile the whole Catholic Church as 'the harlot of Babylon,' as twenty generations of Anglican bishops and clergy did, and then claim her as your mother; separate from the Catholic Church on the ground that she was 'Antichristian,' and claim to be the legitimate descendants of Antichrist?"

But if the Church did not thus err, apostatize, adulterate the pure truths of Christianity, and become antichristian, which most certainly she did not, for to assert that she did, in the face of Christ's own plighted word, "that the gates of hell should not prevail against her," "that He himself would be with her all days," "that the Holy Spirit should abide with her forever and teach her all truth," is blasphemous impiety : then the Reformers broke off from the Church of Christ, severed the bonds of unity, and as schismatics and heretics the reformed bishops never had, as we said before, with Cardinal Wiseman, "any ecclesiastical, hierarchical or Apostolical succession, authority, or jurisdiction whatever, and are in the eyes of the Church illegitimate intruders and usurpers."

V.

WAS MATTHEW PARKER CONSECRATED?

IF Parker was not validly consecrated, the chain of Apostolical succession in the Anglican Church, and, in consequence, in the Episcopal Church of America, is broken, the very first link is wanting, for as Waterworth remarks, "The episcopal sees, and, eventually, the cures throughout England, were supplied by men ordained and consecrated by Parker, and if Parker were not a consecrated bishop, then neither were the Anglican clergy and prelacy episcopally ordained nor consecrated."--(*Hist. Lect., p.* 329.) To realize more fully how the whole episcopate of the Anglican Church hangs on the validity of Parker's consecration, and how true it is that he is the connecting link between the old and new hierarchy of England, we must remember that at the time of Parker's real or supposed consecration, December 17th, 1559, there was but one lawful titular bishop throughout the realm ; every see but one, that of Llandaff, was vacant. —(*Heylin, p.* 114.) Dr. Heylin, a Protestant historian, informs us that there were no more than fifteen living of that sacred order, and that they all, but Kitchen of Llandaff, whom another Protestant historian calls the calamity of his see, refused the oath of supremacy, and were, in consequence, deprived of their sees. There were twenty-six sees within the realm; two of them were archbishoprics. Of these, one archbishopric, that of Canterbury, and nine episcopal sees were vacant by death ; the other archbishop and bishops, Dr. Heylin says, " being called in the beginning of July, 1559, by certain of the lords of the council commissionated thereunto in due form of law, were then and there required to take the oath of supremacy according to the law made in that behalf. Kitchen of Llandaff alone takes it. * * * By all the rest it was refused." After giving the names of every Catholic prelate in the realm who refused, they were not, he says, all *deprived* until the end of September. "But now," he continues, " they had hardened one another to a resolution of standing out unto the last, and were thereupon deprived of their several bishoprics, as the law required. A punishment which came not on them all at once, some of them being borne withal (in hope of their conformity and submission) till the end of September."—(*Heylin, Ref. p.* 114, (1661, *London*) *quoted by Waterwarth, note p.* 330.) "The civil power," says Waterworth, " armed with the oath of supremacy, had destroyed the hierarchy of the Church. The Parliament had thrown down, but how was it to build up? Was the queen or the government to use the same authority which had unbishoped the Church, to create a hierarchy?"—(*Hist. Lect., p.* 331.)

This scrap of English history lets in a world of light on the cradle of the Anglican establishment, and shows that its legal title, " the Church of England by law and Parliament established," *belies the claim to Apostolical origin, stamps it as a royal foundation*, and shows, moreover, how ridiculous and absurd the pretence, that at the Reformation a return was made to ancient rules, and that the Church of England only fell back on her ancient rights. "Let those who pretend such reverence for ancient canons show,"—as Cardinal Wiseman replies to the assertion, that: *On the accession of*

Queen Elizabeth, the true successors of the Apostles in the English Church were reinstated in their rights, "the canons whereby the deprivation of bishops, and the appointment of new ones by letters missive, are granted to the civil rulers. If they allow the authority of Elizabeth to act as she did, then let them be consistent and admit that of Mary to act similarly; and moreover, let them give us their warrant for such authority, in the ancient Church to which they appeal. If they consider it to have been usurpation in Elizabeth, ' of the iron hand and of the iron maw,' as some of them have called her, then is their entire hierarchy based upon an unjustifiable and tyrannical act of power, and they who compose it are intruders."—(*Essays, v. iii. p.* 192.) Who deposed, the same learned cardinal asks, these sixteen bishops, that then formed the hierarchy of the English Church? who reinstated the others? and who were reinstated? We will await a reply to these queries, and in the meantime, we beg to call the attention of that *impartial secular authority* who thinks "that there is a perfect legal and historical identity, so to speak, of person, between the Church of England before the Reformation, and the Church of England after the Reformation," to the historical fact that in the beginning of the month of December, 1559, the Church of England had but one lawful, canonically instituted bishop, and he died in 1563, without attempting to canonically fill the vacant sees or provide for the transmission of the episcopal order, or the legitimate succession of any corporate witness to the identity of the faith and Church of England, nay, absolutely refusing to lend himself to every attempt to keep up such identity and transmit such episcopal succession. "The supremacy of the Pope had been rejected; in the queen had been invested the supreme government of the Church." We quote again Rev. Mr. Waterworth: "Every bond between the crown and the hierarchy, had been broken. England is without a hierarchy, and even if the chain of episcopal succession could be preserved unbroken, what hand could unite the severed link of episcopal jurisdiction? But something must be done; it was an emergency in which ordinary difficulties, if they could not be removed, must be beaten down or passed over; and though the more observing and learned might note the flaw in the episcopal blazonry, the glitter of that dignity, and the actual possession of sees, to which authority had for centuries been attached, would no doubt conceal the defect from the eyes of the multitude."—(*Hist. Lect.*, *p.* 334.)

Parker was elected to fill the vacant see of Canterbury, August 1st, 1559, but who was to consecrate him? The bishops of the realm were obstinate. They were not to be brow-beaten or intimidated; the oath of supremacy had been tendered and refused, the English episcopate had retrieved its honor, redeemed itself from the degrading cowardice and mean servility shown in Henry's reign; many had already been deposed, and sent to the Fleet. Some, as Heylin notes, "were borne withal in hope of their conformity and submission until the end of September." It was all important to the Reformers to have Parker consecrated by some Catholic prelates in order to maintain a semblance at least of episcopal succession and identity with the old Church. The severity exercised towards some would, it was hoped, have its influence on the others, and make them more pliant and submissive to the queen's commands. A commission was consequently issued on the 9th of September to Tonstall of Durham, Bourne of Bath and Wells, Pole of Peterborough, and Kitchen of Llandaff, and to these were joined Barlow and Scorey, returned refugees, legally deprived under the previous reign, who not being then elected to any see were simply styled bishops.—(*Vide note, p.* 329, *Hist. Lect.*) This commission failed; doubtless because the Catholic bishops refused to become *participes criminis* by assisting to consecrate Parker. Mackintosh, in his "History of England," says: "These prelates, who must have considered such an act a profanation, conscientiously refused." (*Hist. of Engl.*, iii., *p.* 16.) Canon Estcourt remarks, "It is difficult now to understand how any one could expect that a commission would be executed which bore so gross an insult on the face of it. Not merely to require them to consecrate a married priest, notoriously suspected of heresy, but to join with them two suspended, excommunicated ecclesiastics, calling themselves bishops, relapsed heretics, and apostate religious, was sufficient of itself to prevent the execution of the mandate."—(*The Question of Anglican Ordinations, E. C. Estcourt, M. A., F. S. A., p.* 85, 1873, *London.*) Shortly after, and most probably in consequence or in punishment of this refusal, Tonstall, Bourne and Pole were *deprived*, leaving as we before mentioned, only one see in the whole realm, with a legitimate incumbent, one legal titular bishop in the whole English Church, Kitchen of Llandaff, and he presumably, because, it was hoped, as he had owned the queen's supremacy, he would yet yield obedience to her commands and consecrate her newly appointed archbishop. This brief chapter in the history of the Anglican establishment we deem important, as showing the straits to which the queen and Parliament were reduced to secure a legitimate episcopate in the nascent royal establishment, and how long and painfully Elizabeth and her ministers travailed in giving birth to the new hierarchy. It may also help us to understand the importance attached to the question of fact, and that of the legitimacy and validity of the consecration of the first-born of the new Church, the first link in a new line of prelates, the parent stock to which the clergy of the Anglican and Episcopal Churches must trace their pedigree, and from which alone they can prove their legitimacy, their mission, or orders. One attempt to get a lawful bishop for the Reformed Church, to weld on to the old, venerable chain of Apostolical succession, in the see of Canterbury, this new link forged by the masculine hand of a Tudor queen, to engraft this suckling scion of royalty on the original Catholic stock, from which alone it could draw sap, vitality, fecundity, failed, proved an utter abortion. Whether the next attempt succeeded better we will examine presently.

We come now to the facts regarding Parker's consecration and the validity of the act, but we wish it distinctly understood that this is a secondary question, as far as the Catholic Church and her doctrine are concerned, for on the principles on which the primitive Church has always acted, and which are so clearly and distinctly enunciated by her in the early and Apostolic ages and which are in fact recognized by Anglicans and acted on by all religious denominations, the Anglican Church, and therefore the Episcopal Church of America, have, and can have, no connecting link with the Apostolic Church, no Apostolic succession. This being the case, we need go no further, to disprove the claim of Anglican succession. But we are willing to go further, and absolutely deny the validity of Parker's consecration, and thus, "strike at the very root of all pretensions in the Anglican and Protestant Episcopal Church of America to Apostolical succession." Premising again, what we have already said, that the validity of consecration and the Apostolical succession of the Anglican bishops are quite different questions, we will now carefully and dispassionately examine and discuss the vexed question of the validity of Parker's consecration, a question of vital importance to Anglican orders, a question of life or death to the Episcopate of the Protestant Episcopal Church of America. For though Catholics may refute and disprove Anglican and Episcopalian pretensions to Apostolical succession, even conceding valid consecration of their bishops, the case of the latter is hopeless, their position untenable unless they can prove to a demonstration, and show beyond the shadow of reasonable doubt, that the first Anglican bishops under Elizabeth were actually and validly consecrated.

All the Catholic bishops, as we have seen, refused to participate in the sacrilege, refused to lay hands on the would-be prelate; and now in the whole realm there is but one bishop with jurisdiction, but one bishop holding a see, and him, Camden styles the calamity of his see. Surely, then, the succession is in imminent peril; this is a critical juncture for the royal establishment of the English Church. How was the crisis got over? We are naturally a little curious on this subject, and we can well imagine the state of suspense and anxiety of those whose whole religious system, orders, mission, prelacy and priesthood hang in the balance, depend on the satisfactory solution of the question: Was Parker validly consecrated? For Anglicanism and Episcopalianism, the issue is life or death. Our strenuous advocate of Anglican succession concedes as much, for although he demurs somewhat to the assertion that if Parker was not consecrated, and validly consecrated, the Anglican succession fails, yet he is willing to let it be assumed, "for if Parker was not duly consecrated, it is certain no bishop in Christendom can prove his orders." This is a strange proposition. What does it mean? surely all the bishops in Christendom do not derive their orders from Parker. All the Anglican and Protestant Episcopal prelates do, and it may most truly be said, that if Parker was not validly consecrated, it is certain no bishop in the Anglican Church or Episcopal Church can prove his orders, or rather, that there is no such thing as a bishop in these denominations. This we assert, notwithstanding the puerile claim made by some Anglican writers, that the apostate De Dominis, or a pretended Irish archbishop assisting at a consecration of some Anglican bishop in the 17th century would suffice to restore the broken line of succession in the Anglican Church. Can they really be serious in making such assertions, or is it not trifling with the intelligence and conscience of those who look up to them for instruction in Christian faith and Church organism? If in the 17th century there were no validly ordained priests in the Anglican church, how could bishops be consecrated or succession communicated? But there could be no such priests if there were no genuine bishops prior to these pretended consecrations. Does it not seem puerile trifling to assert that "the pope sent Archbishop Bedini to America to remedy the first defective succession?" and again, "the succession communicated to us, in two instances, by De

Dominis, archbishop of Spalatro in Dalmatia, in the seventeenth century, transmits of itself, a better and more valid sucession than the Nuncio Bedini conferred on Dr. Bayley, the present Roman Catholic metropolitan." To Catholics this is simply ludicrous. In the year 1853, three new sees were regularly and canonically erected in the province of New York, viz. : Newark, N. J. Burlington, Vt., and Brooklyn, N. Y., and Bishops Bayley, De Goesbriand and Loughlin were regularly and canonically appointed by the Holy See to fill the same. The usual rescript for the consecration, empowering any duly consecrated bishop in communion with the Holy See to consecrate them, was forwarded to the metropolitan, Archbishop Hughes, of New York. Availing himself of the presence of the illustrious Archbishop Bedini, who happened to be in New York, having come to this country on a special mission having absolutely no reference to the consecration of bishops or the introducing of a new succession, Archbishop Hughes requested him to officiate at the consecration of the new bishops, much in the same way as Dr. Brownell had commissioned Dr. De Lancey to act for him in the case of Dr. Coxe's promotion to the see of Western New York. Yet this, we are gravely told, was all designed by the Pope *to introduce a new succession, and remedy a defective one*, when every one knows that the Pope had nothing to do with the matter, and presumably knew nothing of the nuncio officiating and consecrating until after the consecration had actually taken place.

And so little idea had the American hierarchy of any need of an amended succession to be derived from this illustrious prelate that although since the year 1853, many new bishops have been consecrated in the

United States, and among them the present bishop of Buffalo, until very recently not one of the bishops consecrated by Mons. Bedini was called upon to transmit the new succession. In the year 1873, indeed, Archbishop Bayley, as metropolitan of the see of Baltimore, to which he had been transferred from Newark in 1872, did consecrate bishop Gross of Savannah, so that we must congratulate our esteemed friend and brother of Savannah at whose consecration Apostolical succession has been revived, after it had lain dead or dormant for nearly twenty years.

Yet with characteristic hardihood we are referred to the *Civilta Catolica* as authority for this absurd and puerile statement. The *Civilta Catolica*, an able and generally very correct periodical, edited by Jesuits, naturally took notice of the very solemn ceremony which took place in the Cathedral of New York, but that it gives any ground for these inferences and absurd assertions that *the first consecration was so defective that the Pope tried to mend it by a second succession*, or *that by the second or Bedini consecration a second Roman Catholic succession started in New York*, we absolutely deny. But when a church dignitary outrages common decency by echoing the gross calumnies of infidel revolutionists, and maligns the character of one of the most amiable, gentle and gentlemanly of men, an illustrious and estimable prelate, now gone to his reward, by calling him a *butcher* and *virtual murderer*, and when those publicly and triumphantly refuted charges and lying assertions against *the character*, forsooth, *from which the second Roman Catholic succession started in New York*, are rehashed and served up manifestly for the purpose of damaging and vilifying the Catholic episcopate, may we not retort in his own language, and ask, *where is the morality of throwing out such monstrous*, not *blunders*, but downright falsehoods, *in assaulting the spiritual character of others?*

But to return. Was Matthew Parker, then, ever validly consecrated? What was the issue of subsequent attempts after the first failure?

This, as we have seen, is the all-important question for our Anglican friends. On its solution hangs the fate of the whole Anglican system, for on Parker's valid consecration depends the validity of orders in the Anglican Church; and without valid orders there can be no shadow of a claim to Apostolical succession, or legitimate descent from the Apostles, or corporate identity with the primitive Church of Christ. Please to remember, dear readers, what we have already demonstrated, that this question, so vital to Anglicanism and Episcopalianism and to all their vaunted claims, is of little consequence to the Catholic Church, and in no wise affects the Catholic argument against the pretensions and claims made by them to Apostolical succession, or identity with the Church of the Apostles. We discuss this question, then, not through any necessity to make good our argument, or to refute their claims, but to meet them in their last trench, and entirely cut the ground from beneath their feet; to take away their last shadow of a claim to Apostolicity. To prove this, without going over the whole ground again, to show that, even with valid orders, they have no mission, no legitimate authority to teach, because they themselves are not sent, it is only necessary to remember that there was in the whole realm of England only one legitimate bishop, occupying a see, exercising jurisdiction, and he refused to participate in the ceremony of Parker's consecration.

Not one of those who are said to have consecrated him, and who are named in the Lambeth Register, had any jurisdiction. Barlow, Scorey, Coverdale, and Hodgkin are designated without any title, even in the register, and such of them as were afterwards confirmed and appointed to sees, were so confirmed by Parker himself, showing that they had no jurisdiction until after Parker's consecration, and could give none, *nemo dat quod non habet*. But how could Parker give to them, or any others, what no one gave to him? What a miserable subterfuge, then, it is to trace through Bauchier, Neville, and Chicheley, succession to a Roman Pontiff, when nobody denies that the Church of England had valid orders and legitimate succession, down to the time of the Reformation. In the see of Canterbury from Augustine, sent, confirmed and commissioned by Gregory, down to Cardinal Pole, sent, commissioned and legitimately appointed to that venerable archiepiscopal see, by the Sovereign Pontiff, Julius III., there was a continuous line, an unbroken succession of corporate witnesses, succesors of the Apostles. The whole difficulty, then, is in Parker's succession. How has he been linked on to the chain coming down from the Apostles? No Catholic bishop would consecrate him, no bishop exercising, or possessing authority, mission, jurisdiction, or a see, would lay hands on him; there is not only no concurrence of the sovereign Pontiff, of the Patriarch, which concurrence the canons of the Council of Nice make essential to a canonical consecration; there is not only no confirmation of a metropolitan, or approbation of the bishops of the province, nay; the pretended consecration was in direct opposition to the Sovereign Pontiff and every legitimate bishop in the realm ; so that the attempt to preserve Episcopal succession violates every precedent, and every canonical regulation of the Christian Church, and as Rev. Mr. Waterworth, whose valuable lectures we have freely used and made our own, says, the new bishops of the Anglican establishment separated themselves, not only in faith, from the episcopacy of Christendom, but broke through those ordinances which their predecessors had for centuries regarded as Apostolical, authoritative and binding. —(*Hist. Lect., p.* 337). This, moreover, shows how consistent they are in their appeals to the canons and the ancient councils, when in order to get an archbishop, or the first link in the new episcopal chain, they had to violate all ecclesiastical law, run counter to Apostolical precedents, and cast to the winds the canons of Nice. Yet, though they have hopelessly lost Apostolical succession, they have valid orders, if Parker was vaildly consecrated.

Before this can be positively, and with certainty asserted, it must be proved beyond the possibility of doubt or cavil, (1), that the consecration of Lambeth chapel actually took place, and as the chief proof of this is the Lambeth register, its authenticity, or genuineness must be demonstrated ; (2), that Barlow was himself consecrated ; and (3), that he used a valid form in Parker's consecration. The learned Dr. Kenrick, in his exhaustive treatise on Anglican ordinations, to which we have before referred, and from which we have freely borrowed, states the whole question so intelligently and clearly, that we make no apology for the length of the following quotation :

" Matthew Parker was chosen to be the first Protestant archbishop of Canterbury. It is not pretended that he was consecrated by any of the Catholic bishops.

According to the advocates of Anglican orders, he received episcopal consecration from Barlow, who had been made bishop by Henry VIII., and who, on this occasion, is said to have used the form of ordination known as King Edward's form, in whose reign it had been introduced.

" With regard to this important fact, there are three questions—all of which must be satisfactorily answered in the affirmative, before those who trace their orders to Matthew Parker can conclude that they are validly ordained. First, Was Parker truly consecrated by Barlow, in the manner declared? Second, Was Barlow himself consecrated? Third, Was King Edward's form a valid form?

" If these three questions can be satisfactorily answered, then the ordinations of the English Church are valid; its bishops have the same episcopal character as the Catholic bishops; its ministers are priests, equally as those who minister at Catholic altars; in a word, the ecclesiastical hierarchy has been preserved in the English Church, although, of course, being separated from the communion of the Catholic Church, they are withered branches, through which the vivifying sap of Apostolical jurisdiction does not circulate, and which, consequently, instead of bearing fruit, impede the rays of light and grace from reaching the deluded people that repose under their scanty shade.

" But if a single one of the above three facts be disproved; if a single one of them be not absolutely certain, although somewhat probable; if positive and unsuspicious testimony be not at hand whereby *all three* can be established; then the validity of the Anglican ordinations is either positively disproved, or not absolutely certain; and consequently, there can be no obligation to listen to men, who cannot prove that they have received a participation of the Apostolic ministry, whereby they are empowered to preach the Gospel, and minister at the altar. Nothing short of certainty on this point, can, in such a case, justify priest or people in admitting the validity of such ordinations."—(*Anglican Ordinations, pp.* 21, 22, 1841, *Philad.*)

Parker's and Barlow's consecrations are questions of fact, and not of doctrine, questions of history, matters of opinion to be determined by historical research, and on such evidence as would suffice in any other question or fact of history. "But whatever opinion we may form on either or both these questions, it is absolutely certain that, on account of the form said to be used in the consecration of Parker, that devised by Edward VI., Anglican, and consequently Protestant Episcopal orders, are vitiated and invalidated." This, after all, is the only important point: Anglican orders are invalid on account of the invalidity of the form invented by Cranmer, or, as the act has it, *devised* by Edward VI., and used, if any was used, or if there was anything more than the Nag's Head farce, in the consecration of Parker. To this point we would prefer to confine ourselves, as it would simplify the whole controversy, as Canon Raynal intimates in his admirable little treatise on "The Ordinal of Edward VI.," to concede "that Barlow was a true bishop, and that he consecrated Parker on the seventeenth of December, 1559."—(*Chap.* 1, *p.* 2.) There is no necessity for us, and can be little advantage in following Drs. Mason, Lee, and other Anglican writers, in their laborious attempts to prove the reality of Barlow's and

Parker's consecration. With them failure to prove either is fatal to their cause, whilst the most complete and satisfactory demonstration of both will avail absolutely nothing towards the solution of the real question at issue, for without a valid form no sacrament can be conferred, and if the form used in the consecration of the first Anglican bishop, on whom confessedly the Anglican hierarchy depends, from whom Anglican orders are admitted to be derived, was radically defective or invalid, then there are no orders, no priesthood, no hierarchy in the Anglican or Episcopal Church. We feel then that it is only to entangle and complicate matters, to discuss these historical questions, which, from the nature of the subject and the contradictory testimonies of opposing and interested witnesses, can never be satisfactorily and conclusively settled. Yet as such stress has been laid on these comparatively unimportant points, and so much cavil over some statements of ours, we must turn aside again from the main issue, and after correcting some misrepresentations, we shall briefly notice some of the grounds on which Parker's consecration and the Lambeth Register and Barlow's episcopal character have been questioned or impugned; grounds which, even if they fail to convince, will hardly fail to satisfy the reader that it grates harshly on believing ears, nay, sounds almost like blasphemy to assert that "the canon of Scripture rests on no better evidence" than the consecration of Barlow or Parker. And yet this, by implication, at least, is asserted by those who assume that the succession in the Church of England "rests on the same kind of proof by which we receive the canon of holy Scripture." We maintain that even if the

Lambeth Register be genuine, and the consecration of Parker took place, as asserted, at the hands of Barlow, an apostate monk, it is very doubtful that Barlow himself was ever consecrated, or anything more than bishop elect. And even if Barlow was a regularly consecrated bishop, and went through the rite of consecrating Parker, the form used, viz.: that *devised*, as the act has it, by Edward, was notoriously insufficient and invalid.

But what will you, what can you think, of the honesty, or truthfulness, or *morality*, of any person who quoting freely from Dr. Lingard, and presumably with Dr. Lingard before him, makes that author testify to the validity of Parker's consecration ? " Dr. Lingard," we are told, " shows that this act of itself proves the consecration of Parker to have been in all respects regular and validly performed, according to the reformed Ordinal." Now, Dr. Lingard, in the very correspondence referred to, expressly says, that he confines himself to the fact of Parker's consecration, but whether it was valid or invalid was a question with which, as a writer of history, he had no concern.—(*Lingard's letter to Editor of Birmingham Cath. Magazine*, 1834, *Validity of Ang. Ord., p.* 113.) Dr. Lingard, like many other Catholic writers, investigated the fact of Parker's consecration, and hesitated not to acknowledge his belief therein, but Dr. Lingard did not, and no Catholic can without rashness, acknowledge its validity.

Though Dr. Lingard, and some other respectable Catholic authors concede the reality of Parker's consecration, and believe Barlow was a bishop, and acknowledge the Lambeth Register as a genuine document: and although we, for argument's sake, and to eliminate unimportant side issues, that serve only to complicate, embarrass, and obscure the main question, would prefer to concede the same, yet in order to prove that "somebody has not cruelly imposed on us, in the matter of the Nag's Head fable," and that "all respectable Roman Catholics do not dismiss the story of the 'Nag's Head' with contempt," we shall cite names as respectable, perhaps, as even those of Dr. Lingard, and the Anglican defenders of the Lambeth consecration : and authorities, perhaps, as grave and trustworthy as those produced by them, disowning and disproving, or what in our case is equivalent to that, seriously questioning, and throwing grave doubts upon, (1), the fact of Parker's consecration at Lambeth ; (2), the register on which the proof mainly rests ; (3), and especially, on Barlow's own consecration. Yet we do not pretend to settle these questions ; proofs *pro* and *con*, must be weighed, and each one must decide for himself ; to us, and to our argument, and our cause, the decision is immaterial, for we hold, and think we can prove, that even conceding all these points, the consecration of Parker was certainly invalid, for reasons to be given hereafter, showing that a legitimate, and recognized sacramental form, as well as a due intention in the minister are requisite for the valid administration of orders.

Now, as to the Nag's Head story, which we are told, "all respectable Catholic writers dismiss with contempt,' Dr. Kenrick, "a respectable prelate," adduces quite an array of respectable Catholic names, not only not dismissing the story with contempt, but vouching for its truth. We are indeed told that, "the late Hugh Davey Evans, a profound and learned

ornament of the Maryland bar, has not left a shred
of Dr. Kenrick's cause untwisted or unrent," but
we beg to be excused for not accepting this bare
assertion, for, although we have not been able to pro-
cure a copy of Mr. Evans' *able essay*, we have seen the
second edition of Dr. Kenrick's valuable work, revised
and agumented, in which he replies to Mr. Evans' criticisms, in a most masterly manner, and we still find *untwisted* and *unrent*, intact and unimpaired, every substantial link, every strand in his chain of unanswerable
arguments against the "Validity of Anglican Ordinations and Anglican claims to Apostolical succession."
We may, moreover, unhesitatingly affirm that the perusal of Mr. Evans' essay will not "force on any candid mind the conviction that so *respectable* a man as
Dr. Kenrick could hardly have undertaken such a
task, except under some compulsion of superiors to
which, as in the later matter of infallibility, he pros-
tituted his own convictions, under the remorseless dictation of Jesuits." We are satisfied, in the second
place, that no *profound and learned ornament of the
Maryland bar, or any other bar*, in fact very few besides
the writer whom we are reviewing, would have the im-
pertinence to charge a respectable prelate, a high-toned
gentleman, with such cringing servility and baseness
of soul, as to prostitute his talents, at the dictation of
any man, or set of men, to disseminate error, or write
in any cause against his own convictions. We are satisfied, in the third place, that the independence of character, uncompromising firmness, and stubborn self-asser-
tion born of conscious intellectual endowments, which
may at times carry a man to extremes, or at least make
him appear to occupy a false position, and which, unless

safe-guarded by genuine humility, and rare Christian piety, may be perilous to faith, are at the same time surest guarantees against sycophancy, and servile prostitution of talents or mean pandering to human power. Such characteristics belong rather to those who rebel against a divine authority, or refuse submission to a divinely authorized and infallible teacher.

An "Old Catholic" bishop, like Reinkens, may profess absolute dependence on, and unreserved submission to civil rulers, and the will, and good pleasure of those in power, for the hireling, whose own the sheep are not, fleeth when the wolf cometh to snatch, and scatter, and devour the sheep, *because he is a hireling, and hath no care for the sheep;* as an able, eloquent Catholic deputy in the Reichsrath said, commenting on Reinkens's first would-be charge to an unknown, and undetermined flock; but the Catholic prelate will not betray his trust, or compromise his conscience, or degrade his manhood, at the bidding or dictation of any man, or any merely human authority, whilst he freely submits to God, and vindicates his God-given freedom and manhood, by the most implicit and unreserved submission of himself, his intellect, and will, to the authority and law of God. Some cannot understand this, and hence, whilst they wonder at our not accepting the dictum of *our own Catholic historian, Dr. Lingard,* they are indignant and even abusive, because a Catholic bishop acknowledges an infallible Church, and an infallible Pope, and bows a willing and cheerful obedience to the decisions of an infallible œcumenical council. We are, moreover, satisfied, that howsoever a lawyer may, by special pleading, assail the arguments of Dr. Kenrick, or differ with him, in regard to the true interpretation and force of legal documents, or demur to some of his principles or criteria for determining what records are genuine, and what spurious, or even controvert some of his particular conclusions, yet any unbiased man, who reads his "Anglican Ordinations," and ponders seriously his replies to objections urged by Anglicans against the so-called Nag's Head fabrication, and his answer, paragraph by paragraph, to Dr. Lingard's arguments, must admit that he has vindicated, as he proposed to do, the old English Catholic divines, who, according to Dr. Husenbeth, *for, at least, upwards of two centuries, regarded the Nag's Head consecration as a fact, the certainty of which was sustained by stubborn evidence,* from the charge of blind credulity, or a determined will to deny the best authenticated facts. He did not undertake—he tells us himself, and we say the same for ourselves—" to establish the truth of the Nag's Head consecration; but merely to examine whether it be so entirely destitute of probability or proof, as has been pretended; and whether the vindicators of Catholic faith, who publicly avowed their belief in its reality, at a period when they had better opportunities of ascertaining the truth than we now can possibly be supposed to have, were imposed on by an absurd tale."—(*Validity of Ang. Ord.*, chap. VI., p. 77.)

Among those distinguished divines is Dr. Talbot, archbishop of Dublin, who in a treatise on " The Nullity of the Prelatic clergy in England," says: "It is now a century of years since the Nag's Head story happened. It has constantly been related, and credited by wise men, as certain truth, ever since the year 1559 (the year it was acted in): it was never contradicted by any, until it was imagined by our adversaries that the new registers (Mason's), might contest with our ancient tradition, and make the Nag's Head story seem improbable in the year 1613, of which no man doubted, for the space of fifty-two years before. The Catholic bishops and doctors of Queen Mary's time were sober and wise men; they believed the story; and recounted it to Parsons, Fitzherbert, Dr. Kellison, Holiwood, Dr. Champney, Fitzsimmons, etc. Parsons believed it, Fitzherbert and the rest above named, gave so much credit to it, that they published it in print."—(*Validity of Ang. Ord.*, *chap. VII.*, *p.* 88.) We find in an appendix to "Dodd's Church History of England," a dissertation containing a summary of the arguments employed to support both sides of the controversy concerning the Nag's Head ordination. Dodd cites Dr. Champney, who, after a lengthy account of the whole transaction, how they met at the Nag's Head; how the old man Kitchen of Llandaff, feigning blindness, refused to consecrate; how they then turned upon him as an old fool who imagined that they could not be bishops unless *greased;* how Scorey took the Bible, and laying it on their shoulders and saying, "take authority to preach the word of God sincerely," they rose up bishops, concludes thus: "This whole narration, without adding or detracting any word pertaining to the substance of the matter, I have heard, oftener than once, of Mr. Thomas Bluet, a grave, learned, and judicious priest; he having received it of Mr. Neal, a man of good sort and reputation. * * * Again, Mr. Bluet had other good means to be informed of this matter, being a long time prisoner with Dr. Watson, bishop of Lincoln, and divers other men of mark, of the ancient clergy, in whose time, and in whose sight, as a man may say, this matter was done. Of this narration there are, I think, as many witnesses yet living, as there are priests remaining alive, that have been prisoners with Mr. Bluet, in Wisbeach Castle; where I also heard it of him."—(*Dodd's Ch. Hist.*, v. 2, *App. XLII.*) The historian then gives the names and dates and works of the authors, who have handed down to posterity and published the Nag's Head consecration; and referring to Dr. Talbot's "Nullity of the Prelatic clergy," anno 1659, he says: "Wherein the learned author produces several proofs, in confirmation of the account given by Champney." Again, after giving the opposite views of writers of the Church of England at considerable length, he subjoins: "It would exceed my designed brevity to make a distinct reply to these exceptions Protestant writers have made against the Nag's Head story. But Dr. Talbot, the Catholic archbishop of Dublin, having considered them very fully and learnedly, in his treatise on the *Nullity*, etc., I remit the reader to that work, where he may be more fully informed of all the particulars belonging to this controversy." "From which," says the Rev. Mr. Tierney, F.R.S., F.S.A., "it is evident that Dodd was inclined to favor the story of the Nag's Head consecration," though he (Mr. Tierney) felt compelled to adopt the opposite opinion.—(*Ibid. note, p.* 267.) Champney, in his treatise, *De vocatione ministrorum*, positively asserts: "That not only Catholics of unquestionable integrity, who were eye-witnesses of the affair, testify to the solemn meeting at the Nag's Head: but also John Stowe, that most famous chronographer of England, a professor of the reformed religion, is witness of the same, who diligently inquired into all circumstances of this action, though he feared to relate them in his chronicle." It is evident that Dr. Milner, F.S.A., who is not an ignorant man, nor one that would write hastily, or without consideration, on so important a subject, as Dr. Lingard charges, had no faith in the Lambeth consecration; and with these names, and these authorities, may we not venture to hold an opinion concerning an historical fact contrary to that of Dr. Lingard, able and reliable though he be, as a Catholic historian, especially when, as Dr. Kenrick remarks: " The arguments brought forward by him on this subject were derived from authorities, the authenticity of which had been long and publicly questioned, and he was urging the objections which Courayer had, more than a century ago, put forward, and which had been triumphantly refuted at the time by the learned Hardouin, and in the celebrated work of Father Le Quien." —(*Validity of Ang. Ord.*, *chap. IX. p.* 119.) But enough, and more than enough, about the Nag's Head. We must hasten to conclude what we have to say on the Lambeth Register, and the consecration of Barlow, so as to come to what we regard as the point on which the whole question of the validity of Anglican and Episcopalian orders hinge, viz.: the invalid form devised by Edward VI., including the probable absence of due intention in the consecrating would-be prelates.

VI.

THE LAMBETH REGISTER.

HAVING now sufficiently discussed the historical question of Parker's consecration, and shown that it was questioned and positively denied by respectable, learned, and distinguished writers and divines, and that from the year 1559 until 1613 the first bishops of the *reformed* Church had been repeatedly taunted with the Nag's Head story, without any attempt being made, for upwards of fifty years, to produce any documentary evidence of a regular consecration, or any *public reference* to the Lambeth Register, we must now, as briefly as possible, examine the authenticity of this Register on which Anglicans mainly, if not entirely, rest their proof of Parker's consecration at Lambeth ; to whom, consequently, clearest evidence of its authenticity is of paramount importance.

We must again, however, remind our readers that this is a historical question, not materially affecting the main issue of Anglican succession or Anglican orders, so that, whether, after a careful weighing of authorities and documentary evidence we regard the Register as authentic, or spurious, we must not, as Canon Raynal warns us, "attach undue importance to a mere historical fact, and overlook the main point of the controversy, viz. : the invalidity of the forms invented by Cranmer and inserted into the Rite, which is said to have been used at the consecration of Parker." —(*Ord. of Edwd. VI., p.* 2.) Dr. Lingard and other Catholic writers may declare " they see no reason for pronouncing the Register a forgery," whilst disavowing any intention of deciding the question of the validity of the act, nay, expressly and openly flouting Anglican claims to valid orders or a legitimate episcopacy. For ourselves, we would not even stop to consider this point at all, were it not to convince certain writers that the charge of forgery is not a desperate artifice gotten up by Jesuits to impugn the Anglican succession, and to show that, notwithstanding the "*proverbial purity of law and legal processes in England, and the care taken of public records and facts made historical in printed pages, and thrown open to the eyes and inquiries of the most intelligent and truth-loving nation of the world,*" the public records are not above suspicion, or to be accepted with unquestioning credulity, that forgery was not uncommon, and that the Lambeth Register, if not a forgery, is at least a very suspicious document, and that, as Canon Estcourt admits, "there are grave doubts with regard to the authenticity of the Register itself, as an original and contemporaneous document, or record of the facts as they occurred."—(*Quest. Ang. Ord., p.* 101.) This Register, then, publicly referred to for the first time, in a work published in the year 1613, by Francis Mason, chaplain of Abbot, archbishop of Canterbury, testifies that Matthew Parker was consecrated on the 17th of December, 1559, by Barlow, Scorey, Coverdale and Hodgkin. It was at once denounced as a fabrication by Catholic writers. Fitzherbert, "a man of great learning and holy life," hearing with astonishment that one Mr. Mason was attempting to prove the consecration of the first Protestant bishops in the reign of Queen Elizabeth, by a register testifying that four bishops consecrated Mr. Parker, writes: "This is not a new quarrel, lately raised, but vehemently urged, divers times heretofore, by Catholics many years ago, yea, in the very beginning of the queen's reign, as namely, by the learned Doctors Harding and Stapleton, against Mr. Jewel and Mr. Horn, urging them to show how and by whom they were made bishops." And he continues : "What trow ye was answered thereto ? Were there any bishops named who consecrated them ? Were there any witnesses alleged of their consecration ? Was Mr. Mason's register, or any authentic document, produced either by Jewel or Horn ?"—(*Quoted in Validity Ang. Ord., p.* 107.) Kellison, with a like feeling of wonderment at the inexplicable silence of the Protestant clergy, during more than half a century, during which they were repeatedly and tauntingly told that their bishops, Parker, Horn, etc., had not been consecrated, thus expressed himself : " But as for your registers, I know not whence you have exhumed them; they are at least on many accounts suspected by us. For, first, when in the beginning of the new Church of England it was objected that these ministers and bishops were neither truly nor lawfully ordained, they would have easily silenced them (those objecting), and yet they dared not bring forward those acts or refer to them. This much increases our suspicion that they were so late produced after having remained hid so long; although they had been so often called for by our doctors."—(*Examen novæ Reformationis, p.* 131, *quoted ibid, p.* 110.) With the learned and critical author of "Anglican Ordinations," from whom we have borrowed the above extract, slightly abbreviated, we repeat: "Whatever explanation may be given of the non-production of the Register before the year 1613, it is evident that the fact is calculated to awaken suspicion; and, therefore, those Catholic divines who called its authenticity into question, may have been influenced by other motives than those assigned by their adversaries."— (*Valid. Ang. Ord., p.* 109.) " The authenticity of the Lambeth or Parker's register," says Rev. Mr. Waterworth, in a note to his sixth historical lecture, " has been ever since the time of James I. matter of dispute. This is not the place to enter into any details on the question: and I will merely add, that not having met with, or discovered any solid reasons for denying its genuineness, I shall appeal to it in the text as a document, which, though I see no reason to believe it spurious, others may not choose to admit as evidence." —(*Hist. Lect. p.* 334.) To this his American editor appends the following note:

"The author of these valuable Lectures, with that spirit of liberality which distinguishes his work, has followed, in the text, the view most favorable to the Anglican ordinations. His authorities will be found below. With every wish to be equally impartial, we confess that, to our mind, the authenticity of the Lambeth, or Parker's Register, is more than suspicious —its fabrication is next to a certainty. To discuss the subject in a brief note is not our intention; it would moreover be foreign from the character of these Lectures, intended, as they are, to be historical and not controversial. Viewing the question, then, merely as a debated point of history, the following are some of the heads of argument which have led us to the conclusion that the Lambeth Register *cannot* be admitted as evidence of Parker's consecration, and that the Anglican ordinations are null.

" 1st. The Anglican ordinations were contested from the very infancy of the established Church, and by several of the most distinguished of the Catholic writers that the 16th century produced. The very title of Mason's work, published in 1613, himself a Protestant, places this fact beyond a doubt.

"2d. *Fifty-three years* passed away between the supposed consecration of Parker, and the *first* public reference by Mason to the Lambeth Register. If the Register existed before, why were the Protestant clergy silent for half a century, amid the taunts of their Catholic adversaries—that these ministers and bishops, although mitred, were not truly nor lawfully ordained? This silence, considering the importance of the question, and the religious excitement of the times, is almost conclusive evidence that no such register then existed.

" 3d. Had Parker been consecrated in the chapel at Lambeth, according to the form prescribed by the ritual of Edward VI., and as described in the Register itself, the affair must have been notorious. How then, again, shall we account for the repeated public denial, not only of the *validity*, but of the *fact* of his consecration, by the earliest Catholic writers, and for the suspicious silence of Protestants?

"4th. It is not true that the Protestants appealed to the Register, on the first publication by Sacrobosco in 1603, of the story of Parker's consecration, etc., at the Nag's Head tavern. It was only ten years afterwards, in 1613, that the world was informed of the existence of such a document.

"5th. Had the Register been referred to before—had its existence been a matter of public notoriety, would six bishops, with Abbot, archbishop of Canterbury, at their head, have thought it worth their time to assemble, for the purpose of showing it to a few Catholic priests, brought from their prisons to look at it? and when from their prisons they asked for a *second look* at the Register, why was it refused them? Was it, *indeed*, from fear they might destroy the document? their manacles might have been easily tightened. To us this so-called "examination" is almost proof positive that the Register was a forgery.

"6th. The wording of the record in the Register is suspicious, in as much as it is different from that of all the entries that precede and follow it : its circumstantiality, so uncalled for in such documents, is scarcely less suspicious.

"7th. *Mason* was chaplain to the archbishop of Canterbury; as such, it was both in his *power* to falsify the records at Lambeth, and his *interest* to do so; two circumstances, considering the temper of those times, which greatly invalidate his evidence ; especially when such evidence was so long and so vainly called for, before, by the Catholic writers.

"Goodwin's work, *De Praesulibus Angliae*, appeared first in English, in 1601, and afterwards in Latin, in 1615. The first edition, published *before* the appearance of Mason's work, says not a word about Parker's consecration at Lambeth : the second, published two years *after*, repeats Mason's tale. Such being the case, it would be safer for Episcopalians to let Goodwin pass; his previous silence is again almost conclusive evidence that he knew nothing of the Lambeth Register, nor of Parker's pretended consecration.

"*Camden's Annals* also appeared in 1615, two years *after* Mason's work: to copy Mason was no difficult task, and was the most likely course to please the court and his patron, James I.

" As for the work on the antiquities of the British Church, ascribed to Parker himself, it is in the same predicament, and has altogether too much the air of testimony 'got up for the occasion,' to outweigh the serious objections, suspicions, etc., which on every side beset the question of Anglican ordinations. Indeed, the more we study this subject, the more decided is our conviction that the Lambeth Register of Parker's consecration will find its proper place among the mass of documents to which the Protestant historian, Whitaker, refers in the following candid though painful acknowledgment: ' Forgery—I blush for the honor of Protestantism, while I write it—seems to have been peculiar to the reformed.' "—(*Vindication of Mary, vol. iii., p.* 2; *also pp.* 45-54, *quoted by Waterworth, p.* 335.)

This Protestant divine repeats the same more than once in his vindication of Mary, the murdered queen of Scots: " Forgery appears to have been the peculiar disease of Protestantism," and again, "I look in vain for one of these accursed outrages of imposition among the disciples of Popery." We beg, moreover, to direct the attention of our friends who extol with so much pride and apparent self-complacency the stainless and unimpeachable *public records* of England, and the *proverbial purity of law and legal processes of the most intelligent and truth-loving nation of the world*, to the evidence furnished by a clause in a general pardon granted by James I., in the first year of his reign, that public documents even in that model truth-loving land, were not only liable to falsification, but that frequent forgeries and interpolations had been perpetrated in his own reign, and that of his immediate predecessor: "We also pardon, remit and release by these presents, to the aforesaid A. B., all and every offences and transgressions, by erasing and underlining of any rolls, records, briefs, warrants, recognitions or other documents of ours, or any of our predecessors, or progenitors whatsoever, in any court or courts of ours, or of any of our predecessors, or our progenitors, done or perpetrated before the aforesaid 20th day of March."—(*Rymer XVI.*, *p*. 534, *quoted by Kenrick, Validity Ang. Ord.*, *p*. 64.) But is it not playing on the ignorance or credulity of his readers, when a controversialist not only so boldly refers to the sacrosanct, untainted English records, but says that "any flaw in the titles and legislative rights of Anglican bishops, would undoubtedly have been challenged by statesmen, on account of the jealousy with which, for three centuries, every step in the Anglican communion was watched by active enemies?" thereby insinuating that no flaw was found, that the titles and legislative rights of the Parliament bishops were unchallenged, when he knows, and the fact is patent on the open page of history, that at the commencement of the reign of James I., after the death of Elizabeth, the tradition of the ordination made at the Nag's Head tavern in Cheapside, was loudly invoked by Catholics and Presbyterians.

"The Presbyterians said that the pretended bishops were mere priests like themselves, having only been ordained by the imposition of Parker's hands, who himself had received it from a simple priest, Scorey, at the tavern, and consequently, if they had seats in Parliament, the Presbyterians should not be excluded from them." For the same reason the Catholics maintained that, "the episcopacy and priesthood had ceased in England." And he can hardly be ignorant, that among the pleas put forth by Bishop Bonner, of London, in answer to the indictment by Horn, for refusing the oath of the queen's supremacy, was the following: "That the said Mr. Robert Horne, not being lawful bishop of Winchester, but an usurper, intruder and unlawful possessor thereof, for that, according to the laws of the Catholike Churche, and the statutes and ordinances of this realme, the said Mr. Robert Horne was not elected, consecrated, etc."—(*Vide Canon Estcourt, Quest. Ang. Ord., p.* 118.) Which plea of Bonner, says Canon Estcourt, seems to have caused no little alarm and excitement among the Anglican party; and Randolph wrote from Edinburg to Cecil, March 30th, 1565: "The tale is, that Bonner in his defence at his arraignment said that there was never a lawful bishop in England, which so astonished a great number of the best learned, that yet they knew not what answer to give him; and when it was determined he should have suffered, he is remitted to the place from whence he came, and no more said to him." " Bonner's objections," says Rev. Mr. Waterworth, " were both statutable and canonical. He denied Horn's right to administer the oath, because Horn had been consecrated by a form not legally established, and by a metropolitan who was himself no bishop. And this latter assertion he defended on these two grounds: first, Parker was consecrated by King Edward's ordinal; and secondly, that Parker's consecrators were both legally and canonically disqualified from officating at that consecration, being deprived of their benefices." —(*Lect. VI., note p.* 342.) We call attention then again, to the glaring recklessness of assertion, insincerity or ignorance, whichever it may be, manifested by those maintaining that "no imaginable flaw could be found in the title of the Anglican bishops, that their rights as bishops were unchallenged, that the law requiring the consecration of bishops to be absolutely conformed to the Anglican Ordinal, and the fact that in perpetuating the Anglican succession nothing was done in a corner, rendered the succession in the Church of England more demonstrably canonical and regular, in all particulars, than any other succession in Christendom." This is indeed amusing; and we cannot help applying to these writers what Dr. Champney says of Mr. Mason: "He doth well to be bold in affirming, for a good face sometimes helpeth out an ill game."

But we are quite willing to take the Register from Mr. Mason's hands, and still maintain that it is not an original, trustworthy, truthful, contemporaneous record of Parker's consecration. For proof of this, we refer to Canon Estcourt's valuable treatise on "Anglican Ordinations," which we recommend particularly to those liable to be imposed on by our Buffalo defender of Anglican orders, or his implicitly trusted authorities, Courayer, Mason, Haddan and Lee.

We now proceed to give a brief statement of the opinions of Catholic writers, who admit the consecration of Parker, by Barlow & Co., and the Register as genuine, if you will, though evidently not the original record, truthfully detailing the transaction, but a document framed and cunningly devised for a purpose, to meet an exigency, to forestall anticipated difficulties, and answer

Catholic objections. This short historical review may perhaps throw light on some of the most salient points of the controversy, and show how little comfort the defenders of Anglican orders can derive from the most favorable view of the question, and the most liberal interpretation of disputed records. The Princess Elizabeth was proclaimed Queen of England, November 17th, 1558. January 14th was fixed for her coronation, but Heath, the archbishop of York, and all the Catholic bishops, refused to crown her, or lend the sanction of their presence to the ceremony, "until with much ado they obtained the bishop of Carlisle (Oglethorpe), the inferior almost of all the rest, to do that ceremony."—(*Allen's answer to English justice.*) In the year 1559, the first of Elizabeth, all the bishops of the realm in convocation declared, "The supreme power of feeding and governing the militant Church of Christ is given to Peter, the Apostle, and to his lawful successors in the See Apostolic, as unto the vicars of Christ" (*Heylin*); and all except Llandaff refused to take the oath of supremacy: "Only one bishop conformed himself to the queen's commands, and was continued in his place, viz.: Anthony Kitchen, *alias* Dunstan, of Llandaff" (*Fuller*); and before the end of the same year they were all deprived. (*Dodd.*) Elizabeth and her advisers are not blind to the *exigency* of the occasion. A hierarchy obsequious to the queen and favorable to the new doctrines must be created. Matthew Parker, a priest, who had been chaplain to Anne Boleyn, the queen's mother, and was on terms of intimacy with her chief advisers, Cecil and Bacon, and who—notwithstanding his priestly vow of celibacy, in violation of the law of God and of the realm, "that priests, after the order of priesthood, as afore, may not marry, by law of God" (31 *Hen. VIII., chap.* 14), and before the act (2 *and* 3 *Ed. VI., c.* 21) legalizing the marriage of the clergy—had taken to himself a wife, was selected by Elizabeth to be her first bishop. The vacant archiepiscopal see of Canterbury was offered to him, and a peremptory order from the queen decided his acceptance of the proffered, but not coveted dignity, and brought him to London in the beginning of June, 1559. Although cathedral chapters had been deprived in the reign of Edward VI. of the right to elect their bishops, and the right of appointment of the same had been vested exclusively in the king, "from henceforth no *congé d'elire*, shall be granted, nor election of any archbishop or bishop by the dean or chapter made" (1 *Ed. VI., c.* 2), a *congé d'elire*, is said to have been issued to the chapter of Canterbury, July 18th, of the same year. There was one vacancy in the chapter, and of the eleven prebendaries, only four, with Dean Nicholas Wotton, answered the citation and put in an appearance. The election was by way of compromise left with the dean, whose choice, as was fully understood, was the choice or nominee of the queen.—(*Quest. Ang. Ord., p.* 83.)

This singular *congé d'elire* and election by the chapter were deemed sufficient for Parker to assume the episcopal style and title, which he does in a letter to the council, dated Aug. 27th, 1559. From this date until the 17th of December, the date assigned in the Register for his consecration, there is great confusion and even contradiction in the official documents. In some, the full title of bishop is given to him, in others he is designated bishop "elect." A commission dated October 20th, is addressed to Parker, Grindal and Coxe with their full titles as bishops, and on the 26th of the same month, October, we find among the State papers, an official document issued by the queen, asserting that, "The archbishop elect of Canterbury, and the other elect bishops of London, Ely, Hereford and Chichester remain unconsecrated." If any weight is attached to this document, then Scorey and Barlow, the elect of Hereford and Chichester, are on 26th of October, 1559, *unconsecrated.—(Quoted by Can. Estcourt, p.* 84.) Yet we know that Barlow was bishop elect of St. Asaph's and St. David's in Henry's reign, and afterwards of Bath and Wells, though there is strong reason to doubt that he was ever consecrated, as we shall see in the sequel, and Scorey was consecrated by Cranmer according to King Edward's Ordinal, and unlawfully thrust into the see of Chichester, from which Bishop Day had been deposed, because he refused to exchange the altar for the communion table, the sacrifice of the Mass, for the Lord's Supper. If it be by mistake that Parker gets at one time his full title of bishop, and afterwards is styled archbishop "elect," and declared to be unconsecrated, and if, as Canon Estcourt is willing to allow, it be by a clerical error that Scorey, whose register of consecration is extant, is put on the same footing with Parker, Grindal and Coxe, who are certainly unconsecrated, and Barlow, of whose consecration there is great reason to doubt, we at least are justified in concluding that the public records of England were not so carefully kept, and so trustworthy, as some would have us believe. But to proceed.

The so-called election of Parker by Dean Wotton occurred on the 1st of August, and "on the 9th of September, the great seal was put to a warrant for his consecration, directed to the bishops of Duresme

(Tonstall), Bath and Wells (Bourne), Peterborough (Pole), Llandaff (Kitchen), and to Barlow and Scorey (styled only bishops, not being then elected to any sees), requiring them to consecrate him."—(*Burnet, quoted by Waterworth, Hist. Lect., p.* 329.) This commission failed, most probably because the Catholic prelates, "who," as Sir Mackintosh in his "History of England" owns, "must have considered such an act a profanation, conscientiously refused;"—(*Ibid. p.* 331), just as the Catholic prebendaries of the chapter of Canterbury had refused to take part in his election. We are certainly justified in believing Mackintosh, that the Catholic prelates refused, through conscientious motives, to unite with such men as Barlow and Scorey, apostates from the faith and their religious vows, in consecrating Parker, who himself had broken his priestly vow of celibacy, and joined the so-called reformed party, and who, irregularly elected, at the bidding of the queen, had been forced into the episcopal dignity by the civil ruler, and secular power, in contravention of canon law, in defiance of all the spiritual authority and ecclesiastical powers, as well of the universal Church, as of the Church of England; had been named a bishop despite the Pope, despite the patriarch, despite the metropolitan, despite all the laws and traditions of the Church hitherto held sacred. Our belief is strengthened when we find three of these four Catholic prelates suffering the penalty of their non-compliance with the royal wishes in the deprivation of their sees—Tonstall before the 16th of the same month of September, Pole before the 11th of November, and Bourne, on his refusal to take the oath, tendered by a commission issued October 18th.

Yet, a hierarchy must be created for the royal foundation, the new or reformed Church; Elizabeth must have bishops, Parker must be consecrated. The bishops refuse to consecrate him, and they are all, save one, in consequence deprived of their sees. The law requires (25 *Henry VIII.*) for the confirmation and consecration of an archbishop, another archbishop, or four bishops, within the king's dominions. Now, there is no archbishop, and only one bishop, who answers the description of a bishop within the realm. Cecil, the chief adviser of the queen, is sorely puzzled, and in a marginal note in his own handwriting to a state paper detailing the legal steps to be taken for Parker's consecration, he states: "There is no archbishop nor IIII. bishops now to be had. Whereupon, Querendum." —(*Canon Estcourt, p.* 87.) Accordingly, eminent canonists, four clergymen, and two civilians are consulted, and in accordance with their advice a second commission is issued, dated December 6th, "to the bishop of Llandaff; Barlow, bishop elect of Chichester; Scorey, bishop elect of Hereford; Coverdale, late bishop of Exeter; Hodgkin, bishop suffragan of Bedford; John, suffragan of Thetford; and Ball, bishop of Ossory; that they, or any four of them, should consecrate him." We may well repeat with the historian Mackintosh: "Whoever considers it important to examine the above list will perceive the perplexities in which the English Church was involved by a zeal to preserve unbroken the chain of Apostolical succession."—(*Quoted by Waterworth, Hist. Lect., p.* 336.) That the perplexities were grave, indeed, may be inferred not only from the inspection of the names and doubtful character of those mentioned in the commission, but also from the unusual and very strange clause inserted by these canonists, in this commission, with which they asserted it could be lawfully acted on. By this clause the queen, by her supreme authority, dispenses with all disabilities, and supplies all irregularities and deficiencies to any of the persons to whom it is addressed, arising from " their condition, state, or powers, from the laws of the Church, or the statutes of the realm, the urgency of the time and the necessity of circumstances requiring it."—(*Waterworth, Hist. Lect., p.* 337.) Here indeed is a stretch of the royal supremacy and spiritual prerogatives of the crown, but the exigency of the time demanded it. Parker must be consecrated: a new reformed hierarchy must be created; even though the parties had no canonical rights, jurisdiction or faculties to consecrate a bishop, Elizabeth surely can and does supply the want; though they may not possess the *condition* of bishops within the realm required by the law, the queen can dispense with that, nay, even if not bishops at all, the royal prerogative can supply the want of the episcopal character and ecclesiastical state; in fine, no laws of the Church or statutes of the realm must be a bar to the execution of the wishes of the queen, to the establishment of an Anglican episcopate, to the consecration of Parker, and the last forlorn hope is ordered out at this most critical juncture to save the imperiled hierarchy of the Anglican establishment. Yet strange, though thus armed and fortified by these extraordinary royal powers, Kitchen, the only bishop exercising jurisdiction and answering to the description of a bishop within the queen's realms, and Ball of Ossory, and the suffragan Thetford, " either hindered by sickness," says the Protestant historian Heylin, "or by some other lawful impediment, were not in a condition to attend the service."—(*Heylin, p.* 121, *vide Waterworth, ut supra.*)

Verily, perplexing difficulties thicken around poor Parker's path to the episcopacy, unlooked for obstacles obstruct his way to Canterbury. The Fates, it would seem, oppose his elevation to a see rendered illu trious by a line of saintly prelates. However, she "of the iron hand and iron maw" is not to be foiled; she has made up her mind to establish prelacy, that the Church of England as by law, by queen and Parliament established, may have prelates, her iron will is determined to place Parker in the see of Canterbury, and through him fill the other sees, which her despotic will had made vacant. As Kitchen a second time refused to become accessory to the crime and sacrilege of consecrating a bishop without canonical warrant or ecclesiastical authority, Barlow, the next mentioned on the commission, with his worthy compeers, Scorey, Coverdale and Hodgkin, are said to have assembled at the church of St. Mary-le-bone on the 9th of December, to confirm Parker's election, and on Sunday, 17th December, in the chapel of Lambeth house, to have gone through the ceremony of his consecration according to the ordinal of Edward VI., the service beginning "about five or six o'clock in the morning." This is the testimony of the Register, and as to its authenticity and the collateral proofs and authorities, adduced in its support, we need say no more, though, as Mr. Waterworth remarks: "they appeared about the time that the forgery of documents is said to have been so prevalent as to be made a source of fiscal gain. Pardons were issued at a small charge, and ran thus: '*Perdonamus falsas fabricationes chartarum, scriptorum monumentorum, ac publicationes corum.*' "—(*Hist. Lect.*, note, *p.* 338.) Though, then, with the American editor of Waterworth's lectures, we feel it to be " certainly somewhat perplexing, that the commission dated December 6th, 1559, in consequence of which the consecration of December 17th took place, should have no mark by which Rymer could distinguish it from a spurious document"—(*Waterworth*, note, *p.* 339), we must again remind our readers that this is a subject which they must examine and decide for themselves on its own merits, and the documentary evidence adduced. Canon Estcourt hesitates not to say : " We may indeed believe the alleged facts—viz., of the ceremony having taken place at Lambeth on the 17th of December; of Parker and the other persons named having taken their several parts in it, and of the Rite in the book of 1552 having been followed, except in one particular—to be as certain as any other facts in English history. But this belief will not lead us to accept the existing Register as an authentic and contemporaneous record of the facts as they occurred. On the contrary, there are circumstances of considerable suspicion attached to it."—(*Quest. Ang. Ord., p.* 101). Again he says: " The other copies which are constantly referred to as evidence in support of the Register, so far from adding to its credit, rather detract from it."—(*Ibid.*) He then points out the discrepancies between the Register and the two principal documents, usually styled copies or transcripts of the Register, but which are rather original drafts, viz., that of the State Paper Office, and that kept in Corpus Christi College, Cambridge, and.

which is said have been given to the college by Parker himself. The learned Canon proves that "the Register as it stands is a remarkable departure from the usual form," and whilst attesting that Edward's ordinal was used, records an important deviation from its prescription.

He refers to an important document among Foxe's MSS. in the British Museum, and placing it side by side in parallel columns with Parker's Register, asserts: " This MS. to be in the writing of a contemporary, and not an unfriendly hand, and preserved among contemporary papers, of which a part is taken exactly from the Register as it stands, and another part is widely different."—(*Quest. Ang. Ord., p.* 107.) How he accounts for this difference we shall see presently, when we speak of Barlow, whom it seems the early Anglicans were ashamed to acknowledge as the consecrator of their first archbishop, the root and stem of the Anglican hierarchy. In fact, as we said before, it is very doubtful that Barlow himself was ever consecrated, was ever anything more than bishop "elect," and even if the defender of Anglican succession could have an absolute certainty—which after what we have said he cannot have—of Parker's consecration and of the authenticity and trustworthiness of the Lambeth Register, the validity of the consecration would still be doubtful.

VII.

WAS BARLOW EVER CONSECRATED BISHOP?

TO be certain of the validity of Parker's consecration, we must have an absolute certainty of Barlow's episcopal character. We propose now to show that his friends have not cleared up the doubts thrown around Barlow's consecration, and that no positive, conclusive proofs thereof can be adduced. "All are agreed," says Dr. Kenrick, "that Barlow's consecration cannot be established by *positive* evidence, and may, at most, be inferred from the circumstances of his history. In other words, the fact is not *certain;* but according to the most sanguine advocates of English orders *highly probable."—(Valid. Ang. Ord., chap. X., p.* 155.) We asserted in our lecture, " Even if the Lambeth Register be genuine, and if the consecration took place, as asserted, at the hands of Barlow, an apostate monk, it is very doubtful whether Barlow himself was ever consecrated, or ever anything more than a bishop elect." In reply to which Dr. Lingard is cited as testifying the direct reverse, thus: "Is there any postive proof that he (Barlow) was no bishop? None in the world. Why should we doubt the consecration of Barlow and not that of Gardiner? I fear that *the only reason* is this: Gardiner did not consecrate Parker, but Barlow did." This is put down as *directly the reverse* of what we affirmed, yet we never asserted or pretended that there was any *positive* proof that he was no bishop. What we asserted, and re-assert is, that there is no *positive* proof that he was a bishop, or anything more than a bishop *elect*. This is all that is necessary for our contention, that his consecration is doubtful; doubtful, then, too, is the validity of Parker's consecration, and consequently, there can be no absolute certainty of the transmission, not only of legitimate succession, but even of valid orders through the Anglican episcopate, or the bishops of the Protestant Episcopal Church of the United States. It is then not only rash, but a mockery of truth, and an insult to an intelligent public to aver and publish that, "Succession in the Church of England is more demonstrably canonical and regular, in all particulars, than any other succession in Christendom," and—we reluctantly repeat what must grate so harshly on Christian ears— "the canon of Scripture rests on no evidence more explicit." This putting of the succession in the Church of England on the same footing with holy Scripture, or comparing and identifying the evidence on which both rest, strikes us as grossly irreverent to God's Holy Word, and as an unintentional indeed, but most unkind and dangerous thrust at the authenticity, and unimpeachable, absolutely certain, and infallible authority of the inspired Scriptures. We are quite willing to accept the following test of legitimate succession and share in the corporate witness, and applying it to Barlow and Parker we find them wanting. " In any given case," says our Episcopalian divine, "a bishop must be able to prove his own succession by the highest moral evidence. In doing this he must show that his consecrators derived their episcopal order from some ancient Apostolic line. If he can do this by undoubted registers, known and read of all men like other legal documents, by which the succession is carried up to a period antecedent to modern controversy," etc.

Now, let Barlow or Parker prove by undoubted registers, known and read of all men, that his consecrators derived their episcopal order from some ancient Apostolic line. We challenge our Buffalo divine to apply this test in Barlow's case. He knows well that this would be fatal to Barlow's claims to a share in the corporate witness or the episcopal character, and yet he attempts to throw dust in the eyes of the public by boldly setting forth what every Catholic would acknowledge as full and ample evidence of a legitimate title, and thus unfairly insinuating, without a shadow of proof, that the title of the first archbishop and his consecrator rests on such evidence. Again, Dr. Lingard asks: "Why should we doubt the consecration of Barlow and not of Gardiner?" We answer, first, because Gardiner's consecration was never questioned, whereas that of Barlow was openly doubted, and denied; and secondly, because in Gardiner's case, and in every other case, but Barlow's, where the register of a diocesan bishop is wanting, collateral evidence of the consecration is supplied, as Professor Stubs shows in his "Registrum Anglicanum," from the diocesan registers, from Rymer, or elsewhere. But in Barlow's case, there is no such collateral evidence, either from diocesan record, from the calendars of the Church books in which the dates of the entrance and death of successive bishops were kept, or from chapter books, for none of these, strange as it may seem, are to be found at St. David's. Dr. Lingard says again, "I fear that *the only reason* (for denying Barlow's and not Gardiner's consecration) is this: Gardiner did not consecrate Parker, but Barlow did." This is no doubt partially true, for whether Gardiner or Cardinal Pole, or " the other bishops," as Dr. Kenrick justly remarks, "whose record of consecration no longer appears, were, or were not, consecrated is a matter of comparatively minor importance; but it is of most serious importance for the Anglicans to establish, by positive proof, that the man through whom they claim orders, had himself received them."—(*Valid. Ang. Ord., p.* 136.) It is no doubt, then, true that Catholics weighed and examined so carefully the question of Barlow's consecration, and not finding sufficient vouchers or positive proofs thereof, denied the same, because on Barlow, as Mr. Ward declares, "*must be built as on a foundation,* the whole episcopacy and priesthood of the Church of England."—(*Letter of Dr. Milner to Dr. Elrington, ibid. App. p.* 209.) Our Buffalo divine will of course demur to this, for he says: "It must be remembered that it is of no real consequence whether Barlow was or was not a bishop, as he was only one of four bishops, who laid hands, all pronouncing together the formula of ordination." Of the worth and theological soundness of this opinion we will speak hereafter, but we really do not blame Anglicans for being reluctant to own Barlow as the father of their hierarchy, or the laying on of his soiled hands the means of communicating the ecclesiastical spirit and Apostolical commission to their Church. "Of all the bishops," says an Anglican writer, " who were created from the date of 1533 to the end of Edward VI.'s reign, Barlow is perhaps entitled to the palm for abject servility. He seems to have been a mere weathercock, changing perpetually. He was retained in the service of Anne Boleyn as early as 1530, and was soon employed as an agent whom she, the king, and Cromwell, might be sure of to do their pleasure. He had *de facto* contracted a marriage in spite of his profession as a religious." (*Saturday Review, quoted by Estcourt, pp.* 62-3.) On the accession of Queen Mary he made a submission which was equivalent to a recantation, resigned his see, or was deprived, and fled into Germany. His sentiments regarding the necessity of episcopal consecration we have already recited, but not only on this subject were his sentiments lax and his expressions profane, but he was regarded by his contemporaries as a clerical buffoon and scoffer at holy things. Returning to England on Elizabeth's accession he was by her named to the see of Chichester.

It was whilst thus only bishop *elect* of Chichester, without any jurisdiction, he is said to have consecrated Parker on the 17th of December, and on the very next day he himself is confirmed and obtains episcopal jurisdiction from the hands of his grateful, new-born child, Matthew Parker, the episcopal fledgling of a day, whom he presented the day before to Elizabeth and the English Church as the first fruit of the queen's supremacy, the first begotten of a new race of bishops, the first link of a new chain of corporate witnesses. Verily, the *succession in the Church of England is the most demonstrably canonical and regular in all Christendom!* Still his own personal unworthiness, moral degradation, uncanonical conduct, and lack of jurisdiction would not invalidate, though they would render illegitimate and irregular, his conferring of orders, if he were himself. a validly consecrated bishop, and with a proper intention used a valid form. Was then Barlow a consecrated bishop? Buffalo's divine says he was: "Barlow was consecrated bishop of St David's in the 28th year of Henry VIII." But would not the gentleman be kind enough to give us the date more precisely, the day and the month? It would save us a world of trouble searching through historic records and dusty folios; besides it would be so satisfactory, and withal so convincing. Would he not, too, condescend to tell us where he was consecrated, and who were his consecrators? these are the tests which he himself—waiving, of course, the undoubted registers, which cannot be had —demands of every bishop in order to prove his episcopal character. But no, he will deign no reply; but simply affirms Barlow was consecrated in the 28th year of Henry VIII. That must suffice; his *ipse dixit* settles the question. As, then, he will not condescend to gratify our now awakened curiosity, or try to satisfy incredulous and inquiring minds, we must turn to others, we must prosecute our inquiries regarding Barlow's consecration elsewhere, in the pages of English history, and in doing so, we find that we have to tread our way through a mass of conflicting authorities and contradictory statements.

At the outset we find that Courayer, the most earnest advocate of the validity of English orders, contradicts our friend, for he says, Barlow was confirmed by proxy, bishop of St. Asaph, on the 23rd of February, 1535, and most probably consecrated in the country, by virtue of the archbishop's commission: "We know for certain that he was confirmed, and *as it is reasonable to suppose* also consecrated, yet nothing further appears with regard to the see of St. Asaph." This again is contradicted by a royal act, dated May 29th, 1536, allowing the chapter of St. Asaph to proceed to fill the seat made vacant, "by the voluntary exchange of William Barlow, the last bishop *elect* of that place." This also is confirmed by a document found in an appendix to Courayer, in which it is said that, " Barlow was one of the only three bishops translated to new sees within the last two hundred years, without having been consecrated for those to which they were first elected." According to Godwin, he was consecrated on the 22d of February, 1535, whilst Wharton, in his "Fasti Ecclesiæ Anglicanæ," places his confirmation, which naturally precedes consecration, on the 23d of February, 1535. A mandate of King Henry to Cranmer, dated 22d of February, 1536, empowers him to proceed to the consecration of Barlow, though according to Strype, he was confirmed the 15th of September, 1535, and of course the ceremony of confirmation could not take place until the royal mandate for his consecration had been issued. "All these contradictions," as Dr. Kenrick, from whom we have condensed these facts, remarks, " are evidence that nothing certain is known of the period of Barlow's consecration." —(*Valid. Ang. Ord., chap. X., pp.* 136-146.) Canon Estcourt, from data furnished mainly by Mr. Haddan, makes it, if not certain, at least most probable, that Barlow resigned the see of St. Asaph before he was consecrated, and was elected bishop of St. David's on the 10th of April, 1535-6, and took possession of that see in person on the 1st of May. He also shows from authentic original documents that he was styled on the 12th of June, "the bishop elect of St.

Asaph, now elect of St. Davyes," and on the 30th, in pursuance of a writ of summons issued on the 27th of April, in consequence of an exceptional and extraordinary grant of the custody of temporalities made to him, not to " the said elect and confirmed," the usual form, but to " the same now bishop for his life," he assumed the style and title of bishop, and took his seat in the House of Lords. Referring our readers, who may wish to study this question more thoroughly, to Canon Estcourt's most valuable work on, *"Anglican Ordinations,"* we will now with the learned Canon sum up Barlow's case. " All the *a priori* arguments used by Bramhall and Elrington, such as the *præmunire*, the grant of temporalities, the seat in the House of Lords, are shown to be either groundless or contrary to the fact; all the dates assigned for his consecration, viz., the 22d of February by Godwin, the 23d of April by Dr. Lee, and the 11th of June by Mr. Haddan, are contradicted by the testimony of records—and the whole time left for him to be consecrated in is reduced to a period of nineteen days, viz., between the 12th and 30th of June, exclusive."—(*Quest. Ang. Ord., p.* 79.)

The author shows that Mason gave a wrong reference to the record attesting the extraordinary grant of temporalities, and this fact does not enhance our opinion of Mason's honesty nor increase our confidence in registers, which it would be to his interest to tamper with and falsify. " An error in the reference would be of little consequence if he had given a correct description of the document, or if he printed it so as to show its real nature and operation, instead of passing it off as the restitution usually made to a bishop after consecration, and printing only so much as would not betray the deception he was practising."—(*Ibidem, p.* 72.) In the document found among Foxe's MSS., and referred to above, we discover a note concerning Barlow, Scorey, and Coverdale, which seems greatly to strengthen the opinion that Barlow was never consecrated. The writer, evidently in the confidence of the Reformers, writing in their favor, having access to registers, though he states when and by whom the other two were consecrated, is as dry and indefinite about Barlow as his Buffalo defender himself, merely stating, "William Barlow was consecrated in the time of Henry VIII." May we not reasonably conclude that he was unable to tell the date of the consecration, or the names of the bishops who consecrated him? We are, then, surely justified in the conclusion that, although we cannot establish with absolute certainty and by positive evidence, that Barlow was never consecrated, the probabilities are against him, and "with so many circumstances of suspicion, arising from different quarters, yet pointing the same way, it is impossible to admit the fact of his consecration without more direct proof of it."—(*Ibid. p.* 81.) It is then and must remain very doubtful that Barlow was anything more than a bishop elect. Anglicans and Episcopalians can never be certain of their orders, not to speak of succession, unless they can have an absolute certainty of Barlow's consecration, and yet it is boldly affirmed that the " canon of Scripture rests on no evidence more explicit."

VIII.

FUTILE ATTEMPTS TO BOLSTER UP OR SUPPLY FOR BARLOW'S DEFICIENT OR DOUBTFUL CONSECRATION.

WE will now examine what we must regard as a mere subterfuge, a last and very poor shift to escape the consequences of the very grave doubts concerning Barlow's episcopal character. "It must be remembered," says the Buffalo defender of Anglican succession, "that it is of no real consequence, whether Barlow was or was not a bishop, as he was only one of four bishops, who laid hands, all pronouncing together the formula of consecration." In this he follows the lead of such Anglican writers as Mason and Bramhall, who taking it from the Register that all four imposed their hands and said the words of the Rite together, argue that all four were really consecrators, and, therefore, it would be sufficient if only one of the four had been a bishop. Mr. Haddan too, declares that Barlow presided at Parker's consecration, but the position occupied by him does not answer to that of the consecrating bishop, for all joined throughout and equally, both in the imposition of hands and the words. All this we learn from Canon Estcourt, and it will, we think, be evident to any one who weighs carefully and without prejudice, all the documents and authorities he adduces, that "tne Anglican party finding out what a mistake they had made in allowing Barlow to act as consecrator," tampered with the register, "had it wholly or partially rewritten so as to gloss over Barlow's being the principal in the function," (*Quest. Ang. Ord.*, *p.* 108) with a view of meeting the damaging charges of laxity of faith and morals made by Catholics against Barlow himself, and the doubts and difficulties about his consecration. As we have already remarked, in this Register produced by Mason, there is a remarkable departure from the usual form. In all other instances, the Register records the name, either of the archbishop or of some bishop commissioned by him, as taking the principal part, and two other bishops assisting him, but in Parker's case the Register makes no mention of a consecrating bishop and assistants, stating simply that all four imposed hands, and said the words of the form, without saying that they, or any one of them, consecrated him, or that he was consecrated by them, and Mr. Haddan himself remarks "that in other cases a distinction is made between the consecrating and assisting bishops, which is not made here."—(*Quoted by Estcourt, note, p.* 104.) This exceptional form of registration and singular deviation from the customary style of records, coupled with the fact that in the MSS. already referred to, and found in the British Museum, Barlow is expressly named as consecrator, and the others as assistants, show· that if Parker's Register be not an entire forgery, the original record has been falsified, tampered with, for a purpose. That purpose we can easily conjecture from the labored attempts to sustain the opinion which Mr. Haddan thus expresses: "The absence of Barlow's consecration, if it were so, would not invalidate that of Parker." An extreme and hazardous opinion, indeed, but drowning men catch at straws, and the Anglicans seem ready to embrace any opinion or broach any theory that may save them from the alternative of resting their orders and hierarchy on the doubly doubtful Barlow.

But supposing the opinion tenable, that all four were consecrators, and that even if Barlow, the presiding prelate, were not a consecrated bishop, had no episcopal character, Parker would still be validly consecrated, because the three others joined with Barlow in imposing hands and reciting the form; who are these others on whom we are forced to fall back? Scorey, Coverdale and Hodgkin. Scorey and Coverdale were consecrated by the form devised by Edward VI., but that form is notoriously invalid and insufficient, as we shall see presently, and therefore they were not bishops at all, and consequently will not help Anglicanism out of the dilemma into which Barlow has brought it. Its last resort and only dependence are now on Hodgkin, the suffragan of Bedford. But so poor is this dependence, so weak and rickety this last prop, that Dr. Elrington himself admits that, "if Ward could prove that Scorey and Coverdale (in addition to Barlow) were *not truly bishops* it would then follow that *Parker was not a bishop*, and the succession of the English clergy would be destroyed." (*Quoted by Dr. Milner, vide Val. Ang. Ord. p.* 209.) Yet Hodgkin, though only a suffragan and without jurisdiction, was a real bishop, having been validly consecrated, with a valid Catholic form, by Stokesly, bishop of London, in 1537, and hence, if the Register can be relied on as detailing the real facts as they occurred, and the opinion of certain Anglican writers such as Mason, that all four were equally con-secrators, and that it would be sufficient if only one of them were a bishop, can be maintained, Parker may still be a bishop, though Barlow most probably, and Scorey and Coverdale certainly, were not. We are, however, inclined to think that any one who will take the pains to examine this question, and study the contemporaneous documents now within reach, will come to the conclusion that this presenting of all four as equally and individually consecrators is an after-thought, and that Barlow and the others using Edward's ordinal followed its prescriptions, and did not devise something new and exceptional. Now Edward's ordinal and the rubric of the Pontifical, and the invariable and immemorial usage in England, as is evident from every register extant, except this one, suppose and prescribe that there shall be one consecrating bishop, and two assistants. Hodgkin was then most probably present, but took no part in the ceremony, just as now, and at all times in the Catholic Church, prelates come by their presence to add solemnity and *eclat* to the consecration of a brother bishop, but only the officiating prelate, who really consecrates, and the two assistants, take any active part in the ceremony, so that we think Dr. Elrington was quite right in saying, that if Scorey and Coverdale, in addition to Barlow, were no bishops, then Parker was not a bishop.

Now as to the theological soundness of the opinion that all are equally consecrators, certain Catholic theologians are quoted as maintaining that the bishops present are not only witnesses, but co-operators. "*Omnes qui adsunt episcopi non tantum testes, etiam co-opera-tores esse citra omnem dubitationis aleam asserendum est.*"

—(*Martene.*) This by no means implies that they consecrate either separately from him or equally with him, but that they assist and co-operate with the consecrator, and invariably in the rubrics one is called the *consecrator*, the others, *assistants.* The consecrator is spoken of as effecting and completing the whole consecration, the others as "aiding," "co-operating," "giving testimony and approval." Numerous grave authorities and learned theological writers might be adduced, asserting with Filliucius, "Although there are three who consecrate, one of them alone completes the consecration, even though the others pronounce the words, for of one sacrament there is but one minister."— (*Quoted by Estcourt, p.* 112). We are quite willing to coincide with the very modest and moderate views of Canon Estcourt: "Without venturing to express an opinion on either side of these disputed points—that is to say, whether the assistant bishops are only '*testes*,' or also '*co-operatores*,' and if *co-operatores*, in what sense they co-operate; or whether the consecrator alone is the minister of the sacrament, and alone completes the consecration, or whether the others are joint consecrators with him, or whether it could be maintained, that all the bishops present are equally and separately and individually consecrators,—it is obvious that in a point touching the administration of a sacrament, such a defect as the absence of the episcopal character on the part of the principal consecrator would throw a very grave doubt on the validity of the consecration. It is quite sufficient to cause the doubt that various authorities should have taught that 'one bishop alone effects the whole consecration.'"—(*Ibid. p.* 113.) Under no possible theory, then, can the episcopal character of Parker or the validity of his consecration be more than doubtful on the score of his consecrators, whilst on the score of the form used, as we shall soon see, there was most certainly no valid consecration, even on the supposition that everything was done as the register supposes, and as the Anglicans themselves claim. As, however, some persons are not a little exercised over the number of bishops essential to a valid consecration, and seem not able to distinguish between canons of discipline, and doctrines of faith, declaring Roman Catholic succession in America and Ireland disfigured, and in some measure vitiated because the *canonical number of three bishops* has been sometimes wanting, whilst owning that, " without this condition, the ordination may be valid, but it is irregular and defective," we purpose here to lay down from Van Espen the true Catholic doctrine, and the teaching and practice of the Christian Church on this subject. " By the canons of the Nicene and other councils the discipline was established, as well in the Greek as in the Latin Church, that besides the ordaining bishop, two others ought to attend at the consecration of a bishop, and personally assist him.

"The reason of this discipline was assigned by Pope Innocent I., writing in his epistle to Victricius, that 'one bishop singly should not presume to ordain a bishop, lest the benefice seem to be conferred by stealth. For such was also the constitution defined in the Nicene Council!' As if he would say the council would not have a bishop to ascend *furtively*, or *like a thief* into the fold of Christ, but *publicly*, that is to say, with the universal Church, represented by the bishops of the province, approving and assenting.

But neither by the Pope, nor by other authorities, is a consecration rejected as null and invalid, if done without the right number of bishops, but only censured as clandestine, and performed without legitimate approval; for the presence of those bishops is required, not so much for the substance and validity of the consecration, as for having it well considered and approved. And therefore, in case of necessity, the consecration can be given by a single bishop, since the presence of three, or even of two, appears to belong to discipline, and not to the substance or essence of the consecration."—(*Quoted by Estcourt, pp.* 111-112.) We do not then deny that, " Ancient as well as modern canons prescribe that three bishops should be present at a consecration." But this is barely a *precept*, not an *essential condition*, and it appears by the form used in the Church of England, as well as in the Catholic Church, that only one prelate is considered as the consecrator. —(*Dr. Kenrick.*) We might even introduce our friend to a Pope who lived and governed the Church before the Council of Nicea, in the time of the Emperor Trajan, who established this discipline, and decreed that a bishop should be consecrated by not less than three bishops. This at least some affirm of Anacletus, though we do not care to vouch for the authority on which this is affirmed. But surely this Apostolical authority and this venerable Catholic Church, which established these wise regulations, and disciplinary canons, are competent to interpret them and carry them out in the spirit, and for the purposes that inspired them. She surely must be authorized to relax these, her own laws, when necessity requires it, in times of persecution, or conversion of pagan countries, and the evangelization of nations. And most undoubtedly in the establishment of the American hierarchy, and the consecration of the first bishop of the American colonies, to which our friend takes exception, there was nothing hostile or repugnant to the spirit of the Apostolical canons or the practice of the Christian Church, there was nothing done furtively or clandestinely, or without the knowledge, approval and assent of the clergy of the province and the universal Church. Dr. Carroll, "a most worthy prelate," (though, by the way, a Jesuit), was elected by his brethren of the clergy. Their choice was approved and confirmed by the Sovereign Pontiff, who in the usual form and style authorized him to receive the episcopal consecration from any Catholic bishop in communion with the Holy See. And if there was at that period no regular and canonical hierarchy in England, and if bishops were scarce and convened with difficulty in that once eminently Catholic island, devoted to the Holy See and illustrated by saintly bishops, who is to blame, but the persecuting, apostate Church of England? And if Dr. Walmsley, bishop of Rama *in partibus infidelium*, and Vicar Apostolic of the district of London, cannot surround the solemn ceremony of the consecration of the first bishop of the American Church with all the *éclat* and pomp of a numerous attendance of his episcopal brethren, the blame lies at the door of those who sought to crush out the Catholic hierarchy by fire and sword, by the most cruel and tyrannical persecution, and we think Anglicans ought not to force these memories back upon us. The consecration was, however, in all other respects most solemn, regular and canonical, and no one ever dreamed of doubting its validity, or the legitimacy of the succession starting from it, and only a fertile and imaginative, perhaps poetical, brain could invent the new succession from Archbishop Bedini.

This we deem sufficient, in reply to the call made on us "to clear up the difficulties which hang about our own orders," and the strange assertions that "nobody involved in such a consecration is in a position to object to the order of others." But we can hardly forbear a smile, when we read—" But neither the Walmsley nor the Bedini ordination have (*sic*) any validity as establishing a canonical episcopate in this country. Our lawful bishops were already settled in their sees, according to the Catholic constitutions, having been duly elected by their dioceses, and no Italian prelate whatever could give any commission in this country without their consent, except in that defiance of all canons which for many years has been habitual with the Popedom." This is decidedly cool, some might call it impudence. The bishops of the Protestant Episcopal Church are here. Then beware, Catholics, how you intrude! Supreme Pontiff, Bishop of Rome, though the whole flock of Christ is committed to thy care, " Feed my lambs, feed my sheep:" though thou art constituted to " confirm thy brethren," and to sustain as a solid rock and immovable foundation the whole Church of Christ, venture not to send thy emissaries to the free land of America, where "our lawful bishops have already settled their sees." However, the papacy has been for a long time—for well nigh 1900 years—accustomed to disregard such insensate pretensions, and to send its missionaries, priests and prelates, in defiance of infidelity, heresy and error of every kind, to plant the standard of the Cross, to preach Christ crucified, to teach the faith of the gospel in all lands, and this mission it will continue to fulfil to the end of time. But this comes with a singularly bad grace from one who, it will be remembered by all our readers, congratulated, in a note published in all our papers, Reinkens on his consecration, and reached out to him the hand of fellowship as an episcopal brother in full standing, though Bishop Reinkens had gone all the way to Holland to be consecrated by *one* Jansenist bishop, and had come back with what might rightly be called a *roving* commission as universal " Old Catholic" bishop of Germany, or something of the kind, though the Catholic bishops *were already established in their sees*, and all refused to impose hands on him, or admit him to any share in their office, dignity or charge. Kaiser Wilhelm commissions him : Prince Bismarck signs his episcopal brevet; he promises servile obedience to the State. That is warrant enough; no mention of violated canons : of irregular and defective ordination ! O consistency, thou art a jewel! And again, what about the intrusion by Episcopalians into Mexico and the South American States! Who could give *them* commission "except in defiance of all canons" where for ages Catholic bishops "were settled in their sees."

IX.

THE EDWARDINE ORDINAL NOT THE SAME AS THE ROMAN PONTIFICAL—INVALIDITY OF FORM OF CONSECRATION DEVISED BY EDWARD VI.

HAVING seen how vain is the attempt to make Scorey, Coverdale and Hodgkin supply for Barlow's doubtful sufficiency to validly consecrate Parker, we come now to discuss the main question—is the form which Barlow is said to have used in the consecration of Parker a valid form, capable of conferring a valid episcopal consecration? We before affirmed that whatever opinion we may form of the question of fact of Parker's consecration, which, as a matter of opinion and history, is to be determined by historical research, "It is absolutely certain that on account of the form used, Anglican, and consequently Protestant Episcopal, orders are vitiated and invalidated." Again, " Even if Barlow were a regularly consecrated bishop, and went through the form of Parker's consecration, the form used, namely, that *devised*, as the act expresses it, by Edward, was notoriously insufficient and invalid." And again, "The Church established by law seems to have felt this herself, for, in the year 1662, just one hundred and three years too late to save Anglican orders (Parker's consecration, according to the Lambeth Register, was in 1559), convocation changed the form, evidently with the aim of supplying the defect pointed out by Catholic divines." In reply, we are told: "The Roman Pontifical differs from the Ordinal by which Parker was consecrated in nothing which any theologian has ever ventured to pronounce essential." Now, we think it hardly worth our while to waste words with any man who so boldly and unblushingly sets truth at defiance, and contradicts all history. The fact is that every Catholic theologian, and every Catholic writer who has treated of the subject, has denied the validity of all ordinations conferred according to the Ordinal of Edward, and surely that is making an essential difference between it and the Roman Pontifical. Such was the judgment of Cardinal Pole, legate of the Holy See, and archbishop of Canterbury, in the reign of Queen Mary, who, with his sub-delegates, theologians, counsellors, and advisers, investigated the question, when everything was fresh and information easily obtained, when nobody could have any interest in concealing the truth, and when all must have been more than willing to recognize orders conferred according to the new rites, if the orders were valid. How much trouble would have been saved! how many won over by a favorable decision! None knew better than they what discontent and trouble would ensue if men were to be disturbed in the possession of benefices and bishoprics, to which they had been promoted according to the laws of the realm and forms devised by the king, and sanctioned by Parliament. Yet judgment, a solemn and deliberate, disinterested, impartial judgment, was then pronounced against the validity of Anglican orders, and that judgment has never been reversed. The same has been the judgment of all Catholic theologians for three hundred years, and the same is the judgment of the Catholic Church to-day, and yet, here is a writer with some pretensions, too, to position and respectability, and ecclesiastical knowledge, who not only insults truth and candor, but also the intelligence of his readers, by asserting that the 'Roman Pontifical differs from the Ordinal by which Parker was consecrated in nothing which any theologian has ever ventured to pronounce essential."

We might, perhaps, refer, not him, but his readers, to Dr. Milner (" End of Religious Controversy"), Most Rev. Francis Patrick Kenrick ("Theologia Dogmatica"), Most Rev. Peter Richard Kenrick (" Anglican Ordinations"), Dom Wilfrid Raynal, O.S.B. (" The Ordinal of Edward VI."), E. E. Estcourt, M.A., F.S.A. (" The Question of Anglican Ordinations"), as theologians whose works are probably the most accessible, and who, *ex professo*, show the essential difference between the Catholic and the Anglican form of consecration, between the Roman Pontifical and the Edwardine Ordinal, and learnedly and conclusively demonstrate in the language of an able writer in the Dublin *Review* for July, 1873, that " The orders conferred by the bishops who fell into heresy, and who used what is called the Edwardine Ordinal, were held invalid, absolutely null, and unto this day there has been no change in the discipline of the Church." But our Buffalo divine appears to contradict himself, for, in speaking of the different pleas on which Catholics demur to the claim of Apostolic succession in the Anglican Church, he says: "The more decent controvertist tries to prove that the form of words is defective." Who are these more decent controvertists, unless theologians? And how do they try to prove the form defective, unless by proving the Edwardine form insufficient and invalid, and consequently essentially different from the form of the Roman Pontifical? But we are taken to task, for asserting what we have now affirmed, that Cardinal Pole and the Church positively and constantly refused to recognize the validity of Anglican orders, or the valid consecration of bishops, ordained according to the new rites devised by Edward, or the Ordinal which he published and forced on the English Church, as a substitute for the old English liturgies, thus: " Dr. Ryan again quarrels with history, when he asserts that the Popes never recognized as bishops those ordained by the Ordinal of Edward. On the contrary, Pope Paul IV., his legate, Cardinal Pole, and all the papal bishops of England did this in Queen Mary's time, thus barring forever such cavils as Dr. Ryan has collected. Rome never pretended to doubt the validity of the consecrations under the Reformed Ordinal till she lost hope of regaining the Anglican Church."

Now, on this, as on many other points, the gentleman has been imposed upon and misled by Dr. Lee who, himself following the lead of Bramhall, pretends to produce " Roman Catholic testimonies to the validity of Anglican orders." Canon Estcourt, who has entered into an elaborate and critical examination of this point, tells us: " However ambiguous may be the statements of Catholic divines referring to Parker's consecration, there is no doubt with regard to either their opinion or their practice, when they come to deal with ordinations given and received according to the form annexed to the Book of Common Prayer in 1552, and afterwards confirmed by the act, 8 Eliz. cap. I." —(*Quest. Ang. Ord., p.* 133.) After producing copious extracts from Allen, who states the practice of the English College at Rheims, from Bristow, Parsons and the petition presented to King James on behalf of his Catholic subjects, which declares : " Neither is the Protestant minister nor bishop, coming to our Catholike fraternity (as many come of the first sort), reputed other than for mere laymen without orders," and bringing the tradition of the invalidity of the Edwardine orders down from the time of Cardinal Pole, he makes out an interesting list of Anglican ministers reconciled to the Catholic Church before the year 1704, and ordained in the Catholic Church after their reconciliation. He then takes up in detail Dr. Lee's list of Anglican clergymen, who, after having been received into the Church, were said to have declined being ordained, because they believed themselves true priests, and premising that, "it is of very little importance what opinions these persons may have entertained on the subject, having been bred up in heresy, and not having studied a course of Catholic theology, nor having even imbibed Catholic instincts, they were not qualified to form a sound judgment on the question,"(*Ibid. p.* 143) he shows that Dr. Lee has no foundation for many of his statements ; is incorrect in regard to others, and that many of the cases have no bearing on the controversy, and sums up the whole as follows: " On review of these several cases it may be confidently asserted that there is an unbroken tradition from the year 1554, to the present time, confirmed by constant practice in France and Rome as well as this country (England), in accordance with which Anglican orders are looked upon as absolutely null and void; and Anglican ministers are treated simply as laymen, so that those who wish to become priests have to be ordained unconditionally. Not a single instance to the contrary can be alleged. The only case in which any discussion appears to have arisen, is referred to by a contemporary writer as an illustration of the accustomed rule. And the statements made of objections having been raised by various converts to being ordained in the Catholic Church are shown either to be contradicted by the facts, or to have no theological importance, on account of the persons named being unknown, or married, or of an unsuitable character, or only recently converted, or possessing no clear and certain testimony as to their opinions on the subject."—(*Ibid. pp.* 145-6.) The *Dublin Review*, in the article already mentioned, written by one, in our estimation, fully as much of a theologian as our Buffalo divine, thus continues this subject: "People may dispute if they like, but the fact remains, that in the Church the Anglican orders have never been received, never at any time. Besides, there never was any doubt about them. The Catholics left in England after the persecutions of Elizabeth, and during them, never hesitated; they saw with their eyes and heard with their ears, and not one of them, learned or unlearned, seems to have imagined for a moment that any of the ministers made by Parker could say Mass. It might puzzle a profound theologian to say where the flaw is, but no theologian, whether profound or not, has done anything else but confess the flaw." Of Canon Estcourt, the learned reviewer says: "He has shown by most conclusive proofs that the Anglican ordinations have, in no instance, been recognized; that the practice of the

Church has been uniform and constant from the days of
Cardinal Pole, under whose archiepiscopate the question was first discussed; it could not have been
discussed before. From that day to this, the Anglican ordinations have been regarded as nullities, conveying no spiritual power whatever, and leaving the
recipients as much laymen as ever they were in
their lives." Now, what can we think of a man
who has the hardihood to assert publicly that no theologian has ever ventured to question the validity of
orders conferred according to the Edwardine Ordinal,
or what is tantmount to that, namely, that the Roman
Pontifical differs in nothing that any theologian has ever
ventured to pronounce essential from the Ordinal by
which Parker was consecrated. What confidence can
we place in a writer who, with these facts staring him
in the face, boldly and unblushingly affirms, that
Rome never pretended to doubt the validity of the
consecrations under the reformed Ordinal, till she lost
hope of regaining the Anglican Church? We cannot
forbear branding here another similar, deceitful, assertion: "The Pope did not withdraw the Papists from
the Church of England, until the tenth year of Queen
Elizabeth, and till this all his adherents remained in
communion with their proper Church, and also in his
communion. This fact proves that the Anglican
bishops and clergy were fully recognized at Rome, so
long as the Popes had any hope of regaining power
over them." He refers to the bull of excommunication,
which, he tells us, Pius V. issued against Elizabeth in
1570, to which he evidently attaches little importance,
as he is convinced of the nullity and impotence of the
Pope's spiritual and temporal authority, but when he

talks of the Pope withdrawing the Papists from the Church of England in the tenth year of Elizabeth, and that, until then, his adherents remained in communion with their proper Church and in his communion, he talks silly nonsense, and, wishing to appeal to ignorant prejudices, he simply stultifies himself. But admire at least his logical acumen! " This fact, viz.:—that the Pope did not withdraw the Papists from the Church of England until the tenth year of Elizabeth—proves that the Anglican bishops and clergy were fully recognized at Rome, so long as the Popes had any hope of regaining power over them."

If you cannot see it, so much the worse for you; the fault lies in your dimness of vision, or dulness of perception, not in the argument, particularly when you know that all the bishops and clergy, who acknowledged the royal supremacy, were excommunicated in the time of Henry. We wonder if the gentleman knew this when he elaborated the above argument? We wonder if he ever read how the bishops and the clergy in Mary's reign sued for reconciliation with the Church, and obtained, from the Papal legate, absolution from the excommunication and spiritual censures incurred by various acts of schism and heresy, during the reigns of Henry and Edward, and how the whole kingdom was publicly and solemnly reconciled to the Church, on the 30th of November, 1554, by Cardinal Pole, legate of the Holy See? Yes, he must at least have had some inkling of this. He must have read something of the legatine powers given by the Pope to Cardinal Pole, and the extraordinary faculties exercised by him, in reconciling and absolving and dispensing with the bishops and clergy in Mary's time, because it is from a misunderstanding and misinterpretation of these faculties, and the cases in which they were exercised, that Bramhall, Elrington, Haddan, and Lee erroneously concluded, as he does (for he only repeats, almost *verbatim*, Bramhall's words), that: "King Edward's form of ordination was judged valid in Queen Mary's days by all Catholics, and particularly by Cardinal Pole, then Apostolic legate in England, and by the then Pope, Paul IV., and by all the clergy and Parliament of England." We shall soon show the true meaning of the powers and faculties granted to, and exercised by, the legate, and that they did not, and were never meant, to extend to the Edwardine clergy, and no one ordained by the Edwardine form was allowed to celebrate Mass or retain his benefice, unless after a new ordination. "The fact is," says Canon Estcourt, "the Anglican orders were completely ignored, and those who had received them were, to all intents and purposes, looked upon as mere laymen."

That there is, then, an essential difference between the form of the Roman Pontifical, and that of the Edwardine Ordinal, by which Parker is said to have been consecrated, we have shown, and we named, for the benefit of those wishing to know the truth, some Catholic theologians who wrote expressly and professedly to demonstrate a difference so essential as to make one form valid, and the other invalid, and some theological and popular works easily accessible giving not only the opinion of their authors, but collecting the testimony of a cloud of witnesses, theologians and scholars, all testifying to the unbroken Catholic tradition of the insufficiency and invalidity of all orders conferred according to the new rites devised by Edward, Cranmer, and their worthy compeers. That such has been the Catholic tradition and the unanimous teaching of theologians since the question was first mooted in the reign of Mary, we confirmed from the invariable practice of the Church in ordaining *unconditionally* all Anglican prelates and presbyters who, returning to her bosom and the faith of their fathers, wished to exercise the holy ministry, and were found worthy to receive the priestly character, and discharge the duties of the priestly office. This incontrovertible fact is overwhelming evidence of the mind of the Church regarding the validity of Anglican orders, and the Ordinal by which Parker was consecrated. As, however, this is a vital point, we have thought proper to add to the authorities already given, the testimony of Dodd, the historian, found in Appendix No. 42, "Dodd's Church History of England," by Canon Tierney, F.R. S., F.S.A.: (*Vol.* 2, *pp.* 291-2.)

"Though the consecration of bishops and priests, in Henry VIII.'s reign (after the schism happened, and a general interdict and excommunication was pronounced against the whole ecclesiastical body), was esteemed uncanonical, and annulled as to jurisdiction, yet all the time during the said reign, the validity of these consecrations was never contested by the Catholic party. But, in the succeeding reign of Edward VI., a considerable alteration being made in doctrinal points, and, among other things, a new Ordinal established, their ordination was not only looked upon as uncanonical, but also as invalid, upon account of the errors and omissions, which declared the unsufficiency of their Ordinal. The reformers not only struck out the article of obedience to the See of Rome (which rendered their consecration uncanonical, and deprived them of all spiritual jurisdiction), but the most of them renewed the error of Arius, and made no essential difference between the episcopal and sacerdotal character.

To these errors they added several others, which were directly incompatible with a valid ordination; that, ordination was not a sacrament instituted by Christ, but only a mere ceremony, to appoint a ministry in religious performances: that, all power, both temporal and spiritual, was derived from the civil government, and, namely, from the king ; that, those of the episcopal character could perform nothing effectually towards the validity of their character, without the king's mandate or letters patent ; that, those of the sacerdotal character had no power to offer sacrifice, to consecrate the Holy Eucharist, or to absolve from sin. This was the constant belief of both the consecrators, and of those that were consecrated according to the new Ordinal, to which may be added, that though they had held the orthodox points above mentioned, they made use of a matter and form that was insufficient, and not capable of conferring that power, which essentially belongs to the episcopal and sacerdotal character ; and that, having at the same time no intention to confer any orders, but such as were conformable to their errors, which were destructive of Christ's institution, their ordination was, *ipso facto*, null and invalid.

These are the considerations Dr. Harding and others went upon, when they denied Jewel's character, and represented the whole body of the reformed clergy to be no other than laymen, excepting such as were consecrated in Henry VIII.'s reign, before the new Ordinal, or any other erroneous ceremony of ordination was made use of. For the same considerations, the learned divines of Queen Mary's reign, nay, the convocation, and even the legislative power in Parliament, declared the aforesaid bishops and inferior clergy to be invalidly consecrated; and actually caused all those to be re-ordained, in whom they found any essential defect. In the following reign of Queen Elizabeth, the divines of the Catholic party continued in the same opinion, concerning the invalidity of Protestant ordinations; and all were re-ordained, that came over to them, notwithstanding any pretended consecration among themselves—Parker's Register, and the account there given of the consecrators' qualifications, being insignificant in the case, where an essential defect was alleged in the matter, form, and intention of the persons deputed to perform the ceremony." Now, if to this we add the testimony of Perrone, whom no one will deny to be a theologian, we shall have gathered for our readers data enough to enable them to form their own judgment about the assertion, that no theologian ever ventured to reject, as essentially invalid, the form of consecration used by Barlow in the consecration of Parker, allowing that he did go through the ceremony at all. "Anglican orders are deemed *null* and *void*, not because they are conferred by heretics and schismatics, but on account both of the interruption of episcopal succession in that sect, and of their form having been *essentially* vitiated; *ob vitiatam essentialiter formam.*" (*Perrone, de ord., cap. IV., quoted by Raynal, Ordinal of Edward VI., p.* 134.) And in this connection, Canon Raynal makes the important remark that the "Revised Ordinal was rejected by the Holy See some years before the alleged December consecration of Parker by Barlow."—(*Ibid.*)

And Rev. Mr. Waterworth, in his historical lectures, thus refers to the same subject : " It is not here the place to enter into the validity of the orders conferred by the new Ordinal ; it will be sufficient to observe that it was composed principally by men who considered ordination an unnecessary rite ; and that in the ensuing reign, the statute authorizing the Ordinal was repealed, and the ordinations made, in conformity with it, reputed both by the bishops and Parliament, invalid, principally because the anointing of the candidates, and the porrection of instruments were omitted, and that *no form of words was preserved significative of the orders conferred.*" —(*Lecture IV., p.* 196.) Yet in spite of all this, our " Old Catholic," misled by false teachers, stoutly avers that in Queen Mary's time the Pope and his legate, Cardinal Pole, and all Catholics judged King Edward's form of ordination valid. As the pains-taking Canon Estcourt has proved this false, after thoroughly sifting the whole matter, and investigating every particular case, we refer to it again only to show from the true character and tenor of the faculties granted to Cardinal Pole, how little those dispensations which he granted in virtue of those faculties, can be relied upon to prove that the cardinal recognized not only the ordinations celebrated in the schism under Henry VIII., but those also under Edward VI. The cardinal does, indeed, as seen in Statutes 1 and 2 Philip and Mary, cap. 8., dispense with and receive in their orders and benefices those who should return to the unity of the Church. " *Omnes ecclesiasticas personas* * * * *quæ aliquas impetrarunt dispensationes,* * * * *tam ordines quam beneficia ecclesiastica, pretensa auctoritate supremitatis ecclesiæ Anglicanæ, licet nulliter et de facto obtinuerint, et ad cor reversæ ecclesiæ unitati* *restitutæ fuerint, in suis ordinibus et beneficiis, misericorditer recipientes, secum super his opportune in Domino dispensamus."*—(*Dodd's Ch. Hist., App. XXV., p.* 135.) Yet this proves nothing, as the same author shows, because only those are or could be received back in their orders, who had orders, and this is apparent from the tenor of the faculties which he received, and which he distinctly explains and interprets himself. In exercising his faculties, as well as in granting to the reconciled bishops the extraordinary powers which as legate he held he expressly distinguishes two classes of persons, viz., those who had been ordained during the schism, *even unduly*, by heretical and schismatical bishops, yet according to the ancient Catholic rite; and, secondly, those who held benefices without being ordained. The former were allowed "to exercise the sacred orders and the priesthood even, received as aforesaid from heretical and schismatical bishops, even unduly (minus rite,) *provided* that the form and intention of the Church had been preserved"—(*Vide Quest. Ang. Ord., p.* 45), the latter might be ordained, if worthy, and retain the benefices if otherwise canonically conferred, whilst numerous instances are adduced to show that those latter were persons who had been ordained according to the new rites, and were acting as Anglican ministers. These, if unmarried and otherwise qualified, were be to ordained and retain their benefices. "And thus," remarks the Canon, "Dr. Elrington, Mr. Haddan, Dr. Lee, and other Anglican writers, have been entirely mistaken in referring the words ' minus rite' to ordinations after the Edwardine form."—(*Ibid.*)

The fact then remains, and cannot be controverted, or challenged, that the Pope and cardinal wishing to facilitate the return of the English Church to Catholic unity, from which a tyrannical, lustful king had violently torn her, stretched indulgence to the utmost limit, condoned all violations of canonical law and Church discipline, sanctioned whatever was not positively against the substance of God's holy institutions, dispensed with irregularities, and absolved from ecclesiastical censures incurred by receiving holy orders, 'minus rite,' without canonical sanction and approval of the Holy See, from prelates schismatical and heretical, if only what was essential to the validity of the sacrament was observed; and hence all the ordinations in Henry's time were recognized because the old form according to the Catholic Pontifical and the ancient English liturgies was used. But not a single instance can be adduced of the recognition or sanction of any ordinations performed in Edward's time, after the adoption of the new Ordinal, because they were absolutely, intrinsically worthless, and no earthly power could give them force or value, because the sacramental form was substantially destroyed, purposely and wickedly vitiated by men who sought to overturn the whole hierarchical order, by poisoning its very root, men who did not believe in the divine institution of the episcopate or priesthood, the sacrament of the Eucharist or the sacrifice of the Mass. Now, as we are not writing a treatise *de ordine*, or *de sacramentis in genere*, but reviewing and exposing sophistries and refuting false assertions, we must refer our readers, wishing further information on any of the points which we skim over, to the authors and works already named, or to any recognized hand-book of theological science to be found in our Catholic book-stores. Having shown that we did *not* quarrel with history when we asserted that the Popes never recognized as bishops those ordained by the Ordinal of Edward; having nailed the falsehood: "that Pope Paul IV., his legate, Cardinal Pole, and all the Papal bishops of England, did this in Queen Mary's time," and this other: "that Rome never pretended to doubt the validity of the consecration under the Reformed Ordinal, till she lost hope of regaining the Anglican Church;" and having, in our own opinion at least, shown that Popes, legates, bishops, theologians, the whole Church, constantly, unconditionally, without an exception, and with entire unanimity, in teaching and in practice, rejected as worthless the orders conferred by Edward's Ordinal, we may proceed to discuss our next point.

"When Dr. Ryan presumes to object to the Anglican formula of ordination, I have only to reply that it is the same which was used in England *before the Reformation*, and is essentially the same on which his own orders depend—'receive ye the Holy Ghost.'"

Here are three distinct propositions, all equally false and untenable. (1) That the Anglican formula of consecration is the same that was used in England before the Reformation; (2) That it is essentially the same as that on which Dr. Ryan's orders depend; and, by implication, at least, (3) That, "Receive ye the Holy Ghost," is the essential formula on which orders in the Catholic Church depend, or the essential sacramental form of ordination.

Let us examine each of these propositions: (1) The Anglican formula of consecration is the same that was used in England before the Reformation. Did not Edward then appoint a commission composed of six bishops and six others learned in the law to draw up a new Ordinal, to suit and accompany the new liturgy, recently compiled and introduced, enforced by pains and penalties? Is there not on the statute book of England, an act that reads: " For as much as concord' and unity to be had within the king's majesty's dominions, it is requisite to have one uniform fashion and manner of making and consecrating of bishops, priests, and deacons, or ministers of the Church, be it therefore enacted, by the king's highness, with the assent of the lords spiritual and temporal, and the commons in this present Parliament assembled, and by the authority of the same, that such form and manner of making and consecrating bishops, priests and deacons, and other ministers of the Church, as by six prelates, and six other men of this realm learned in God's law, by the king's majesty to be appointed and assigned, or by the most number of them, shall be devised for that purpose, shall, by virtue of this present act, be lawfully exercised and used, and none other, any statute or law or usage to the contrary notwithstanding"? (3 and 4 Ed. vi. c. 12). Were not several Catholic bishops who saw the tendency and aim of this new Ordinal, and the purpose of its framers and compilers, and on that account refused to give their consent or approval to the same, deprived and sent to the Fleet? Or, will any one dare to maintain, that the new Ordinal is the same as the old? Why, then devise a new one? Why did the Bishops, Tonstall, Aldrich, Heath, Day and Thirlby protest in Parliament against the commission appointed to compose it? Why did it require penal laws to force the bishops to use it? Why was Heath punished with inprisonment for refusing to approve it?

But (2) can any one be bold enough to say that the Ordinal, composed by Edward's mixed commission, is the same as the old Sarum Pontifical? or that the meagre, meaningless formula of episcopal consecration: " Take the Holy Ghost, and remember that thou stir up the grace of God, which is in thee by the imposition of hands ; for God has not given us the spirit of fear, but of power and love, and soberness," is the same as that found in the Gregorian Sacramentary, brought from Rome by St. Augustine ? " The traditional forms," says Canon Raynal, "brought from Rome by St. Augustine in the Gregorian Sacramentary, are found in the Anglo-Saxon Pontificals of Ecgberht, and St. Dunstan, and can be traced from the Roman conquests to the very days of the impious Cranmer."—(*Ord. of Edw. VI., p.* 58.) Dr. Pusey, in his *Eirenicon*, convicts somebody either of not knowing what he is talking about, or deliberately falsifying facts. " The form adopted at the consecration of Archbishop Parker was carefully framed on the old form used in the consecration of Archbishop Chichele a century before. * * * The tradition of that consecration was then ' only a century old." Then it was not the formula in use before the Reformation. It had not been used for a whole century. And Dr. Pusey says its use even then was exceptional, "having been resorted to at a time when the English Church did not acknowledge either of the claimants to the Papacy ;" and that the form was wholly different from that used in the consecration of the number of archbishops consecrated in obedience to Papal Bulls. Dr. Pusey's testimony then proves clearly that the Anglican formula of ordination was *not* that used in England before the Reformation, but one whose use was exceptional, and he thinks, " it was of the providence of God that they had that precedent to fall back upon." Now, we need not stop here to tell our readers that the only possible explanation of this assertion of Dr. Pusey is, as Canon Estcourt remarks, that Chichele was consecrated according to the form of the Roman Pontifical, in which the words, *Accipe Spiritum Sanctum* are found, and not according to the old English *Sarum*. Nor need we stop to remind Dr. Pusey that it was one of these claimants to the Papacy, viz., Gregory XII., who consecrated Chichele, bishop of St. David, in the year 1408, and that afterwards, in 1414, when promoted to the archiepiscopal see of Canterbury, he was confirmed by Pope John XXIII. —(*Vide Quest. Ang. Ord., pp.* 115–6) This, by the way, to show how true it is that England did not recognize the authority of the Pope, and that the Pope did not exercise any jurisdiction within that kingdom.

X.

THE INSUFFICIENCY OF THE EDWARDINE ORDINAL, CONTINUED.

HAVING seen that the Anglican formula of ordination is not the same as that used in England before the Reformation, is not the same as that found in the Sarum Pontifical, or the Gregorian Sacramentary brought from Rome by St. Augustine and "used until the time of the impious Cranmer," we come to the second proposition that the "Anglican formula of ordination is essentially the same as that on which Dr. Ryan's own orders depend," we must remark that our objections are to the formula of consecration said to have been used by Barlow in the consecration of Parker, that devised by Edward and found in the Ordinal composed by his mixed commission. We do not, however, wish to intimate that the form now used in the Anglican ordination rite, revised, corrected, and amended as it has been, especially by the addition made in 1662, is a sufficient or valid form, and we do not care to quarrel with the declaration: "the words added in 1662, while they add something to the dignity of the rite, were never supposed by any body in his senses to add anything to its validity." We only wish to avoid confusion by having it understood that in the proposition: "The Anglican formula of ordination is essentially the same as that on which Dr. Ryan's own orders depend," the Edwardine form is meant, for to this alone exceptions are taken, and whether the other is or is not valid, is of no consequence, since it came upwards of one hundred years too late to rehabilitate, or give force or value to, Anglican orders. Dr. Pusey is more candid and more correct than most Anglicans, when he acknowledges that the forms used when bishops were consecrated in obedience to Papal Bulls, were wholly different from that used at Parker's consecration. Now, as, not only all the bishops of England, from the introduction of Christianity into the island were always consecrated in obedience to Papal Bulls until Henry, bullying a weak and servile hierarchy and Parliament, ordained that bishops should be consecrated only in obedience to his royal Bulls, but also, we, and all the Catholic bishops of Christendom of the Latin rite have been consecrated in obedience to Papal Bulls and by the forms found in the Roman Pontifical, the form on which our orders depend, was, to say the least, even according to Dr. Pusey, very different from the Anglican formula. Can they then be essentially the same? We hold they are essentially different and precisely because purposely, *de industria*, Cranmer and his Calvinistic co-laborers, in framing the new Ordinal, modified, altered and omitted what we regard as essential in the ancient rite, and thus made the new, reformed Ordinal, substantially and essentially at variance with the Roman Pontifical. We beg our friend to take the Mechlin edition of the Roman Pontifical, to which he in a foot-note refers, and which he presumably has, or if not, we will cheerfully loan him the one now before us, and compare it with his own Ordinal.

It would occupy too much of our space to show all the points wherein they differ, even all essential points, at least, what we deem essential points, and hence we can here only insist that a careful and critical examination of the Anglican forms of making, ordaining and consecrating bishops, priests and deacons will reveal the fact which the "Question of Anglican Ordinations," draws out lengthily, conclusively, viz.: that they were framed purposely with a view of excluding the idea of sacramental efficacy, or a consecrated character impressed on the soul. They recognize no divine gift of grace or power communicated through the rite, conferred by the sacrament; that, alterations, omissions and novel additions to the liturgy and Pontificals have been made with set purpose and design to introduce the newly invented doctrine of the Reformers, to destroy the spirit and sacramental idea of the holy rite of ordination. Too late the schismatical Bishops, Heath, Day and Tonstall perceived—what Gardiner and Bonner had realized from the start—that Cranmer was bent on the destruction of the English hierarchy, the divine institution of the priesthood and the holy sacrifice, by tampering with the form of the sacrament of the Holy Orders; and they protested against the appointment of a commission to devise a new form of consecrating and ordaining bishops, priests, deacons and other ministers. "The commission, however," says Canon Raynal, "obtained the sanction of the Great Seal for their newly devised forms, and without further trouble forced them upon the bishops. This was in sober truth the dismantling of the for-

tress."—(*Ord. of Edw. VI., p.* 28.) In the form of ordination to the priesthood : " there is no indication of looking for a gift of grace peculiar to the order, nor for any interior consecration, nor for any special power of priesthood ; such a gift of grace as communicated through the imposition of hands, is unasked for, unrecognized, unknown ; it is completely ignored. Those parts of the ancient Catholic rite which indicated such grace are omitted, and the portions of the ceremony still retained are so changed as to exclude any such idea. The forms and phrases used are either new, or else applied in a sense quite different from that understood by the Catholic Church."—(*Quest. Ang. Ord., pp.* 222–3.) In the Edwardine form of consecrating bishops, "the few slight phrases of the Pontifical that are preserved, show that the compilers had the ancient form before them, and that while keeping up a pretence of the same thing, they deliberately altered it, in order to reduce it to the Lutheran and Zuinglian notions of a mere admission to an office and a trial before a congregation."—(*Ibid. pp.* 225-6.) "There is no mention of the functions of a bishop, as in the Pontifical, '*Episcopum oportet judicare, interpretari, consecrare, confirmare, ordinare, offerre et baptizare.*' The functions alluded to in the new Ordinal are, ' to govern, to instruct, to teach, and exhort, to convince gainsayers, to drive away erroneous doctrine, to correct and *punish*,' though in 1662, 'to ordain' was added. But as it stood at first, there was no allusion to administering any sacrament, or to anything requiring the power of order."
—(*Ibidem.*)

Again, as a proof that the Anglican form of consecrating is not the same as that of the Roman Pontifical, please to note the very serious and essential omission in the former of the two prayers of the Pontifical having special reference to the grace of the episcopal order: "Be propitious, O Lord, to our supplications, and turning over on this thy servant the horn (that is, abundance, or plenitude) of sacerdotal grace, pour out to him the power of thy benediction." "And therefore grant, we beseech Thee, O Lord, to this, thy servant, whom Thou hast chosen unto the ministry of the *High Priesthood.* * * * Complete, O Lord, in thy priest the sum (or perfection) of thy ministry." In fact, as Canon Estcourt remarks, whilst "certain expressions are retained and taken from the prayer anciently called '*Consecratio*,' every phrase that expresses a divine power, an authority coming from God, a sacramental efficacy, is studiously omitted. There is no prayer for the gift of the keys of the kingdom of heaven, nor of the power of binding and loosing, nor of the episcopal chair to rule the Church and people committed to him. Almighty God is not asked to be his authority, his power, his firmness. He is to be ready to preach the gospel and glad tidings of reconcilement; but the ministry of reconciliation is not given to him. He is to be the faithful and wise servant, giving the Lord's family meat in due season, but not one whom God sets over his family. Even 'the power which Thou dost bestow' (as the Pontifical has it), is changed into 'the authority given him,' leaving the source of the authority untold. And when we look back in order to know what the authority is, we find only, ' such authority as ye have by God's word, and as to you shall be committed by the ordinance of this realm.' Thus the prayer is only for grace to fulfil certain duties, and it does not ask for, nor recognize any sacramental gift whatever."—(*Ibid. p.* 228.) And this is just what we might expect from the well known, and often and publicly avowed sentiments of the compilers of the Ordinal. This ought to be more than enough to show that the formula of ordination of the Edwardine Ordinal, on which hang the validity of Parker's consecration, and the orders of the Anglican Church, is not essentially the same as that of the Roman Pontifical, on which depend Catholic orders.

But (3,) as some seem to regard nothing as essential but the words: " Receive ye the Holy Ghost," we will now try to prove that this proposition is as false and untenable as the other two ; that " Receive ye the Holy Ghost," cannot be the sole essential form of episcopal consecration. One simple syllogism should be enough to settle this point. That cannot be the sole essential form of consecration, which was not known in the Church, used in ordination of a bishop, or found in any Pontifical earlier than the 13th century. But the formula, " Receive ye the Holy Ghost" was not known in the rite of episcopal ordination, and is not found in any Pontifical or Sacramentary earlier than the 13th century, therefore it cannot be the sole essential form of consecration. Some one, then, has been again misled by his usual blind guides. Mason, an authority for our friend, admits the necessity of a sacramental form in Holy Order, and that for the validity of this form, its words should denote the special order conferred and the power given. But the words, " Receive ye the Holy Ghost," do not express the special office, order or power conferred, therefore they cannot be the sole sacramental form of episcopal consecration. Yet, with strange inconsistency, and a boldness of assertion and disregard of logic, worthy even of some one whom we know, he gravely maintains, that: "if the imposition of hands be the sole essential matter of the episcopate (as all theologians are agreed that the words which are pronounced whilst the matter is used, constitute the form), the words '*Accipe Spiritum Sanctum*,' (Receive the Holy Ghost) must be the sole essential form, and as these are found in the Edwardine form, the bishops of the Anglican Church must be true bishops." Hereupon Canon Raynal remarks: " Mason evidently did not know the fact that the words '*Accipe Spiritum Sanctum*,' were comparatively a recent addition to the episcopal form, and being a recent addition, could not be the sole essential form. Otherwise the episcopate was never validly conferred during a thousand years."—(*Ord. of Edwd. VI., p.* 140.) And referring to the illogical conclusion which Mason draws from his incorrect premises, Dr. Champney says: "It is a marvel to me that he should so peremptorily say, that their bishops are ordained with true matter and form. But he doth well to be bold in affirming, for a good face sometimes helpeth out an ill game."—(*Ibid.*)

Many other reasons might be assigned why these words, " Receive ye the Holy Ghost," as they are found in the Edwardine Ordinal, cannot be the sole essential or sufficient form of episcopal consecration. They do not indicate the order or express the distinctive character or power of the episcopacy; they are vague and indeterminate; they are used alike, and with equal fitness in the ordination of a bishop, a priest and a deacon: and in the form used in the Anglican Church, until 1662, when Cosin and others thought fit to make the change, there was not a syllable in the form for consecrating bishops to determine which order it was intended to confer. In fact it is, as Dr. Milner observes, "just as proper for the ceremony of confirming or laying hands upon children as for conferring the powers of the episcopacy."—(*End of Religious Controversy*, N. Y., *p.* 224.) But let us see how our Buffalo critic maintains the sufficiency of this form, "Receive ye the Holy Ghost." "As these were," he argues, "the only words used by Christ Himself in giving the Apostolic commission, it may be well asked, what more can be needed to continue it?" Here, indeed, is something to astonish us! "As these were the only words used by Christ Himself in giving the Apostolic commission"!! Surely, he must have written that sentence for us, poor benighted Papists, who are not allowed to read our Bibles! or he could not have hazarded such an assertion. However, not trusting our memory in opposition to so positive an affirmation, we turn to the holy gospels to verify what sounds strangely to us. Opening the gospel according to St. Matthew, we find no mention of these words, but we do find our Lord giving the Apostolical commission with authority to teach, and baptize, and discharge all the functions consequent thereon in the well-known words: "All power is given to me in heaven and on earth. Go ye therefore, and teach all nations; baptizing them in the name of the Father, and of the Son, and of the Holy Ghost; teaching them to observe all things whatsoever I have commanded you: and behold I am with you all days, unto the end of the world," —(*Matt. xxviii.* 18, *et seq.*) Most interpreters would take these words as giving the Apostolic commission and assuring its perpetuity.

Coming next to St. Mark's gospel, we again search in vain for the words, which, we are told, are the only ones used by Christ in giving the Apostolic commission. We do, indeed, find such words as these : " Go ye into the whole world, and preach the gospel to every creature. He that believeth, and is baptized, shall be saved, but he that believeth not, shall be condemned."—(*Mark xvi.*, 15, 16.) Once more we turn to St. Luke, and still find no trace of these words, though the risen Saviour declares to His Apostles that " penance and the remission of sins should be preached in his name among all nations, beginning at Jerusalem, and ye are witnesses of these things. And I send the promise of my Father upon you."—(*Luke xxiv.*, 47, 48, 49.) In the gospel according to St. John we find the world's Redeemer on the first day of the week entering where the disciples were gathered together: " He said therefore to them again : Peace be to you: as the Father hath sent me, I also send you. When He had said this He breathed on them and said to them : Receive ye the Holy Ghost. Whose sins ye shall forgive they are forgiven them, and whose sins ye shall retain they are retained."—(*John xx.*, 21, 22, 23.) Now how can the man say in the face of an intelligent Bible-reading community that, " Receive ye the Holy Ghost," were the only words used by Christ, in giving the Apostolic commision? He gave his apostles their commission when he bade them go teach all nations, preach the gospel, and baptize in the name of the Father, and of the Son, and of the Holy Ghost. He gave them power and authority to fulfil the commission, when He sent them, as He had been sent by His Father: He breathed into their souls the grace and power of the Holy Ghost to enable them to execute and perpetuate the divine commission until the end of time, and He clearly intimates among the duties and powers contained in the commission, and communicated to them by the same, the duty and power of forgiving sin in His name, "*whose sins ye shall forgive they are forgiven them; and whose sins ye shall retain they are retained.*" Surely, no man with this page of the gospel open before him, can say that "Receive ye the Holy Ghost," were the only words spoken by our Lord when commissioning His Apostles, or that these, more than the other words spoken on the same occasion were intended by the Saviour as the essential form of the sacrament of orders or the rite of ordination by which that commission was to be continued.

XI.

DISCREPANCIES BETWEEN THE ROMAN PONTIFICAL AND THE ORDINAL OF EDWARD, CONTINUED.

IN establishing our thesis that the form of consecration by which Barlow is said to have consecrated Parker, was altogether an insufficient and invalid form, invalidating all the orders in the Anglican Church, we have had to meet and disprove the assertions: (1) that such was the form used in England before the Reformation; (2) that it is substantially identical with the form of the Pontifical by which we ourselves were conrecrated; (3) that *Receive ye the Holy Ghost* is the essential and the only essential form of episcopal consecration; and that these were the only words used by Christ in giving the Apostolic commission. How very unwarranted and untenable these assertions are must be apparent to every reader who has followed up the discussion, and what amazes us is that such totally groundless assertions could have been published by any one pretending to historical and ecclesiastical knowledge. But there is really no limit to boldness of assertion, and in the interest of truth, and for the sake of the simple and unwary who may have no chance of examining or ever seeing any Catholic authors, we must still further follow up and expose the errors, falsehoods, and fallacies of this writer, pub-

lished here, on the subject of the Ordinal of Edward and the Roman Pontifical. Thus he writes:
"His (our) own Pontifical is certainly less explicit on this point (of the form) than the Ordinal of Edward; for while in both we have the formula, *Receive the Holy Ghost*, there is nothing more in the Pontifical; while the Ordinal goes on *with the very words of the Holy Ghost to a bishop*, thus defining the precise *charisma* bestowed by the laying on of hands." We are inclined to ask, at reading the above extracts, that, *The Pontifical is less explicit than the Ordinal of Edward*, and that : *In the Pontifical there is nothing more than the bare words, Receive the Holy Ghost*, has the gentleman ever seen or read the Pontifical published at Mechlin, to which he refers? If he has, he either does not understand its language, and has merely copied second-hand statements of false teachers, or he is, in bad faith, trying to deceive those who perhaps will never have an opportunity of seeing a Pontifical. Is that fair and honest in a minister of religion? We are then tempted to quote here the most beautiful and appropriate prayers of the Pontifical which immediately follow the "*Accipe Spiritum Sanctum,*" "*Receive the Holy Ghost,*" prayers that really determine and express the order of the episcopacy, the plenitude of the priesthood, the High Priesthood, the sum or completeness and perfection of the ministry, figured in the Levitical law by the priesthood of Aaron; prayers which actually and explicitly define—what the vague and unmeaning form of Edward's Ordinal positively does not —the special graces and precise charisma *bestowed by the laying on of hands*. Though somewhat lengthy, these beautiful prayers of the ordination service in the

Pontifical will well repay a perusal, and, more forcibly than any words of ours, they will evince how utterly unreliable is our Buffalo controversialist.

"Be propitious, O Lord, to our supplications, and as the horn of sacerdotal grace is outpoured upon these Thy servants, do Thou send down upon them the strength of Thy blessing. Through," etc.

"O God of all honors, God of all dignities which in sacred Order minister to Thy glory; O God, in the secret and familiar converse with Thy servant, Moses, amongst other directions for Divine worship, Thou didst prescribe also the forms of the priestly attire, and didst command Aaron, Thy elect, to be vested in mystic robes when offering sacrifice; in order that posterity might hereafter derive knowledge from the usages of the ancients, and the instruction of doctrine might not fail at any time. Mere symbolism won reverence amongst those of old, but to us realities were to be more familiar than mystic figures. Thus the attire of the ancient priesthood is a symbol of the adornment of our mind, and it is no longer the honor of garment, but beauty of soul, that renders Pontifical glory commendable unto us. Yea, even in former times, they looked more to the mystic significance of things than to the pleasure they gave the carnal sight. Wherefore, O Lord, we beseech Thee to bestow Thy grace upon these, Thy servants, whom Thou hast chosen to the ministry of the High Priesthood, that whatsoever was signified in those garments by the brightness of gold, the splendor of gems, and the variety of embroidery, may shine forth in their lives and in their actions. Perfect in Thy priests the fulness of Thy ministry; clothe them with every adornment of glory, and sanctify them with the outpouring of heavenly unguent. May it, O Lord, flow abundantly upon their heads, may it bedew their lips, and overspread their whole frame, that the strength of Thy Spirit may inwardly replenish them, and clothe them outwardly. Let steadfast faith, pure love, and sincere peace abound in them.

"Place them in the Episcopal Chair to rule Thy Church and the whole of Thy people. Be Thou unto them authority, power, and strength; multiply upon them Thy blessing and Thy grace, that rendered worthy by thy bounty to invoke Thy name, they may also become holy through Thy grace. Through," etc.—(*Pontif. Rom. Mechliniæ.*)

These prayers of the Pontifical are identical with those of the Leonine Sacramentary, so called from Pope St. Leo the Great, who sat in the chair of Peter, A. D. 440-461, to whom they are attributed. Even if he be not the author, for some seem to question it, the Sacramentary that bears his name is the oldest liturgical work extant in the Church either East or West, and antedates by centuries the liturgies containing the words, "Receive ye the Holy Ghost;" which, though now an integral part of the form of consecration, are comparatively of recent origin. Courayer himself admits that the form, "*Receive the Holy Ghost* was not observed for many ages in the primitive Church." It is strange, then, but true, as a contemporary author remarks, that "the Reformers, pretending to go back to ancient rites, were misled by a blind adherence to their Popish doctors, the mediæval schoolmen, who taught that the imperative form of ordination, and the delivery of the instruments were essential and of more importance than the prayers from the ancient Sacramentaries. This seems like a retribution for their unauthorized and sacrilegious meddling with the sacred traditions of the Church." But as we have transcribed the prayers of the Pontifical which are most commonly regarded as the form of episcopal consecration, and as we have been speaking of the Anglican form devised by Edward VI., and revised and augmented in the reign of Charles II., we will now place the latter in juxtaposition before our readers, that they may compare them with one another, and with the prayers of the Pontifical given above:

Form of consecrating Bishops devised by Edward VI., in 1549.	*Form of consecration amended by convocation in* 1662.
"Take the Holy Ghost, and remember that thou stir up the grace of God, which is in thee by the imposition of hands; for God has not given us the spirit of fear, but of power, and love and soberness."	"Receive the Holy Ghost for the office and work of a bishop in the Church of God, committed unto thee by the imposition of our hands; in the name of the Father, and of the Son, and of the Holy Ghost. And remember that thou stir up the grace of God, which *is* given thee, by this imposition of our hands; for God hath not given us the spirit of fear, but of power and love and soberness."

"But the Ordinal," says "Old Catholic," "goes on with the very words of the Holy Ghost to a bishop." This again is disingenuous and deceitful. These words are simply the admonition of St. Paul to Timothy, to stir up the grace of God which he had already received, and though they prove, as Catholic divines teach, that grace is conferred in the sacrament of orders, and that, consequently, it has one of the necessary conditions or requisites of a sacrament of the new law, viz.: the conferring of grace, they do *not define the precise charisma bestowed by the laying on of hands;* they do not indicate the communication of the episcopal character, the conferring of the episcopal order; they are consequently insufficient, and the form is still, in spite of them, an invalid form. "Do these words, then," we are asked, "detract from grace?" Not at all. Who ever said or even insinuated that they did?

But he continues: "The words added in 1662, while they add something to the dignity of the rite, were never supposed by anybody in his senses to add anything to its validity." *Transeat*, we are certainly under no obligation to defend the validity of the new rite, but mark now the sophisty: "If the lack of them (the words added in 1662) deprives the older Ordinal of validity, then the same lack must deprive Catholic consecration of validity." That there was a lack of something essential in the Edwardine form was apparent from the commencement to all who believed in the divine institution of the episcopate and the sacramental character of Holy Orders. The reformers were upbraided by the Catholics and Puritans alike with the insufficiency of the new rite to establish episcopacy. The Catholics openly accused its compilers of a design to blot out the episcopacy as a divine vocation conferring, *jure divino*, special powers, and imparting special graces, of making bishops merely "ecclesiastical sheriffs," subject to the orders and bidding of the king, levelling down all the different orders of the hierarchy, thus abolishing all distinction between bishops and priests by making no essential difference in the form of ordaining both. "In nothing," says Dr. Milner, "does Cranmer's spirit of Presbyterianism appear so plain as in his form of consecrating bishops." Thus, we see the Edwardine form, by the express design of its framers, actually did what the Pope and Catholic divines are falsely accused of doing, viz.: it destroyed the episcopal order, and the Presbyterians of the 17th century protested against Anglican bishops being admitted into the House of Lords, to which they had no more right, they maintained, than their own ministers, and they called on the Anglican Church to disavow all episcopal rights and privileges, "*since in the ordination of her clergy, she invariably used forms which established no distinction between the episcopate and the priesthood.*" The Kirk of Scotland openly asserted the existence of bishops in the Anglican Church to be incompatible with the use of forms destructive of the episcopate. Bishop Burnet acknowledges in his " History of the Reformation," that in Edward's Ordinal " there was no express mention made in the ordination of a priest and a bishop of any words to determine that it was to the one or the other office the person was ordained, and that *this* having been made use of to prove both functions the same, and that the Church esteemed them one order, the form was altered of late years as it is now."—(*Vide Ord. of Edwd. VI., p.* 164.) There was then felt to be a lack of something in the Edwardine form, and Bishop Cosin and his associates in convocation in 1662 undertook to supply what was lacking. Whether it was with a view to silence the clamors of the Dissenters, or to meet the objections of the Catholics, or to quiet the scruples of Anglican bishops of the Laudian school, who, after the restoration of the Stuart king, and after having been brought, during a foreign exile, in contact with Catholic bishops, had conceived other and truer notions of their own dubious orders, is of little consequence to us or to our argument, though it looks a little suspicious, that convocation regarded the change as something more than merely adding to the dignity of the rite.

All the circumstances of that change taken together and duly considered, there is no doubt in our mind that convocation *aimed* at supplying essential defects invalidating the form, pointed out by Catholic divines, and especially by a learned convert from Protestantism, Rev. John Lewgar, in a polemical work styled "*Erastus Senior*," published precisely at the time of the sitting of convocation. We conclude then with Dr. Kenrick that, " If the forms *devised* by Edward VI. were sufficient, the convocation of 1662, by changing them, especially in those points in which their validity had been assailed, inflicted a wound on the character of English orders, which it will be extremely difficult to heal or remove. If the forms of Edward VI. were not sufficient, the change came one hundred and three years *too late!* Hence, whichever opinion be adopted, the validity of English orders has been most seriously compromised by those who should have maintained it." —(*Valid. Ang. Ord.*, chap *XI.,p.* 161.) But now, please to note this style of argumentation: " If the lack of these words deprives the older Ordinal of validity, then the same lack must deprive Catholic consecration of validity." What wonderful logical acumen. Who would ever think of asserting that it was the lack of these words, added in 1662, which rendered the older Ordinal insufficient, and the Edwardine form invalid; and that because these precise words, which Bishop Cosin and his brethren in convocation devised to remedy the defects of their *jejune* form of consecration are not found in the Roman Pontifical, therefore, all consecrated by that old and venerable liturgy which dates back for centuries before Cosin lived, or Cranmer apostatized, or king and Parliament arrogated to themselves the right or power to establish the "manner of making and consecrating of bishops, priests," etc., are not validly consecrated. There was indeed a lack, and a patent and fatal lack, in the form of Edward's Ordinal, but that lack originated precisely because Cranmer and his co-laborers, appointed and authorized by act of Parliament to establish "a uniform fashion and manner of making and consecrating bishops," changed and modified and adulterated the form of the Pontifical, and the old English liturgies, of Sarum, York, Lincoln and Bangor, and omitted in their new Ordinal the prayers and form of the Roman Pontifical, already cited, containing what all Catholic antiquity regarded as essential to valid ordination. It is indeed most laughable to be told that we, with the traditional forms and liturgies of the Christian Church from the earliest ages, cannot have what is essential to a valid ordination, and what is lacking in Cranmer's forms, because, forsooth, we have not inserted in our Pontifical, Cosin's corrected and enlarged forms, or the words added in 1662 to the Anglican Ordinal. We are again asked, whether we are ignorant that " the Roman Pontifical is modern in many particulars, and has been often changed?"

The Roman Pontifical is that of Clement VIII. and Urban VIII., revised, as we read on its title page, and corrected by the illustrious and learned Benedict XIV., with additions approved by the Sacred Congregation of Rites. Benedict XIV. was born in 1685, and elected Pope in 1740, and consequently the authorized *edition* of the Roman Pontifical is comparatively modern. But we also know that if at times the Church authorizes a new edition of her pontifical and liturgical works, and adds some words, and prayers, such as, for instance, "Receive the Holy Ghost," which we have shown to be a comparatively modern addition, authorized, and made by the sanction and approval of the Church an integral part of the form, or if she omits some prayers and forms of blessing that have fallen into desuetude, and thus adapts her ritual to the wants and present discipline of the Church, it is not at the dictation of a boy-king, or in obedience to a Somerset and a Warwick; it is not in virtue of an act of Parliament enforced by pains and penalties, or through an acknowledged necessity, because her liturgy was deemed insufficient for the valid administration of the sacraments, rendering her orders doubtful, her ministrations unsafe, her hierarchy insecure. We know, and this lets out the venom of the charge, that, whatever changes, additions or omissions have thus been made by her in virtue of her own divine right, under warrant and sanction of her God-given authority, as a perfect spiritual society having power to regulate her own discipline, manage her own internal affairs, and to enact her own laws, they have never affected the substance of the sacraments, have never materially or substantially altered the sacramental forms. We hold with Benedict

XIV., and the Council of Trent, that Christ has given to his Church power to ordain or change any rites or ceremonies in the dispensation of the sacraments that do not affect their substance, *salva illorum substantia*, but that may contribute to the edification of the people, the utility of the recipient, or the veneration and dignity of the sacraments themselves. The matter and form appertain to the substance of the sacraments, and therefore the matter and form are invariable, and the Roman Pontifical of to-day is substantially identical, as to the matter and form of Holy Orders, with the Leonine, Gelasian and Gregorian Sacramentaries, with the old English Pontificals, and with the Oriental liturgies. King Edward's Ordinal on the contrary is substantially different from all these, and therefore we say: Please, dear sir, to redeem the pledge given in these bantering terms: " His (our) most learned Catholic authors can construct no argument in behalf of the Pontifical's present form, which does not equally cover our case. This I am prepared to show him at large when he presents me with such an argument." We flatter ourselves that *we* have presented such an argument, but we beg the gentleman not to refer us, as he seems inclined to do, to his ordinary authorities for reasons already stated, and which may be found more at large in chap. viii., " Ordinal of Edward VI.," by Dom. Wilfrid Raynal, O.S.B. We want facts, arguments and historic documents, and if we refer to and use freely, both with and without acknowledgment, Catholic authors, particularly Kenrick, Estcourt and Raynal, we wish our readers to attach importance or weight to their writings only as they find their arguments, convincing; their reasonings, conclusive; their con-

-clusions, irresistible ; their assertions, warranted by the records of history; their facts, undeniable. We have, perhaps, spun out too lengthily this point of the inadequacy of the Edwardine Ordinal, and invalidity of Anglican orders, but the vital importance of the subject must be our apology.

We are anxious to conclude this question of Anglican orders, on which we have expatiated at much greater length than we originally designed, but the subject grew on us insensibly, especially as we were in some sort forced into the discussion of several questions in order to expose and refute theological blunderings, historical inaccuracies, erroneous statements and unscrupulous falsifications of facts, connected with the matter in dispute. We need hardly notice again what we find again so positively, yet so falsely asserted and reiterated : " The words added in our Ordinal in 1660 ('62 ?) make the old formula more explicit, not a whit more sufficient, for the formula itself remains as it was in the old Ordinals; and as it is still in the Romish Pontifical." The falsehood of this assertion is already proved and patent, but its reiteration is something amazing, as anyone who will take the trouble to compare any of the old, ante-Reformation Sacramentaries, and the present Roman Pontifical with the unrevised Edwardine Ordinal, will at once see its glaring falsehood. "The words, Receive the Holy Ghost," he continues, "'are used in both (the Roman Pontifical and Edward's Ordinal) as sufficient to complete a solemnity which preceding words have defined to be the consecration of a bishop." Now let us remember that, as we before declared, the words, " Receive the Holy Ghost," were not at all in the older Ordinals, and in the Roman

Pontifical they were not used as sufficient to complete the consecration of a bishop. These words now used in the consecration of a bishop constitute an integral part of the form, and the Council of Trent has defined that the Holy Ghost is given in Holy Orders, and that the bishops say not in vain " Receive the Holy Ghost," but the Council has not defined or insinuated that these words are the form of the sacrament of orders,. nor does the Pontifical teach that these words are sufficent for the consecration of a bishop. The Church has not defined what precise words do consititute the sacramental form of Holy Orders and are positively essential to its valid administration, and theologians have held different opinions on the subject, but all hold that in orders, as in baptism, the sacramental form is contained in the words or prayers used in the application of the matter, and that there must be at least a moral union between them, so that whilst the minister pronounces the words of the form, he may be morally supposed to perform the act denoting the special nature of the sacrament which he confers, and signifying the special effects produced, and determining the special character impressed on the soul, or sacramental grace infused.

It will not do, then, for any one following Courayer and other Anglican writers, to say that words preceding the form sufficiently determine the meaning of the form, and define the solemnity to be the consecration of a bishop. Would he acknowledge, for instance, the validity of a baptism in which the determining words, "I baptize thee," were omitted, on the plea that the preliminary interrogatories, and ceremonies, and prayers, sufficiently indicated that it was the sacrament of baptism which the minister intended to confer? We think not; at least Catholics would not, and Pope Alexander III. has pronounced invalid, baptism in which these words " I baptize thee" were omitted, and merely the words " in the name of the Father," etc., said whilst the water was poured: not, as a learned canonist remarks, because these precise words were omitted, for the Greeks do not use these identical words, but " because the act which is performed by the minister is not regarded as sufficiently expressive," does not sufficiently determine the special object of the sacrament. The same author (von Espen) affirms that Eugenius IV., in his famous decree to the Armenians, " clearly intimates that the expression of the ministerial act in baptism is necessary for its effect: thus anxiously requiring that the act which is exercised by the minister should be expressed." From this Canon Raynal, from whom we largely borrow, argues· " What has been said of the form of Baptism, will hold good in regard to Holy Orders, and an expression of the ministerial act which determines the special character conferred by the imposition of hands, is absolutely necessary for the validity of the sacramental forms of the sacred orders."—(*Ord. of Edwd. VI., pp.* 105-6.) But in the form by which Parker was consecrated, or the words," Receive the Holy Ghost," there is no such expression of a ministerial act determining the special character conferred, or defining the rite to be the consecration of a bishop, and no preceding words can supply for this essential defect in the Edwardine form. Canon Estcourt produces the testimony of Richard Broughton, a Catholic writer, on the Thirty-nine Articles in 1632,which bears so strongly on this subject of the

Anglican form, which is so persistently maintained to be the same as that of the Roman Pontifical, and the same as that on which our own claims to be a bishop must depend, that we cannot resist the temptation of quoting it:

"And these Protestants' form of making their pretended bishops, is also utterly overthrown. * * * For there is not one singular or privileged thing, sign, ceremony, word or act, that may by probable or possible means give episcopal order; * * * for here is no more done or said than was in their making of pretended priests or ministers before, for these, the same were their ceremony, and words: 'Receive the Holy Ghost.' Here is no material difference; a bishop is pretended consecrator in both alike; the ceremony of laying on of hands is the same; the words spoken do not differ, in both there is the same sentence and sense. * * * In the pretended ordination of bishops there is no power at all given, but the party only put in mind or admonished to stir up that grace, which was in him before—the very same words which St. Paul, absent, wrote to St. Timothy, long after he had consecrated him priest."—(*Judgment of Apostles*, etc., pp. 371-2-3, *quoted by Estcourt, Quest. Ang. Ord.*, p. 235.) We do not think it necessary for our purpose, in this little treatise, and to justify our rejection of the Anglican form, to examine the theological question whether these words, "Receive the Holy Ghost," in the mouth of a Catholic Bishop, united in faith, and in full accord with the Catholic Church regarding Holy Orders, the priesthood, and the Holy Sacrifice, and using otherwise a liturgy approved by the Church, and expressing the faith of the Church in the sacramental grace and power of Holy Orders, would be sufficient, or in other words, whether the form used in the Anglican Church, *si nihil aliud obstet*, were there nothing else to hinder it, would be a valid form. Some Catholic writers affirm it. Canon Estcourt is of this opinion, and a writer in the *"Catholic World"* for August, 1874, coincides with Canon Estcourt, that, "so far as the material words of the Edwardine forms go, they are sufficient—*i. e.*, they are words capable of being used in a sense in which they would be sufficient—but the words are ambiguous." These writers have apparently adopted this opinion on the strength of a so-called decree of the Holy Office, in 1704, approving of certain Abyssinian ordinations, in which the abuna, or Abyssinian ordaining prelate, passed hurriedly along a line of deacons, laying his hands on the head of each and saying, *Accipe Spiritum Sanctum*, Receive the Holy Ghost. "Canon Estcourt," says the writer in the *"Catholic World,"* "has understood the Sacred Congregation of the Inquisition, in their decree of 1704, to have ruled that the form, '*Accipe Spiritum Sanctum*,' understood in the sense of the Abyssinian liturgical books, is valid for the priesthood, although, in the particular case, no further expression is given to this sense, at least no expression within the limits of the form, strictly so called—*i. e.*, " the verbal formula synchronous with the matter." For ourselves, we do not see how this decision or answer of the Sacred Congregation (which Cardinal Patrizi says is not a decree of the Sacred Congregation), in a special case, in regard to a solitary deviation from an otherwise approved liturgy, can be amplified into a general recognition of the validity of the form, *"Accipe Spiritum Sanctum."* The answer can cover only the case, or solve the doubt proposed. Now there is no proof, as far as we can see, that the dubium proposed by the missionaries to the Holy Office had reference to the sacramental form, F. Jones asserting that it turned exclusively on the non-tradition of the instruments, and the fact that the bishop did not lay his hands on each of the deacons during the whole of the form, but hurried along the line, imposing his hands on each only whilst pronouncing a part of the form, or the words, *Reple eum Spiritu Sancto*, which words he thinks the missionaries translate, "*Accipe Spiritum Sanctum.*" This most probably is the correct view and statement of the case proposed to the Sacred Congregation, so that the "*tal modo e forma*" of the dubium may refer to the hurried imposition of hands during one phrase, instead of the whole of the form, *Respice*, etc.

In fact, we do not see how from this so called decree of the Sacred Congregation, dated April 10th, 1704, after the letter of his Eminence Cardinal Patrizi to Cardinal Manning, which we find in "*The Month*," for August, 1875, and which we subjoin, can in any way be construed the sufficiency of the form, "*Accipe Spiritum Sanctum*," the cardinal expressly affirming: "This S. S. C. never, either explicitly or implicitly, declared that the imposition of hands with these only words, *Accipe Spiritum Sanctum*, sufficed for the validity of the order of the priesthood."

I.—LETTER FROM H. E. CARDINAL PATRIZI TO H. E. THE CARDINAL ARCHBISHOP OF WESTMINSTER.

"*Domino Cardinali Archiepiscopo Westmonasteriensi.*

"Eminentissime ac Reverendissime Domine Obs^me

"Litteris diei 24 Augusti, anni nuper elapsi referebat Eminentia Vestra quæstionem isthic exortam inter aliquos Scriptores, circa sensum cujusdam, ut appellat, "decreti," ab hoc Suprema Congregatione Universalis

Inquisitionis die 10 Aprilis, anni 1704, editi, quod valorem respicit ordinationis in quodam Casu Abissinorum expletæ per verba *Accipe Spiritum Sanctum* manuum impositioni conjuncta, ex eoque Anglicanos præsumere ac jactitare nullum jam posse a Catholicis moveri dubium de eorum ordinum validitate. Proinde ad anxietates eliminandas, veritatemque securius defendendam, quærebat eadem Eminentia Vestra sequentis dubii declarationem; scilicet, an, in supra-asserto decreto, explicite vel implicite, contineatur doctrina ad validitatem ordinis presbyteratus sufficere impositionem manuum cum iis dumtaxat verbis *Accipe Spiritum Sanctum*.

"Jam vero Eminentissimi Patres Cardinales una mecum Inquisitores Generales, articulo formaliter ac mature discusso, in feria iv. die 21 labentis mensis, rogationi ejusmodi respondendum duxerunt *Negative*. Atque, ad hujusce decreti justitiam protuendam, pauca, ex mente Sacri Ordinis, Eminentiæ Vestræ innuisse sufficiat. Scilicet, ex ipso Coptorum ritu, ut in eorum libris Pontificalibus habetur, manifestum esse, illa verba *Accipe Spiritum Sanctum* non integram formam constituere, nec sensum documenti, quod ex anno 1704 profertur, quodque non est decretum Sanctæ Congregationis, uti ex ejus Tabulario patet, alio modo intelligendum esse nisi quod, penes Coptos, ordinatio presbyteri cum impositione manuum Episcopi, et prolatione formæ, in antiquo eorum ritu præscriptæ, valida sit habenda: nunquam vero Sanctam Supremam Congregationem, sive explicite sive implicite, declarasse ad validitatem ordinis presbyteratus sufficere manuum impositionem cum his dumtaxat verbis, *Accipe Spiritum Sanctum*.

"Post hæc, cum me jam mei muneris partes implevisse sciam, superest ut, eo quo par est obsequio, Eminentiæ Vestræ manus humillime deosculer.

"Eminentiæ Vestræ—

"Romæ, die 30 Aprilis, 1875.

(*Sig :*) " Humillimus et devotissimus Servus,

"C. CARD. PATRIZI."

This so-called decision does not then, as the learned Canon Estcourt supposes, establish the principle that the words, *Accipe Spiritum Sanctum*, are sufficient as a form of ordination to the priesthood. Cardinal Patrizi expressly declares that from the rite of the Copts, as found in their Pontifical books, it is manifest that those words, *Accipe Spiritum Sanctum*, do not constitute the integral form, and that the sense of the document published in 1704 is to be understood in no other way than that among the Copts the ordination of a priest with the imposition of the bishop's hands and the pronouncing of the form prescribed in their ancient rite is to be held valid.

However, no one pretends that the Sacred Congregation sanctioned the form, *Accipe Spiritum Sanctum*, taken by itself simply, but specificated in the sense of the Abyssinian liturgy, as the "*Catholic World*" justly interprets the mind of Canon Estcourt. But the learned canon expresses this himself so strongly and clearly that we must give his own words: " It is perfectly well known that even if the prayers prescribed by the Abyssinian sacred books are not said, yet that the faith and doctrine of the Abyssinian Church is expressed by those prayers, and that it is the same with the faith and doctrine of the Catholic Church regarding Holy

Orders and the priesthood. There is no addition made to the words which excludes the due and proper sense from them, and therefore no doubt can exist about the sense in which the words are used in an Abyssinian ordination, though the practice is so far short of the theory. There is also a certain faith and doctrine expressed in the Anglican forms of ordination; and it is not the faith and doctrine of the Catholic Church, but that of Luther and other reformers. It is impossible to take the words, *Accipe Spiritum Sanctum*, separately from the context in which they are found. And the context does exclude a due and proper sense, and fixes and determines the sense to be contrary to that of the Catholic Church. Thus the Abyssinian abuna, though he repeats no more than those three words, yet, following the traditions of his Church, expresses his faith with respect to the sacramental grace and power of the order conferred in a manner agreeable with that of the Catholic Church. On the other hand, the bishop who uses the Anglican form in ordaining, is not only prevented from attaching a right sense to those words, but openly declares and professes that he does not repeat them according to the sense in which the Catholic Church receives and uses them."—(*Quest. Ang. Ord., p.* 244.) So that even if the material words, "Receive the Holy Ghost," were sufficient in connection with an otherwise approved liturgy and authorized ordination rite, the Anglican form would be invalid, because the Catholic liturgies and the Catholic Ordinals were vitiated for the purpose of introducing error.

"It is a settled principle with Catholics," says Archbishop Kenrick, "that no error about the nature or efficacy of a sacrament, no positive disbelief of its divine institution, or any other personal unworthiness on the part of him who administers it, can deprive such a sacrament of its effect, provided sufficient matter, valid form, and due intention concur in its administration.

"But if the matter be omitted, or curtailed of any essential part ; if the form be vitiated, or if ambiguity be introduced, for the purpose of introducing error, it is no longer a valid means of producing sacramental effects."—(*Valid. of Ang. Ord., p.* 175.) Dr. Newman in a note, since his conversion to the Catholic Church, on an essay written whilst a leading spirit of the Anglican communion, says: " The consecrations of 1559 were not only facts, they were acts, those acts were not done and over once for all, but were only the first of a series of acts, done in long course of years; these acts, too, all of them, were done by men of certain positive opinions and intentions, and none of these opinions and views, from first to last, of a Catholic complexion, but on the contrary, erroneous and heretical. And I question whether men of those opinions could, by means of a mere rite or formulary, however correct in itself, start and continne in a religious communion, such as the Anglican, a ministerial succession which could be depended on as inviolate. I do not see what guarantee is producible for the faithful observance of a sacred rite in form, matter, and intention, through so long a period, in the hands of such administrators."—(*Essays, vol. II., p.* 76, *London,* 1871.)

I will now adduce one more testimony in confirmation of the view of the nullity of the Anglican form, on account of the bad faith and heterodoxy of its framers. Dr. Lee, one of the Buffalo divine's most trusty guides and reliable authorities, alleges the celebrated Franciscus a Sancta Clara, as an authority in favor of the validity of Anglican orders. Him, then, we shall summon, as our last witness to confound Dr. Lee, and to demolish the forms of Edward's Ordinal. After asserting in explanation of the 36th Article, that: their (the Anglican) ordination, for as much as concerns their form and matter, will be valid, "*si nihil obstet,*" "*if there be nothing else to hinder ;*" he subjoins: " Notwithstanding all this, after a serious and sincere examination, I must put this final resolution as a most indubitable conclusion: *according to the clear sense of the ancient and present universal Church, their ordinations are, ipso jure, invalid.*"—(*Quoted by Estcourt, Quest. Ang. Ord., p.* 236.) After showing that: " The judgment of the whole Catholic Church was and is, that baptism administered by an Arian intending to oppose the Church's sense, that is, not to do what the Church doth, by that their imperfect form, would be invalid, and by consequence, his ordination, though not differing essentially from the Catholic form, provided that he should hereby sufficiently manifest his depraved sense to be against the truth of Christ's institution," he continues: " The application of this, or this explication, is easy to the question of ordination, ministered by our Protestant bishops; for though we should suppose these forms not to be substantially changed, or their derivation of episcopacy to have been originally from ours, as they seriously pretend, yet since they have changed the church forms, *de industria*, as the second sort of Arians did, to declare that they do not what the Church intends, and in pursuit thereof have solemnly decreed against the power of sacrificing and consecrating, that is in the sense of the old and present Catholic Church, of changing the elements of bread and wine into the body and blood of Christ, our Lord, as appears in the 28th and 31st Articles, it evidently concludes that they never did or could validly ordain priests, and consequently bishops, having, as I say, expressed clearly the depravation of their intentions in order to the first and principal part of ordination, which consisteth in the power, *super Corpus Christi verum*, of sacrificing and consecrating his true body, by them professedly denied, and the sacrifice declared *a pernicious imposture* (a strange expression) in their articles, never repealed or mitigated in any synod."--(*Ibid. p.* 239.)

After ridiculing the pretension that, even if there were a flaw in the first consecration, a valid succession was transmitted in after times, as if "they could derive a succession *per saltum*, as from a great grandfather, without a father," he concludes with this argument: "All ordinations, celebrated in a form different from the Church, with an intention, sufficiently expressed, of opposition to her sense, are invalid according to the definitions of the general councils cited (Nice and Arles). But their ordinations are such, ergo."—(*Ibid.* 240.) From this extract it is plain, as Canon Estcourt remarks, from whom we have abridged it, that this would-be witness to the validity of Anglican orders, rejects them most explicitly and roundly, even when conceding that the forms may be sufficient in themselves, "yet, as they have been changed, *de industria*, to declare that the ordainers do not intend what the Church intends, the ordination cannot be valid." We have now done with the main question at issue, the legitimate succession and valid orders of the Anglican and Protestant Episcopal bishops, having demonstrated fully, at least we think so, that Anglicans have no claims to either. Dr. Lee himself, the champion of Anglican orders, is too fair and too conversant with the subject to simply pooh-pooh the objections of Catholics. We will then let him have the closing words on Anglican ordinations. "There are," he says, in his late work, "certain difficulties, which, it must be frankly allowed, have always been felt by learned Roman Catholics and Orientals, with regard to the fact of Parker's consecration and which must be duly faced and removed, before any recognition of the validity of English ordinations can be reasonably expected from the Eastern or Western Churches. Anglicans must not remain contented with assertions, which appear to satisfy themselves, but be prepared with arguments and conclusions, which will convince their opponents." (Vol. 1. p. 99). "The modern Easterns," continues the same frank and able writer, "though personally civil and polite enough, frequently repudiate our ordinations with scorn. The late archbishop of Syros and Tenos, even more civil than some of his brethren, reordained absolutely the Rev. James Chrystal, an American clergyman of the Protestant Episcopal Church; while the Servian archimandrite, who once gave Holy Communion to a London clergyman, the Rev. Wm. Denton, who had rendered good service to the Servian Church, was most severely reprimanded by authority, and made to give a promise in writing, that he would never repeat that, his canonical offense; and this in a formal document, which described the Church of England as 'unorthodox,' and Protestant, and the clergyman in question as 'without the priesthood.'" We are not alone, then, in questioning Anglican and Protestant Episcopal orders.

Nor is it owing to the gross ignorance of Roman

Catholic theologians, that succession and orders in the Anglican establishment are rejected, for Dr. Lee, with praiseworthy candor, asserts: "At Rome every care is taken to arrive at the truth, so that the inadequate defences regarded as sufficient and satisfactory by some at home, will never pass muster, in presence of the skilled theologians of the eternal city. A huge assumption, as Roman Catholic theologians maintain, that all was right in Parker's case, is of course easily enough made; but detailed proof of facts, and satisfactory replies to objections often give trouble, entail research, and yet remain insufficient for the purpose." (Vol. i. p. 200.) And yet, in spite of his close study of facts and patient research, Dr. Lee is forced to fall back on what he styles the *moral* argument in favor of Anglican orders. But let us hear him further: "Of course to any English churchman, of the Oxford school, the proceedings in question will no doubt be read with some pain. It is no easy task to show that the revived doctrines and Catholic practices, now so largely current in every diocese of our beloved country, and, many of them, so generally popular, were utterly repudiated by the dismal prelates, whose violent and heretical language is so awful in itself and so disquieting to dwell upon; and whose destructive labors it is so distasteful to put on record. Men who in a spirit of self-sacrifice now repair churches, cleanse the font, rebuild the broken-down altar of the Lord, beautify His sanctuary, adorn with pictured pane and mosaic representation the chancel wall—who open the restored churches for the daily office, who—in the face of secular and senseless 'judgments'—believe in baptismal regeneration, practise confession, pray for the departed, and have been led, step by step, to restore the Christian sacrifice and Eucharistic adoration; and who, furthermore, look upon themselves, now clothed in sacerdotal garments, and standing facing the crucifix at lighted altars, as sacrificing priests of the New Law—can surely have but little in common with the vulgar anti-Catholic bishops of Queen Elizabeth's day, whose profane and awful words, when read at a distance of three centuries or more, make a reverent person shudder; and the dark records of whose blasphemies and active wickedness, when calmly faced, sends a thrilling shiver through the heart of a Christian, and makes every decent Englishman—unparalyzed by indifference, and not choked by false science—blush for shame that such officials ever belonged to so moderate and respectable an institution as the Church of England by law established now appears." (Vol. i. p. 272-4.)

The above we have borrowed from an able article in the "*Liverpool Catholic Times*," and although somewhat lengthy we will allow the writer to continue his review of Dr. Lee's work in his own words:

"From these data, Dr. Lee, in several places, but especially in his introductory essay on 'The present position of the Established Church,' draws a 'moral' argument in favor of Anglican Orders. 'It is seif-evident,' he writes, 'that the moral argument in favor of their validity is very strong, perhaps stronger than either the theological or historical argument. When the frightful state of degradation into which the National Church during Elizabeth's reign had been brought, is honestly contemplated; and when the striking contrast between its position then and its altered state now is duly realized—the manner in which so much that had been then cast away as valueless is now sought after and has been once more secured ; we may reasonably infer (though there be no exact precedent nor perfect parallels in past history for the complex character and unique position of the Established Church of England) that, as divine grace has never been withdrawn from her crippled rulers, so an inherent and essential distinction between clergy and laity has been in the main consistently and continually remarked and admitted.' (Pp. 51-52.)

" We give the argument in the writer's own words, so as not to deprive it of any weight which may legitimately attach to it. But we cannot but think that Dr. Lee's own volumes are its completest refutation. Anglicans are in the habit of assuming that the 'Reformation' in England essentially differed from that on the Continent and in Scotland in certain respects, and, *inter alia*, in the retention of a belief in, and respect for, the grace of Holy Orders; and *then* (when historical difficulties are raised) they fall back upon the sentiment that God would never have permitted the lapse of sacramental grace through the accidental oversight of any essential. Dr. Lee makes short work, however, of any such assumption. He shows the authors and abettors of the New Church as being to the full as blasphemous and sacrilegious, as coarse, as immoral, and altogether as satanic, as the Continental, 'Reformers,' with the superadded malice of abominable and anti-Christian subserviency to the crown. So far, then, the moral argument against Anglican orders is as strong as against Presbyterian or Lutheran ones. In other words, as, upon Anglican equally as upon Catholic principles, we know that God permitted the Kirk of Scotland and the Continental Protestant Communions to have lost the grace of orders and sacraments, there is no reason (in the absence of direct proof) to believe that He dealt otherwise with the equally guilty and sacrilegious rulers of the Elizabethan Church. The weight of probability is that God should, rather than that He should not, have withdrawn His sacraments from the sacrilegious grasp of men who were wont to style the Blessed Sacrament—*horrescimus referentes*"—(We cannot bring ourselves to quote the low and shocking language used by the reformers towards the Blessed Sacrament): "who in all things were the subservient tools of a monster who, whilst claiming more than Pontifical honors, caused the Corpus Christi canopy to be borne over her at Cambridge, and who ended by making the hearing or singing of Mass a crime punishable by fine, imprisonment and death.

"But the moral argument *against* Anglican orders is still stronger when we consider the attitude of the Elizabethan bishops themselves towards orders. One and all they repudiate any such belief in ordination as obtains among Ritualists, or even among moderate Anglicans. They denounced the sacrament of order as fully, as consistently, and as vehemently as they denounced the Mass, the Real Presence, or Extreme Unction. Again and again they admitted men to cure of souls who had never received episcopal ordination, and allowed preachers to occupy benefices who refused to administer either Baptism or 'the Supper,' and were known as 'no sacrament ministers.' They were quite content to hold their posts solely from the queen, to be 'bishops by act of Parliament.' And when, later on, an attempt was made to claim for them some kind of spiritual jurisdiction as successors of the Apostles, they were promptly told that their jurisdiction was derived from the crown, and that any attempt to claim independent jurisdiction would lay them open to the penalties of *præmunire*. Even Hooker, whom Dr. Lee rightly praises as 'the first person among the English ministers who, by the general soundness of his principles, the clearness of his thoughts, and the ability with which he set them forth, began to stem the tide of confusion, innovation, and novelty,' never adopted the Catholic belief as to orders, and actually regarded Dr. Adrian de Saravia—'ordained abroad by presbyters, if at all,'—as a fit and capable confessor, and so employed him upon his death-bed, receiving also the Communion at his hands. No doubt the Caroline divines, like their successors of the Oxford school, succeeded in raising the standard of sacramental belief, but like the changes in the Ordinal, due, no doubt, to the influence of their teaching, such improvements came too late to affect the main question."

XII.

CONCLUSION.

WE have now come to the end of our little work, and it only remains for us to summarize the main points on which we touched, and the conclusions which we reached. We have endeavored to show, with what success our readers will judge, that the line of Apostolical succession has been hopelessly broken between the Primitive Church, and the Anglican and Protestant Episcopal Churches, and that every attempt to bridge the chasm between Catholic England under the supremacy of the Popes, and the Anglican establishment under the Tudors, between Cardinal Pole, last Catholic archbishop of Canterbury, and Matthew Parker, the first link of the new line forged by the despotic, iron hand of Elizabeth, has been vain. Supposing the Lambeth Register to be a genuine, authentic document, the form used at Parker's consecration was confessedly that of the Edwardine Ordinal, devised towards the end of the year 1549. The form prescribed in the Roman Pontifical was abolished by act of Parliament (3 Edward VI., c. 2), and the newly devised form made obligatory after April 1st, 1550, and added to Book of Common Prayer by another act of Parliament in 1552 (5 and 6 Edward VI.). According to the Lambeth

Register, Parker was consecrated by this form, which was so plainly inadequate and invalid that acts of Parliament were deemed necessary to supply its defects, and in the year 1662, one hundred years later, the form was again changed, obviously to remedy deficiencies pointed out by Catholics and Dissenters, and perhaps, too, to satisfy a reactionary movement inside the establishment itself towards Catholic doctrine and practices, though its defenders stoutly affirm that the change was not made to add to the *validity*, but to the dignity of the rite. Be that as it may, the form was intrinsically insufficient to confer valid consecration. Matthew Parker, therefore, never was a bishop, and consequently could not validly consecrate others. Besides, grave doubts and suspicions attach to the Lambeth Register, and still graver doubts are entertained as to the fact of Barlow's consecration, and the slender thread on which Anglican orders rest must be painfully apparent to those who claim that the assistant bishops at Parker's consecration, and at some subsequent consecration, would even suffice to supply for Barlow's non-consecration.

What thick mists and dark clouds of suspicions, doubts and uncertainties hang over the orders of the Church of England, even if it could be conceded—which it cannot consistently with the doctrinal teachings of the Christian Church—that the form was a valid one. But Apostolical succession requires not only valid orders but lawful mission; this has been proved from the teaching and practice of the early Christian Church; this is held by Anglicans and Episcopalians. This must, however, be ever carefully borne in mind, that the power of order, and the right to exercise that order, jurisdiction, mission, the assignment of charge or people over which that power may be exercised, are very different things, and do not necessarily go together. A bishop from the time of his appointment, even before his consecration, has jurisdiction over his diocese, though he may exercise no exclusively episcopal functions, do no act requiring the episcopal order and character. He may govern his flock as a legitimate pastor, and administer his diocese and empower other bishops to ordain priests and officiate in episcopal functions. And a validly and lawfully consecrated bishop may be without episcopal jurisdiction, may have no actual charge, or diocese to govern. Auxiliary and co-adjutor bishops have only such limited jurisdiction as the titular bishop or ordinary of the diocese may grant them, and not unfrequently, in case of the absence or death of the titular bishop, the administration is in the hands of a priest, a vicar-general, for instance, and he gives jurisdiction to the lawfully consecrated auxiliary bishop. How often do I here ordain priests for other dioceses and confer on them all the powers of their priestly order, but I cannot give them jurisdiction. That belongs to their own bishop. Only, then, a lawful ecclesiastical superior can impart ecclesiastical jurisdiction, and only valid orders and jurisdiction, transmitted in an unbroken line from the days of the Apostles to our own time, can constitute Apostolical succession.

Granted, then, that Barlow was a regularly consecrated bishop, and that he, in the Lambeth chapel, actually consecrated Parker with valid matter and form, even with the intention of the Church, and agreeably to the Roman Pontifical, from whom does he

(Parker) get jurisdiction? What ecclesiastical superior assigns him a charge? gives him the right to exercise the power of his episcopal order? who gives him charge of the diocese of Canterbury? Not Barlow, nor Scorey, nor Coverdale, nor Hodgkin; one, according to the Register, bishop elect of Chichester; one, bishop elect of Hereford; one, bishop elect of Exeter, and the fourth suffragan of Bedford. What right had they in the diocese of Canterbury? How could they confer jurisdiction on the archbishop from whom they themselves were to be confirmed and to receive a mission and right to exercise their episcopal orders? Not from the Pope, who utterly rejects his pretensions, and excommunicates him, can he derive jurisdiction. Not from the Pope, whose authority he repudiates and forswears. From Queen Elizabeth, then? Yes, this is his only and last resource. Here, then, comes the claim of royal, spiritual supremacy or headship over the Church of England, started by her royal father, asserted by her royal brother, and now exercised by herself, and thus, in virtue of the powers conferred by queen and Parliament, is Parker first Anglican archbishop of the Church by law established, and thus from the commencement is the fatal defect, the disastrous break in the chain of Apostolical succession. And it is well said: " that as original sin is not done away with by distance from Adam, so this original defect of jurisdiction cannot be supplied by length of time, *quod ab initio nullum est tractu temperis non convalescit.*"

MISSTATEMENTS OF CATHOLIC FAITH

AND

NUMEROUS CHARGES

AGAINST THE CHURCH AND HOLY SEE,

CORRECTED AND REFUTED.

BY

S. V. RYAN, BISHOP OF BUFFALO.

PART II.

CONTENTS.

I.—INTRODUCTORY. 1
II.—THE EPHESINE SUCCESSION. 4
III.—HENRY VIII.—TO WHOM HE BELONGS. 11
IV.—THE NEW LITURGY—BOOK OF COMMON PRAYER. . . 16
V.—NEW ANGLICAN ORDINAL. 19
VI.—CLEMENT'S DISPENSATION TO HENRY. 21
VII.—EQUIVOCATION—AUTHORITY OF SAINTS AND DOCTORS OF THE CHURCH. 23
VIII.—PAPAL INFALLIBILITY. 32
IX.—POPES LIBERIUS AND HONORIUS. 47
X.—HONORIUS VINDICATED. 52
XI.—ST. GREGORY THE GREAT CLAIMING AND EXERCISING PAPAL SUPREMACY. 62
XII.—CATHOLIC BISHOPS NOT SIMPLE PRESBYTERS OR MERE VICARS OF THE POPE. 74
XIII.—TEACHINGS OF THE ANCIENT FATHERS VINDICATED . 81
XIV.—CANONS OF NICE AND EPHESUS. 86
XV.—THE CATHOLIC DOCTRINE REGARDING ECCLESIASTICAL JURISDICTION. 93

MISSTATEMENTS OF CATHOLIC FAITH

AND

NUMEROUS CHARGES AGAINST THE CHURCH
AND HOLY SEE, CORRECTED AND REFUTED.

I.

INTRODUCTORY.

I HAD fully resolved not to notice the many irrelevant questions, groundless and false assertions profusely scattered through the pages of the little pamphlet, "Catholics and Roman Catholics," by "An Old Catholic," to which the articles substantially reproduced in the preceding pages, and originally written for the "*Catholic Union*," were intended to reply. However, as the specious and misleading statements, put forward with a certain air of plausibility and confidence might, if left unchallenged, impose on those who have no access to original documents or works of reference, I have, on second thought, deemed it incumbent on me, in the interest of truth and Catholic faith, to rectify the principal misstatements of "Old Catholic," even at the risk of swelling this little publication to unexpected proportions.

The discussion of these matters will, in my opinion, prove how easily people may be imposed on by ungrounded assertions, how cautious we should be in giving credence to authorities cited at second-hand, and how sadly deficient in accurate information regarding the doctrines, traditions and history of the Church even intelligent and otherwise well-educated Churchmen often are, whose reading and studies, ministerial labors and professional duties seem to be directed to the single point of obscuring the claims of the Catholic Church, or deterring others from the calm, dispassionate, thoughtful investigation of the same. Of such we can only say, in the language of one whom the grace of God and light of the Divine Spirit enabled to rise above the prejudices of his early education: "Prejudice is always obstinate, but no prejudice is so wilfully stubborn as that which is professional. It is bad enough, in any case, that the mind should be settled in opposition to the truth, but when a man has made it the special business of his life to oppose and controvert that truth, his intelligence becomes so fortified by his will, as to be almost inaccessible. The citadel of his heart is well nigh impregnable. * * * His mind is systematically warped. He is trained to reason from false principles. He becomes, perhaps, by sheer habit, the champion of untruth."—("*The Invitation Heeded:*" *Dr. Kent Stone. Part III., Chap. I., p.* 207.) This may explain, and if not excuse, in some degree extenuate the blind, unreasoning prejudices of men who are schooled into bitter hostility to the Catholic Church, and forced by their position and professional duties to repudiate her as the true and legitimate spouse of Christ, to reject her authority and deny her identity with the Apostolic Church, simply because these claims annihilate all their own titles, brand them as illegitimate, spurious, counterfeit. Yet we do not presume to judge how far they are responsible for errors which they have inherited and prejudices which they have unconsciously imbibed, religious predilections and affinities naturally springing from circumstances over which they could have no control, and hence we disclaim any personal feeling, most sincerely profess to be actuated by motives of Christian charity and love of truth. And if in anything we say we appear to be pointed and personal, it is because of the necessity of meeting particular charges, or misleading and injurious insinuations against Catholic faith and practice.

II.

THE EPHESINE SUCCESSION.

"THE first archbishop of Canterbury was consecrated at Arles in France (597), and thus introduced the Ephesine succession from St. John, through Irenæus and Photinus."—(*Note* 1, *Catholics and non-Catholics.*) We have answered already that Augustine was consecrated bishop at Arles by Virgilius, acting as legate and vicar of Pope St. Gregory, but the title and privileges and jurisdiction of archbishop were afterwards accorded to him by Gregory, Pope of Rome, not by Virgilius of Arles, who had, as we shall presently see, only such jurisdiction as Gregory granted him in Gaul. Lingard, in his " Antiquities of the Anglo-Saxon Church," says: " Gregory, whose zeal already predicted the entire conversion of the octarchy, commanded it to be divided into two ecclesiastical provinces, in each of which twelve suffragan bishops should obey the superior jurisdiction of their metropolitan."—(*Amer. edition, Ch. II., p.* 40.) Again, as clear proof that not only the new Anglo-Saxon converts with their bishops and archbishops, but also the ancient British Church, acknowledged the authority of the same Roman Pontiff, Lingard says: " Gregory, treading in the footsteps of his predecessor, Celestine, who two centuries before had appointed the monk Palladius to the government of the Scottish Church, invested Augustine with an extensive jurisdiction over all the bishops of the Britons."—(*Ibid. p.* 41-2.) To show still further what little truth there is in the assertion that the Pope "could never assert even a patriarchal authority over England," let us hear Dr. Lingard still further: "Augustine himself preferred Canterbury to London; and the metropolitical dignity was secured to the former by the rescripts of succeeding Pontiffs."—(*Ibid. p.* 44.) Again, Pope Vitalian placed Theodore, an aged monk, in the see of Canterbury, and " invested him with an extensive jurisdiction, similar to that which Gregory had conferred on St. Augustine."—(*Ibid.*)

But let us now see how the archbishop of Arles, who consecrated Augustine, acknowledged the authority and supreme jurisdiction of the Pope, Gregory the Great, over the churches of Gaul. In the year 595, two years before he consecrated Augustine, Virgilius wrote, and had King Childebert II. write, to Gregory, asking the pallium and the dignity of vicar of the Apostolic See, with which the greater part of his predecessors had been honored. In the month of August of the same year, Gregory writes to him (*L.* 5, *Epist. liii.*) granting his request, and among other things says: " I am very far from suspecting that in asking the use of the pallium and the vicarship of the Apostolic See, you thought only of procuring for yourself a passing power and an exterior decoration. I prefer to believe that knowing—for no one can ignore it—whence the faith was propagated over Gaul, you wished in addressing yourself to the Apostolical See, according to ancient custom, to act like a good son, who has recourse to the bosom of the Church, his mother." He concludes his letter thus: " We establish your fraternity our vicar in the churches of the kingdom of our most excellent son, Childebert, without prejudice to the rights of the metropolitans. We send you also the pallium, which you will make use of only in the church and during the Mass. If any bishop wishes to take a long journey, he will not do it without permission of your holiness. If any question of faith, or any other difficult affair come up, you will assemble twelve bishops to take cognizance of it. If it cannot be decided, you will refer the judgment to us." He wrote at the same time, in the same sense, to the bishops, exhorting them to submit to the new vicar of the Apostolic See, as the Angels of Heaven, though without sin, are subordinate one to another; and to King Childebert, begging him to support by his authority what he had regulated in favor of Virgilius, and for the sake of God and St. Peter to cause the decrees of the Apostolic See to be observed in his states.—(*Works of S. G., L.* 5, *Epist. liv. et lv.*) This, I should say, would make the great St. Gregory, in the 6th century justly styled the Apostle of England, a good enough Pope of the 19th century. But of this we will have more to say hereafter. Now we are prepared to examine the question of the " Ephesine succession from St. John, through Irenæus and Photinus." *We* should have said, through Photinus and Irenæus, for the latter succeeded the former in the see of Lyons, A. D. 177.

Now, we would greatly desire to see any one trace the succession of Virgilius of Arles to St. Photinus of Lyons, and then trace St. Photinus to St. John, in order to bring the Ephesine succession down to the bishop of Western New York. It is simply ridiculous to talk about the Ephesine succession, and no one familiar with ecclesiastical history, or with those saintly and historic names of the ancient Church of Gaul could commit himself to such an absurdity. The see of Arles was founded by bishops sent directly from Rome. St. Trophimus, its first bishop, was sent, according to St. Gregory of Tours, from Rome to Arles in the year 250, during the reign of Decius, and the Pontificate of Pope Fabian. Later French writers maintain that he was sent by St. Peter himself, during the reign of the Emperor Claudius, and in proof hereof, they cite a letter of nineteen bishops, written to Pope Leo, praying him to restore to the metropolitan see of Arles the privileges which had been wrested from it. "It is a matter well known," the letter goes on to say, "to all Gaul, and to the Holy Roman Church, that Arles, the first city of Gaul, has the honor of having received the faith from St. Peter through Bishop Trophimus, and that it spread thence to the other provinces of Gaul." These particulars we have taken from the excellent English translation of Alzog's "Universal Church History," by the lamented Dr. Pabisch and Rev. Thos. S. Byrne (*vol. i., page* 246). Whether the translator's learned observations will convince the reader that Arles owes its foundation to the Prince of the Apostles or not, the discussion proves conclusively that Arles does not derive its succession, its orders or its mission from Lyons or from Ephesus, but from Rome, and that Virgilius goes back through Trophimus to either Fabian or Peter, and not through Irenæus or Photinus to St. John. But now, suppose we get to Lyons, and to Irenæus, who succeeded St. Photinus, martyred in 177, how can we find our way to Ephesus and St. John?

Rev. Alban Butler tells us, on the authority of St. Gregory of Tours, that Polycarp, bishop of Symrna, and disciple of St. John, and ordained by him, sent St. Irenæus to Lyons. (*Life of St. Irenæus, June* 28.) But he was not yet a priest, but was ordained a priest of the Church of Lyons by St. Photinus, its first bishop, to whom he succeeded. Though a disciple of St. Polycarp, from whom he derived his doctrine, there is not the slightest proof or pretence that he exercised his orders, or his mission under other authority than that of Rome, and as an unanswerable proof that even then, in the second century, the Churches of Gaul, and the Church of Lyons in particular, acknowledged the supreme authority of the Bishop of Rome, St. Irenæus was actually sent by the Church of Lyons, as we learn from Eusebius and St. Jerome, to entreat Pope Eleutherius not to cut the Orientals off from communion with the Church on account of their difference about the celebration of Easter. But does St. Irenæus himself appeal to the Ephesine succession to prove the truth of his doctrine and the Apostolicity of his faith and his lawful descent from the Apostles? In his third book (*Contra hæreses, chap. iii.*), he says that most assuredly the Apostles delivered the truth and the mysteries of faith to their successors, and to them we must go to learn the same, but especially "to the greatest Church and most ancient and known to all, founded at Rome by the two most glorious Apostles, Peter and Paul, which retains the traditions received from them and derived through a succession of bishops down to us. For with this Church, on account of the more powerful principality, it is necessary that every Church, that is, the faithful who are in every direction, should agree."—(*S. Iren., L. 3, c. iii.*)

He then enumerates the Pontiffs from Peter to Eleutherius, then reigning, and to this succession in the See of Rome, and not to the Ephesine succession, does Irenæus appeal. To the same did St. Augustine appeal. To the same Apostolic See do we appeal, repeating again that the See of Rome is the only Apostolic See, whence it is at all possible for Christian prelate or priest to trace his Apostolical pedigree and descent. Happy, then, for our episcopal claimant of Apostolical succession if he can "show his line going direct to Rome, by many points," even if, as he confesses, "it is just there that the greatest confusion occurs; so that we do not think much of it."

LINKS OF ANGLICAN SUCCESSION OF UNSAVORY ODOR.

Of course, since he must recur to the Popes for his succession, it will be his business, not ours, to determine which of the three rival Popes was the true Pope when Gregory XII. consecrated Chichele. As he cannot again claim succession through Arles to Ephesus, he must go to Rome for all his right and title to be a "corporate witness," and in his desperate attempt to get there, vaulting with a bound the wide and deep chasm separating Parker from Pole, he goes through Scorey (throwing Barlow overboard) and Cranmer to Beaufort, of whom he says: "I have now reached the name of one of the worst characters in the Anglican succession." Strange that he should stop in this unsavory spot, yet he thinks that he ought not be expected to go further, "for Beaufort was just the kind of a man to please a Pope," and hence I suppose a good enough man to transmit Anglican orders. As, however, he mentions, and very earnestly, that : "The succession by which Christ himself 'came in the flesh,' is disfigured by many unworthy names, besides that of Rahab; and the Scriptures have reached us through many unworthy hands," I am saved the trouble of defending or justifying those Popes "whose abominable lives," he tells us, "were the by-word of their times." Impartial history has done tardy justice to many of the maligned Pontiffs of the middle ages, but the subject matter under discussion debars me from entering more lengthily into the history of these ages and these Pontiffs, nor have I the slightest inclination to shield any of the very few unworthy occupants of the Pontifical throne from merited censure. But neither the Church nor the Papacy is responsible for their personal vices, nor is the purity of Christian doctrines blackened or defiled by the unchristian lives of those who neglect the teachings of the Church, whether they be of high or low degree, whether simple faithful, or masters in Israel. "The Scribes and Pharisees have sitten on the chair of Moses. All things, therefore, whatsoever they shall say to you, observe and do, but according to their works, do ye not; for they say and do not."—(*Matt. xxiii.*, 2, 3.) At least after the admissions made above, objections of this kind will come with very bad grace from those who own descent from immoral characters, and from a line disgraced by Pontiffs "compared with whom Henry VIII. is almost pure."

III.

HENRY VIII.—TO WHOM HE BELONGS.

JUST here we may as well remark that "Old Catholic" is not in love with the first royal *Head* of the Anglican Church, and has "no disposition to take him off of the hands of those to whom he exclusively belongs—the Roman Catholics." Well, we confess he was once a Roman Catholic, and a staunch champion of the Papacy, and from a Pope received the title of "Defender of the Faith," and that "he never fully deserted his faith; but he allowed his passion to blind his eyes and impel him to the greatest of scandals."

Then he severed himself from Rome, *then* he rejected the authority of the Pope, *then* he started the "Church of England as by law established," and had himself proclaimed its head by a subservient Parliament and a weak, servile clergy; he threw off spiritual allegiance to the Pope, imposed the oath of royal supremacy on the English realm, and thus started what Edward and Elizabeth afterwards worked into shape; and that *impartial secular authority* in the "*Saturday Review*," who ventures to write that, "there is a perfect legal and historical identity, so to speak, of person, between the Church of England before the Reformation and the Church of England after the Reformation," goes very near establishing in our minds his own identity with the gentleman who quotes him, and who says, "that Henry merely continued the Church as he found it," and "as for her (Queen Elizabeth) establishing the Church of England in any sense other than that in which it was the law of the land under the Plantagenets and the Papacy, is a very ignorant mistake." In both, there is such assurance, such defiance of history, and implicit reliance on the ignorance of their readers, that we can hardly go wrong in tracing them to the same source, and assigning them the same paternity. Queen Mary, we are again told, "established the Roman hierarchy by law, 'by queen and Parliament,' while Henry never did anything of the kind." True, indeed, Henry never did anything of the kind, because he found the Roman hierarchy existing in England not only since Augustine came from Rome to convert the Angli, but ever since a Pope sent the first missionaries to convert the ancient Britons—a Roman hierarchy, exercising its authority under the jurisdiction and in the communion of the holy Roman See, until by legal enactment, by king and Parliament, he and his son Edward severed that communion cemented by the tradition of ages, by immemorial usages, arrogating to themselves spiritual jurisdiction over the realm, and not only appointing, but confirming, empowering, and even by newly-devised forms consecrating a new hierarchy, thus establishing a New Church, whose very legal title, the name imposed on it at its birth—not Church of England, which St. Gregory recognized, and of which he is justly styled the Apostle, but "Church of England by law established,"—belies its claim to Apostolical origin, stamps it as a royal and parliamentary foundation, a modern invention, a sect.

Mary's attempt was then, not to erect the Roman hierarchy by law, but to repeal the laws enacted in the two previous reigns, and to restore the Church of England to the condition in which it was before "Henry's passions blinded him and impelled him to the greatest of scandals." "Henry belonged to the Roman Catholics." True, so did Cranmer once, so did Calvin, so did Luther, so did Pelagius, so did Donatus, so did Arius, so did all the heretics of ancient times, but they fell away, they apostatized, they left the only ark of safety, the One, Holy, and Apostolic Church. The infamous traitor Judas was once a disciple, nay, even a chosen Apostle of our Lord, and you may as well charge our Lord and His Apostles and the Christian name with the infamy and fearful crime of that arch-traitor, as to make the Catholic Church responsible for the crimes of Henry after he severed himself from the communion of the Holy See, and had himself proclaimed Supreme in spirituals as well as temporals. It is true, and no Catholic, as far as we know, will deny what the late Welby Pugin asserts, that England presents "a fearful example of a Catholic nation betrayed by a corrupted Catholic hierarchy. Henry is declared the *Supremum Caput* of England's Church; not *voce populi*, but by the voice of convocation; the Church is sacrificed, the people are sacrificed, and the actors in this vile surrender are the true and lawful bishops and clergy of England." It is also true that, "all the terrible executions of Henry's dreadful reign were perpetrated before the externals of the old religion were altered," but it is not true that it was before the system of Protestantism was broached, or the *essentials* of the Catholic Church denied. For the wretched system was broached, and the Catholic faith in its essentials was rejected when the authority of the Church and the primacy of the Pope were rejected and denied. It is also true that by his will he ordained that masses should be celebrated for his soul, for the externals of the old religion, the ancient liturgy, the old Catholic Missals and Pontificals were not yet altered, and the masses that were said by an Augustine, a Cuthbert, a Wilfrid, an Anselm, a Dunstan, a Bede, and thousands of saints of the English Church, were still said in Henry's time, and even Cranmer himself, who is applauded as a model reformer, offered Mass for the repose of the soul of Francis I., King of France, on the 19th of June, 1547. "The archbishop of Canterbury, Cranmer, with eight other bishops in their richest Pontifical habits, sung a mass of Requiem."—(*Collier ii.*, 229, *as quoted by Dodd, part ii., p. 6.*)

Let me quote the same historian, Dodd, in answer to the charge that Henry's evil conduct may be laid at the door of the Catholic Church. "To charge the scandalous part of Henry's life upon his popish education, is so groundless an aspersion, that it is inconsistent with every circumstance of the facts. While he lived like other princes, in due subjection to the See of Rome in all spiritual matters, no one had a better character; but as the first step of unfortunate children is disobedience to their parents, this seems to have been the origin of Henry's disorderly life; who no sooner had broke out of the pale of the Church, but he ranged without control through all the paths of vice. Perhaps Catholics will not recriminate so closely in their reflections, as to charge the monstrous crimes he was guilty of upon the reformers' principles, though some of his advisers, who out him on the method of Reformation, were capable of delivering such lessons): yet it has always been an observation, both in private life, and in the fate of nations, that a defection from the Universal Church had two dismal consequences, free thinking as to religion, and a boundless liberty as to morals." (*Part i., Art vi., p.* 323.)

IV.

THE NEW LITURGY—BOOK OF COMMON PRAYER.

BUT is it not strange to hear the objection that Henry belonged to the Catholics because masses were said for him, when it is known that there was in England no other form of public worship, no other liturgy, until the second year of Edward VI.? Is it not known that the commission which he appointed in the year 1554, "pretending to work on the plan of the four Rituals hitherto used in England, viz., Sarum, York, Bangor and Lincoln, compiled the 'Book of Common Prayer?'" Is it not known that at this time the so-called reformers were fearfully mixed up and divided in regard to the holy Mass? "One while they were disposed to retain the names, *sacrifice* and *mass*, and as a necessary consequence also the word *altar*."

Now, the altar was to be called a table, which was removed some distance from the wall, again placed in the middle of the chancel, and once more restored to its original place, where the high altar stood. "On which occasion, Dr. Hugh Weston merrily said, 'The reformation was like an ape, not knowing which way to turn his tail.'"—(*Foxe, iii. 76.*) This new liturgy entitled "Book of Common Prayer," and made obligatory under pains and penalties by act of Parliament (2 *and* 3, *Edward VI., c. 1*), was thus forced on the English

Church, though the bishops of Norwich, Hereford, Chichester and Westminster, who were on the committee, for drawing up the bill, protested against it (*Collier iii.,* 264); and four other bishops who had been on the committee, namely, those of London, Durham Carlisle and Worcester, were equally opposed to it. (*Lord's Journal* i. 331, *cited by Rev. Mr. Tierney, F. S. A. —Dodd's Ch. Hist., part ii., p.* 29). The act of Parliament providing for " uniformity of service and administration of sacraments throughout the realm," passed January 15th, 1549, became obligatory on the Feast of Pentecost of that year. " On that day," says Rev. Mr. Tierney, "the English service was for the first time solemnly performed in the Cathedral of St. Paul's. As to the clergy, although to escape pains and penalties, they had been induced to conform to the provisions of the act, they were not disposed to abandon the ancient liturgy: the bishop (Bonner) was known, moreover, to be favorable to their views; and accordingly, while the common prayer was recited publicly at the high altar, Mass continued to be privately celebrated in the different chapels of the Cathedral," (*Ibid. note, p.* 31) just the same, we may remark, as Mass is said to-day in the different chapels of our own Cathedral. Thus we see how, and when, and by whom the Mass was abolished in England. Soon after came another order to the bishops from the king, to burn and destroy all the missals, antiphoners, graduals, etc., previously used in the churches, and as the bishops were unwilling to enforce, and the clergy to obey the royal mandate, a bill was passed (3 *and* 4 *Edward VI.,* 10), by which any person refusing to surrender, or any archbishop, bishop, or other officer neglecting to destroy, such books, should suffer fine or imprisonment, as the case might be. This common prayer, established in 1549, was revised and altered in 1552, and again under Elizabeth in 1559, again under King James I. in 1604, and afterwards under Charles II. in 1662. Thus we have a history of the Anglican form of public worship, or Book of Common Prayer, originating with the novelties of the Reformation, forced by king and Parliament upon the Church, revised, altered and modified to suit and give expression to the ever-changing faith of a Church that had broken loose from the chair of Peter, the Reformers thus instinctively and perhaps unconsciously affirming the Catholic principle that a Church's liturgy or form of prayer is the truest expression of a people's faith, which Pope Celestine I. thus enunciates, writing (*Epis. viii.*) to the bishops of Gaul: " *Ut legem credendi, lex statuat supplicandi.*"

V.

NEW ANGLICAN ORDINAL.

HAVING changed the ancient liturgy of the Church, and destroyed the old missals used in the Church of England from time immemorial, and thus insensibly robbed the people of their faith by a mutilated and deceptive form of public prayer, craftily obscuring and implicitly denying the very essence of sacrifice, the next step of the wily reformers, headed by Cranmer, who, together with a wife had smuggled into England from foreign lands many of the errors of Luther and Calvin, was to devise an Ordinal or form of ordination to accompany the Common Prayer Book, which should ignore and obliterate the very idea, character and office of the priesthood. During the first two years of Edward's reign, no essential change was made in the Roman Pontifical. Only the oath of allegiance was changed, and hence all those priests ordained and bishops consecrated during this time, though schismatics, and excommunicated and deprived of all power of jurisdiction, had valid orders, were validly, though illicitly (*minus rite*), ordained and consecrated, and they could be, and were with proper dispensations in the time of Mary allowed again to exercise their orders, recognized as bishops and priests. But in 1550 Parliament passed an act devising a new method and "uniform fashion and manner of making and consecrating bishops, priests, deacons or ministers of the Church," and for not concurring in which at least four bishops were deprived. This new Ordinal, established by authority of Edward's Parliament, was again confirmed in 1552 (5 *and* 6 *Edward VI.*, *c.* 1.), when the Prayer Book was revised. In again examining carefully the history of the introduction of the Prayer Book and Ordinal, we cannot understand how any one can assert that the acts of Parliament innovated nothing, and only made the law of the land what was before the ecclesiastical law. The very reverse is transparent. And we may be allowed here again to quote the historian Dodd, who asserts that this Ordinal of Edward, that by which Parker is said to have been consecrated, "was in the ensuing reign (of Mary) examined and declared to be insufficient and invalid as to the purposes of consecrating a new ministry," because, among other reasons, "there was no form of words specifying the order that was conferred, and particularly, no words or ceremony made use of, to express the power of absolving, or offering sacrifice."--(*Church Hist.*, *v. ii., p.* 38.)

VI.

CLEMENT'S DISPENSATION TO HENRY.

BEFORE finally closing our historic review of this period of the Anglican establishment, I must call attention to a strange error, or shall we call it, fabrication? "The Pontiff did actually give Henry permission to have two wives at once." But, continues our honest controversialist, who, in this instance at least, seems to have descended not to equivocation merely, but to bare-faced falsification: "Bad as Henry was, he had more conscience, it would seem, than this compliant Pope, who, anxious to be on good terms alike with Henry and Charles, could only continue to please them both by authorizing Henry to practise bigamy." There is not a word of truth in it. It is a falsehood, manufactured out of whole cloth, and the pretence of quoting Lingard makes the fabrication all the more glaring. Dr. Lingard ("*History of England*," vol. vi., c. iii.) acknowledges that the Pope, Clement VII., signed a document by which " he granted to Henry a dispensation to marry, *in the place of Catharine*, any other woman whomsoever, even if she were already promised to another, or related to himself in the first degree of affinity." We have italicized the words *in the place of Catharine*, showing it was not *a permission to have two wives at once*, or an authorization *to practise bigamy*. Dr. Lingard, in a note on this same passage, tells the reason why such a dispensation was deemed necessary, and where the Bull of dispensation could be found. Now, as any one may see at a glance, from the words of Dr. Lingard, and more clearly still from the document sent from England and signed by Clement, A. D. 1527, and of his Pontificate, the fifth, that the dispensation was granted conditionally, to authorize Henry to contract a valid marriage with Anne Boleyn, if, in the investigation then going on before a commission empowered by the Pontiff himself, it were found that the marriage of Henry with Catharine was null and invalid. The dispensation was asked, as we read in the document itself: "*in eventum declarationis nullitatis matrimonii*," and granted: "*Si contingat matrimonium cum praefata Catharina, alias contractum, nullum fuisse, et esse;*" Now, how any man can, with these documents before him, assert that the Pope granted to Henry permission *to have two wives at once*, or *to practise bigamy*, is more than I can understand, and I must repeat that it appears to me not an equivocation, but a bare-faced falsification, worthy of those, "who reck not what they do or say to damage an adversary."

VII.

EQUIVOCATION—AUTHORITY OF SAINTS AND DOCTORS OF THE CHURCH.

WHILST thus retorting in his own words, I must, for the sake of truth and in self-vindication, notice and repel the injurious charges and insinuations contained in the following extracts from the same pamphlet, and harped upon in season and out of season by the same writer, to throw discredit on Catholic theology, and our veracity and regard for the truth. " I have no Liguori permitting me by infallible authority to say anything but plain truth:" " His infallible master has commended in a superlative degree the teaching of Alphonsus dé Liguori, by which he is instructed to *violate even an oath*, whenever 'the good of the Church' conflicts with keeping it. It is lawful for a Roman Catholic, ' for a good cause, to use equivocation, in the modes laid down, and *to confirm it with an oath.*' So says the Papal authority." We will not now advert to the questionable courtesy of the expression, *his infallible master*, or the misuse of the words, *Papal authority*, applied to St. Liguori's treatise on moral theology, or the misapplication of the term *infallible*. I purpose simply to show that the gentleman misconstrues the text of St. Liguori, and gives a misleading rendering of the very passage which he cites. Taking it apart from its context, he gives a false coloring to the whole. " I should be sorry to accuse him of wilful mistake," but probably not having the works of St. Liguori, he has been imposed on "by the authors from whom he borrows his statements," and who "freely use a license," which neither *Jesuit* nor *Liguorian morals*, as we know them, would tolerate.

Then we say it is totally false that " St. Alphonsus dé Liguori instructs us to violate *even an oath*, whenever the ' good of the Church' conflicts with keeping it." St. Alphonsus does say—(*Lib.* 4, *Tract.* 2, *de secundo præcepto decalogi*), and this is obviously the passage which our friend pretends to give in an English dress —" *His positis, certum est et commune apud omnes, quod ex justa causa licitum sit uti equivocatione modis expositis, et cum juramento firmare.*" Not, then, whenever the *good of the Church* conflicts with keeping an oath are we instructed to violate it, nor does he say that we may use equivocation and confirm the same with an oath *for a good* cause, but having explained three different ways in which equivocation, or a play upon words, or the use of double meaning expressions, amphibology, may be used, he says simply that it is the certain and common opinion of theologians that when there is a just cause it is allowable to use equivocation in the ways or manner laid down, and before explained, and to confirm the same with an oath. Now, we must here know what is meant by *ex justa causa*, which is a *sine qua non*, and what are the *modes laid down*, or the manner in which play on words, or equivocation, is allowable. When a word or sentence has two meanings, and the speaker uses it in one sense, and allows his hearers to take it in another, or when an expression may be taken in a literal or a spiritual sense, as for instance, when our Lord said of John the Baptist : " He is Elias," and the Baptist himself said : " I am not Elias." Such a play on words, St. Liguori says, is allowable, and when there is a just cause the same may be confirmed with an oath, and a just cause the saint explains as, " *quicumque finis honestus ad servanda bona spiritui, vel corpori utilia.*"

As a recent writer on this subject well says, " The right to plead ' not guilty,' acknowledged in our law, St. Liguori maintains to be, under certain circumstances, a natural right. When a questioner has a right to the truth, then the equivocation is forbidden, and where the saint would allow of equivocation, his Protestant critics would in all probability lie more or less clumsily." To show that this is not a groundless assertion I will take the liberty of making an extract from the admirable work of Dr. Newman, " Apologia pro vita sua," where, whilst affirming that on this point he does not follow the holy and charitable St. Liguori, but rather other saints and doctors of the Catholic Church, he shows that many good Protestant authorities need vindication fully as much as our saint. " Now I make this remark, first—great English authors, Jeremy Taylor, Milton, Paley, Johnson, men of very distinct schools of thought, distinctly say, that under certain special circumstances it is allowable to tell a lie. Taylor says: 'To tell a lie for charity, to save a man's life, the life of a friend, of a husband, of a prince, of a useful and a public person, hath not only been done in all times, but commended by great and wise and good men. Who would not save his father's life at the charge of a harmless lie from persecutors or tyrants?' Again Milton says: 'What man in his senses would deny, that there are those whom we have the best grounds for considering that we ought to deceive —as boys, madmen, the sick, the intoxicated, enemies, men in error, thieves? I would ask, by which of the commandments is a lie forbidden? You will say, by the ninth. If, then, my lie does not injure my neighbor, certainly it is not forbidden by this commandment.' Paley says: ' There are falsehoods which are not lies, that is, which are not criminal.' Johnson: 'The general rule is that truth should never be violated: there must, however, be some exceptions. If, for instance, a murderer should ask you which way a man has gone?' "—(*Apol.*, *pp*. 295-6, *N. Y.*, 1865.) The estimable and learned Dr., now Cardinal, Newman continues: " You must not suppose that a philosopher or moralist uses in his own case the license, which his theory itself would allow him. A man in his own case is guided by his own conscience; but in drawing out a system of rules, he is obliged to go by logic and follow the exact deduction of conclusion from conclusion, and be sure that the whole system is coherent and one." —(*Ibid. pp.* 297-8.) And as Dr. Newman remarks, and as we all know from St. Liguori's life, he who by some is so flippantly paraded as authorizing equivocation, and even lying, was most scrupulous and of singular delicacy of conscience on that very point, so much so, that having been unwarily led into defending a case on false grounds, whilst in the profession of the law, he abandoned his profession and embraced the religious life.

I will then only add what Dr. Newman so well and clearly says on this point in the Appendix to the work already mentioned: " Almost all authors, Catholic and Protestant, admit that *when a just cause is present*, there is some kind or other of verbal misleading, wnich is not sin," and the equivocation and play on words which St. Liguori allows, is precisely such as is not a lie, is not sinful, and therefore *ex justa causa*, when there is a just cause, may be confirmed by an oath. This, after all, is only his opinion as a private theologian, and the Church, (much less the *infallible Pope*,) must not be held responsible for his private theological opinions. Archbishop Kenrick, in his " Theologia Moralis," (*Tract. iii., c. xii.*, § *iv.*) thus speaks of equivocation, or ambiguity of speech : " It is confessed by all Catholics that in the common intercourse of life, all ambiguity of language should be avoided: but whether such ambiguity may ever be allowed, is a subject of dispute. Most theologians give an affirmative answer, provided a grave cause urges, and from the adjuncts or circumstances the mind of the speaker may be gathered, although in reality it is not so gathered." And then he instances examples of Holy Writ, as when Abraham counseled Sara to call herself his sister, hiding their marriage relations, and Isaac would have Rebecca called sister, rather than wife. So our Lord said he would not go up to the festival day—not wishing to go up publicly, with his disciples, and manifest His divinity, though intending to go up afterwards in secret.—(*John vii.*, 8, 10.) He spoke of Lazarus sleeping, and said of the girl that she was not dead. —(*John xi.*, 11.) He declared He knew not the day of the judgment because it was not to be made known. —(*Mark xiii.*, 32.) Meaning His body, He spoke of the temple, so that the Jews understood Him to speak of the temple of Jerusalem.—(*John ii.*, 19.) And the learned author quotes Jeremy Taylor, affirming:

"It is lawful, upon a just cause of great charity or necessity, to use in our answers and intercourse, words of divers signification, though it does deceive him that asks."—(*Theol. Mor.*, vol. 1, *p.* 184, *Philad.* 1841.) This I think is sufficient to show St. Liguori does not even go as far on the subject of equivocation as other learned and esteemed Anglican authors, and that his language is garbled, his meaning distorted, his teaching grossly falsified when he is said to "teach us to violate even an oath whenever the *good of the Church conflicts with keeping it.*" Surely, he "whose teachings have been commended in a superlative degree," would not contradict nor ignore the teachings of Pope Innocent XI., who condemned the following proposition:

"If any one alone, or before others, whether interrogated, or of his own prompting, either for the sake of recreation, or any other end, swears that he did not really do what he did do, meaning in his own mind something else which he did not do, or some other way, from that in which he did it, or any other true circumstance, he does not really lie, is not a perjurer."—(*Ibid. p.* 146.) No matter, then, what may be the opinion of individual theologians and casuits as to the lawfulness of misleading by equivocation or ambiguity of language in certain circumstances and with just cause, or as to cases when untruths are not lies; the teaching of our holy Church is that lying is never lawful, that it is not allowed to tell the slightest venial lie to save the whole world. Not, then, for *the good of the Church*, nor to secure the return to her bosom of the whole Protestant world, could the Church authorize a wilful lie, much less a false oath. A lie is an offense against God, for which no finite good, no conceivable good to the whole human race can compensate; and besides, the catechism of the Council of Trent, which is the Church's authorized hand-book of Christian doctrine, declares: "To none, therefore, can it be matter of doubt, that this (eighth) commandment condemns lies of every sort, as these words of David expressly declare: 'Thou wilt destroy all that speak a lie.'"—(*Donovan's Translation*, *p*. 303, *N. Y.*) And again, "But the evil consequences of lying are not confined to individuals; they extend to society at large. By duplicity and lying, good faith and truth, which form the closest links of human society, are dissolved; confusion ensues; and men seem to differ in nothing from demons."—(*Ibid. p*. 308.) I have dwelt on this point so fully because again and again these same parties have belied ourselves and our Church, charging us with holding doctrines which the Church repudiates and rejects, and, they never tire of throwing in our teeth the "license of Jesuit and Liguorian morals." In addition to misconstruing, distorting and falsifying the teaching of our saints and doctors, they will still insist that these authors, because canonized saints and doctors of the Church, are the very mouth-pieces of the Church, and speak with Papal, and even infallible, authority.

To set at rest forever this false notion so industriously circulated, we will again ask a learned friend to speak for us. Dr. Newman, in the appendix to his "Apologia pro vita sua," says: "It is supposed by Protestants that, because St. Alfonso's writings have had such high commendations bestowed upon them by authority, therefore they have been invested with a quasi-infallibility. This has arisen in good measure from Protestants not knowing the force of theological terms. The words to which they refer, are the authoritative decision that 'nothing in his works have been found *worthy of censure, censurâ dignum*,' but this does not lead to the conclusions that have been drawn from it. These words occur in a legal document, and cannot be interpreted, except in a legal sense. In the first place the sentence is negative; nothing in St. Alfonso's writings is positively approved; and secondly, it is not said that there are no faults in what he has written, but nothing which comes under ecclesiastical censure."—(*pp.* 361–2.) Pope Benedict XIV. says: "The *end* or *scope* of the judgment pronounced on the works of a saint when examined before his canonization, is, that it may appear that the doctrine of the servant of God, which he has brought out in his writings, is free from any *theological censure.*" It can never be said that the doctrine of a servant of God is *approved* by the Holy See, but at most, it can (only) be said that it is not disapproved (*non reprobatam*). Hence a writer of Mechlin, quoted by Dr. Newman, observes: "It is, therefore, clear that the approbation of the words of the holy bishop touches not the truth of every proposition, adds nothing to them, nor even gives them by consequence a degree of intrinsic probability."—(*Ibid. p.* 363.) So much then for the approbation of the writings of canonized saints. Now what about solemnly declared doctors of the Universal Church? I borrow my answer from a well-informed writer in a late number of the *London Tablet.*" "The highest appreciation of the doctrine of doctors is in a quotation made by Benedict XIV. from a decree of Boniface VIII., where we read that for one to be raised to such rank, it should be verified that, by his doctrine the darkness of errors was dispersed, light thrown upon obscurities, doubts resolved, the hard knots of Scripture unloosed." Besides, as the same writer remarks, does not St. Alfonso himself often impugn the opinions and controvert the teachings of other illustrious and sainted doctors, and among others of St. Thomas Aquinas himself, the great scholastic doctor and angel of the schools. And may not we say in regard to St. Liguori what the monk Nicholas is said to have answered, when charged with want of reverence to St. Bernard, who is styled the most lovable of the doctors of the Church: " We may not indeed doubt of his glory, but we may dispute his word." Nay, more, though we are firm believers in Papal infallibility, and always have been, even before its explicit definition and formal promulgation by the Vatican Council, we do not hold that the canonization of a servant of God, or his elevation to the rank and title of doctor of the Universal Church, by the Holy See, invests his writings with infallible, or quasi-infallible, or Papal authority, or decides the truth of every theological proposition which he maintains, though, as Benedict XIV. remarks: "We should speak of him with reverence and attack his opinions only with temper and modesty." More still, Catholic faith does not make the Pope, nor does he himself claim to be, infallible, when, as a private doctor or theologian, he discusses theological questions or writes on disputed points of doctrine or morals.

VIII.

PAPAL INFALLIBILITY.

THIS brings us to the subject of papal infallibility, so frequently mentioned and strangely misrepresented in the pamphlet of an "Old Catholic," reviewing our lecture. I must of necessity be brief on this point, and must confine myself to a statement of the Catholic doctrine and the grounds on which it is based. This will suffice to correct the wrong views taken of it, and the false impressions which unreflecting readers might take from the pamphlet in question. In the last session of the Vatican Council, on the 18th day of July, the following definition of Catholic faith was promulgated:

"Therefore, faithfully adhering to the tradition received from the beginning of the Christian faith, for the glory of God our Saviour, the exaltation of the Catholic religion, and the salvation of the Christian people, the sacred council approving, we teach and define, that it is a dogma divinely revealed: that the Roman Pontiff, when he speaks *ex cathedra*—that is, when in the discharge of the office of pastor and teacher of all Christians, by virtue of his supreme authority he defines a doctrine of faith or morals to be held by the Universal Church—is, by the divine assistance promised to him in Blessed Peter, possessed of that infallibility with which the Divine Redeemer willed that His Church should be endowed for defining doctrine regarding faith or morals; and that therefore such definitions of the Roman Pontiff are irreformable of themselves, and not from the consent of the Church."

No novelty in doctrine then is here introduced, no new article of faith taught, but *faithfully adhering to the traditions received from the beginning of the Christian faith*, it is declared to be a *dogma divinely revealed* that when the Roman Pontiff, in his supreme official capacity of pastor and teacher of all Christians, speaking *ex cathedra*, defines a doctrine touching faith or morals to be held by all Christians, he cannot err in so defining, but through the divine assistance promised to Blessed Peter he is endowed with the infallible magisterium or teaching authority, with which our Lord and Saviour was pleased to invest His Church. We recognize no authority on earth, in Pope or council, to make a new article of faith, to alter, add to, or take from the *deposit* of faith once committed to the saints ; we believe in no new revelation. The question before the council was simply, has this doctrine been revealed? is it clearly contained in the *depositum fidei?* The bishops of the Catholic world assembled in council under the presidency of the Sovereign Pontiff claimed no authority to make a new dogma, no right to impose a new article of faith on the consciences of their people.

They were indeed judges and qualified witnesses of the faith and traditions of the churches wherein the Holy Ghost had placed them pastors. The revealed word of God, the holy Gospels, were reverently enthroned in the council chamber, and the Fathers asked themselves, is this doctrine sustained by Scriptural proof? is it taught in the infallible word of God? is it conformable to the revelation of Jesus Christ? what has been the faith of the Christian Churches? what traditions have been handed down? It was only after the most conclusive evidence, afforded by an elaborate and critical examination of Scriptural authorities, and a patient, thorough, searching investigation of the traditions of all the Christian Churches, that, it was proclaimed a revealed dogma of Christian faith; that, the above decree was formulated, the sacred council approving; that, the explicit formal decision of the question was definitively and authoritatively pronounced. Did the Council of Nicea, in the year 325, under Pope St. Sylvester, make a new article of faith when it defined the consubstantiality of Christ with the Father? Did the Council of Ephesus, in the year 431, under Pope St. Celestine change the Christian faith when it defined that there was but one person in Christ, and that Mary was truly the Mother of God? Does our Supreme Court alter the Constitution of the United States, or add an amendment to the same, when it interprets officially and authoritatively that honored instrument, which Americans love to call the *great palladium of our liberties*, and decides grave legal rights and hotly contested questions to be within the purview of the Constitution of our fathers, or conformable to its provisions? This is all the Fathers of the Vatican Council did, this is all that any Council ever did, or can do. Constituted a Supreme Tribunal of *last resort*, it decides not only definitively but with infallible authority what is of faith, what is conformable to the revealed word of God. This is all the Church has ever claimed, but this prerogative she has ever claimed and exercised, and it is absolutely necessary to her in the fulfilment of her divine commission to teach all nations, all truth, down to the end of time; absolutely necessary for the preservation of oneness of faith; absolutely necessary that we may know what is the faith, which we are bound to believe if we would be saved. And hence our Blessed Lord, in establishing His Church, and requiring us to receive her teaching: " He that will not hear the Church let him be to thee as the heathen and publican," (*Matt. xviii.*, 17), and declaring, " He that believeth not shall be condemned (*Mark xvi.*, 16), must of necessity have made her unerring, absolutely infallible in her teaching, as he did, promising "Himself to be with her forever," (*Matt. xxviii.*, 20), and to send the Spirit of Truth to abide with her forever, to teach her all truth. Since the coming of our Saviour there has been no new revelation. The *faith once delivered to the saints* is unchangeable, and hence with St. Paul we say, if any one, even an angel of Heaven, preach to you any other gospel save that which you have received, let him be anathema.—(*Gal. i.*, 9.)

The Church is then simply the witness among men of the original revelation. Her office is to declare what was contained in that original *deposit*, and in declaring this she is divinely assisted, and thus it is, by the divine assistance of the Spirit of Truth, the integrity and purity of faith, are divinely and infallibly preserved, and as may be seen by the decree itself, and by what may be called the preamble to the decree, the whole text of the fourth chapter of the first constitution of the Church of Christ, she goes back to the teaching of Scripture and tradition, councils and doctors of the Church, and expressly declares: " The Holy Spirit was not promised to the successors of Peter, that by His revelation they might make known new doctrine, but that by His assistance, they might inviolably keep and faithfully expound the revelation or deposit of faith delivered through the Apostles." Indeed I feel impelled to transfer to these pages the full text of that fourth chapter, " On the infallible magisterium, or teaching authority of the Roman Pontiff," and although somewhat lengthy it will well repay perusal, as it shows the mind of the council, the sources whence it drew the doctrine defined, and must forever set at rest the charge of novelty or innovation.

" Moreover, that the supreme power of teaching is also included in the Apostolic primacy which the Roman Pontiff, as the successor of St. Peter, Prince of the Apostles, possesses over the whole Church, this Holy See has always held, the perpetual practice of the Church confirms, and œcumenical councils also have declared, especially those in which the East with the West met in the union of faith and charity. For the fathers of the fourth council of Constantinople, following in the footsteps of their predecessors, gave forth this solemn profession: The first condition of salvation is to keep the rule of the true faith. And because the sentence of our Lord Jesus Christ cannot be passed by, who said: Thou art Peter. and upon this rock I will build my Church (*Matt. xvi.*, 18), these things which have been said are approved by events, because in the Apostolic See the Catholic religion has always been kept undefiled, and her holy doctrine proclaimed. Desiring, therefore, not to be in the least degree separated from the faith and doctrine of that See, we hope that we may deserve to be in the one communion which the Apostolic See preaches, in which is the entire and true solidity of the Christian religion.— (*Formula of St. Hermisdas, subscribed by the fathers of the Eighth General Council [fourth Constantinople*], *A. D.* 869.) And, with the approval of the second council of Lyons, the Greeks professed that the Holy Roman Church enjoys supreme and full primacy and pre-eminence over the whole Catholic Church, which it truly and humbly acknowledges that it has received with the plenitude of power from our Lord Himself in the person of the Blessed Peter, Prince or head of the Apostles, whose successor the Roman Pontiff is; and as the Apostolic See is bound before all others to defend the truth of faith, so, also, if any questions regarding faith shall arise, they must be defined by its judgment.—(*Acts of Fourteenth General Council [second of Lyons*], *A. D.* 1274.) Finally the Council of Florence defined: (*Acts of Seventeenth General Council of Florence, A. D.* 1438) that the Roman pontiff is the true vicar of Christ, and the head of the whole Church, and the father and teacher of all Christians, and that to him, in Blessed Peter, was delivered by our Lord Jesus Christ the full power of feeding, ruling, and governing the whole Church.—(*John xxi.*, 15-17.)

To satisfy this pastoral duty our predecessors ever made unwearied efforts that the salutary doctrine of Christ might be propagated among all the nations of the earth, and with equal care watched that it might be preserved genuine and pure where it had been received. Therefore the bishops of the whole world, now singly, now assembled in synod, following the long-established custom of churches (*Letter of St. Cyril of Alexandria to Pope St. Celestine I.*, A. D. 422, *vol. vi., pt. II., p.* 36, *Paris Edit. of* 1638), and the form of the ancient rule (*Rescript of St. Innocent I. to Council of Milevis*, A. D. 402) sent word to this Apostolic See of those dangers especially which sprang up in matters of faith, that there the losses of faith might be most effectually repaired where the faith cannot fail. —(*Letter of St. Bernard to Pope Innocent II.*, A. D. 1130, *Epist.* 191, *vol. iii., p.* 433, *Paris Edit. of* 1742.) And the Roman Pontiffs, according to the exigencies of time and circumstance, sometimes assembling œcumenical councils, or asking for the mind of the Church scattered throughout the world, sometimes by particular synods, sometimes using other helps which Divine Providence supplied, defined as to be held those things which with the help of God they had recognized as conformable with the sacred Scripture and Apostolic tradition. For the Holy Spirit was not promised to the successors of Peter that by His revelation they might make known new doctrine, but that by His assistance they might inviolably keep and faithfully expound the revelation or deposit of faith delivered through the Apostles. And indeed all the venerable fathers have embraced, and the holy orthodox doctors have venerated and followed their Apostolic doctrine; knowing most fully that this See of holy Peter remains ever free from all blemish of error, according to the Divine promise of the Lord our Saviour made to the Prince of His disciples: I have prayed for thee, that thy faith fail not, and when thou art converted confirm thy brethren.—(*Luke xxii.*, 32. See also acts of Sixth General Council, A. D. 680.)

This gift, then, of truth and never-failing faith was conferred by heaven upon Peter and his successors in this chair, that they might perform their high office for the salvation of all; that the whole flock of Christ, kept away by them from the poisonous food of error, might be nourished with the pasture of heavenly doctrine; that the occasion of schism being removed, the whole Church might be kept one, and, resting on its foundation, might stand firm against the gates of hell.

But since, in this very age, in which the salutary efficacy of the Apostolic office is most of all required, not a few are found who take away from its authority, we judge it altogether necessary solemnly to assert the prerogative which the only-begotton Son of God vouchsafed to join with the supreme pastoral office."

" Therefore," continues the council, " adhering to the tradition received from the beginning of the Christian faith," etc., as above. To demonstrate that this same tradition was held in the Church of England before the so-called Reformation, Card. Manning calls up two archbishops of Canterbury. St. Thomas in a letter to the bishop of Hereford: "Who doubts that the Church of Rome is the head of all the churches, and the fountain of Catholic truth? Who is ignorant that the keys of the kingdom of heaven were entrusted to Peter? Does not the structure of the whole Church rise from the faith and doctrine of Peter?"—(*Pastoral on Papal Inf.*, 1870.) And the illustrious St. Anselm, who died in 1107, writes to a Pope of his day:

"Forasmuch as the Providence of God has chosen your Holiness to commit to your custody the (guidance of the) life and faith of Christians, and the government of the Church, to no other can reference be more rightly made, if so be, anything contrary to the Catholic faith arise in the Church, in order that it may be corrected by your authority."—(*Ibid.*) In further proof, if indeed that be needed, that the dogma is no novelty, let us take a short extract from a pastoral which seventeen of the archbishops and bishops of Germany addressed to their clergy and people from Fulda after the Vatican Council in 1870: "Wherefore, we hereby declare that the present Vatican Council is a legitimate General Council, and moreover that this council, as little as any other General Council, has propounded or formed a new doctrine at variance with the ancient teaching; but that it has simply developed and thrown light upon the old and faithfully preserved truth, contained in the deposit of faith, and in opposition to the errors of the day has proposed it expressly to the belief of all the faithful; and lastly, that these decrees have received a binding power on all the faithful by the fact of their final publication by the Supreme Head of the Church, in solemn form at the public session."— (*Vat. Coun.*, App. p. 247, *N.Y.*, 1871.) Thus, what was always contained in the deposit of faith, by the formal explicit definition of the council, and solemn promulgation by the Sovereign Pontiff, became of binding force on all the faithful; what was before matter of implicit faith became thenceforth of explicit faith. What then becomes of the objection of "*Keenan's Catechism*," and *Bossuet*, of the *want of unanimity in the council*, etc.?

Before the final ruling of the Supreme Tribunal and

the explicit decision of the question at issue, Catholics could take sides, and as the German prelates say: "As long as the discussions lasted, the bishops, as their consciences demanded, and as became their office, expressed their views plainly and openly, and with all necessary freedom; and as was only to be expected in an assembly of nearly 800 Fathers, many differences of opinion were manifested."—(*Ibid.*)

That religious questions would arise, and differences of opinion, eighteen hundred years after Christ, as well as in the first age of the Christian Church, our Lord well knew, and he provided for the solution of these questions and the settlement of those differences, and thereby for the integrity and purity of Christian faith by establishing an ever-present, living, speaking authority in His Church, who would be His own mouthpiece, and make His people, the world over, and down through the ages, *unius labii*, and thus save them from the Babellike confusion into which those sects necessarily fall who reject the authority of an infallible teacher.

The Bible is the word of God, but without the living voice of an authorized teacher it is wrested to the destruction of faith and to the endless divisions of Christianity. What anarchy and endless disputes, and bitter, bloody feuds, to say nothing of wild revolutionary schemes, would have ensued before the first centennial of our independence, had the wise fathers and founders of the Republic left each man to judge for himself of the true meaning, scope and intent of the constitution, without a tribunal, whose decisions were to be final and possessed of a certain legal infallibility. And can we believe that our Lord, in giving a constitution to His Church, which was to spread over the habitable globe, from ocean to ocean, and from pole to pole, and to continue to the consummation of ages, would have left us without some such resource, the hopeless victims of interminable divisions, doubt, uncertainty and error whilst, too, obliging us under penalty of exclusion from the kingdom, to believe His doctrine, to be His disciples, and to observe all those things that he had commanded? But thanks to His infinite love and mercy, He has not thus abandoned us. He has established a Church with authority to teach, and it is His own mystical body, which cannot exist without a head, and which, animated by the divine Spirit, becomes the organ of infallible truth and divine life to man United with that head must the members be, would they share that divine life; around that head were the bishops of the Church of God gathered in love and reverence, and bearing witness to the unfailing faith of ages: through the voice of Pius they proclaimed that the Sovereign Pontiffs were still the successors of blessed Peter, and by the divine assistance promised to that privileged Apostle, when defining faith or morals, *ex cathedra*, as doctor of all Christians, are possessed of that infallibility with which our Divine Redeemer wished his Church to be endowed.

Such, then, is the true doctrine of Papal infallibility, to which at once all bow submission, and cry out with the Apostles of our Lord : " Lord, to whom shall we go, but to thee? Thou hast the words of eternal life." (*John* vi., 69.) How different from the so-called Church of *freedom*, that dares not define its own belief, because conscious of no divine authority to teach, for "how can they teach if they be not sent?" But how unjust and ungrounded the charge of crouching servility, made so recklessly against Prelates, ready to sacrifice liberty and life rather than compromise principle, who have shown themselves not only men of pure elevated character, but intrepid heroes and martyrs in defence of religion, and the rights of conscience. If our own testimony on this subject be not taken, whose privilege it was to be present in the venerable council, and to have had an inside view of all its proceedings—and I will during my whole life cherish it as the greatest honor of my life, to have been thus brought into friendly, social, fraternal relations with many of the most estimable, highly cultured, and saintly of men—if the plain language of the learned and independent German Prelates be not enough to vindicate the honor of that council against the aspersions of an anonymous writer who, ashamed, as well he might be, to make himself known, concealed his identity under the title of "Janus," I beg to refer to "Anti-Janus," by Dr., now Cardinal, Hergenröther, or to the "True Story of the Vatican Council," by Cardinal Manning. I have dwelt so long on this point, because of the misunderstanding and misconception, and either ignorant or wilful misrepresentation of the doctrine of Papal infallibility, and the so-called innovation in doctrine by the Vatican Council. This may show also how easily some people can say: "*I have shown* that not even the Roman Church held this doctrine of infallibility four years ago ;" and: "*I have shown* that Pius IX., on the 18th of July, 1870, taught a new doctrine," when they have *shown* no such thing, nor can they show anything more than that four years ago, (from the time the person wrote,) that is, until the 18th of July, 1870, there was not an *explicit* positive decision, or an official ruling of the Supreme Tribunal of

God's Church; but the doctrine of Papal infallibility was implicitly contained in the deposit of faith revealed by Christ, and committed to the keeping of the Church.

In civil affairs doubts arise as to the legality of certain acts, or to the constitutionality of certain legislative enactments, and men take sides and are free to hold different opinions, because as yet the case has not been authoritatively and definitively decided, but when the case has been submitted to the Supreme Court, and the decision has been handed down, there is no longer question. That decision is appealed to as a final settlement of the question, though no one in his senses would say that the fundamental laws of the country have been changed, or a new article added to the constitution by such a decision. Now, there is just one more point in this connection to which I wish to call attention. I asserted in my lecture that in the ancient Church, communion with the See of Rome was a conclusive proof and crucial test, not only of legitimacy of succession, but also of orthodoxy of faith, to which our "Old Catholic" reviewer replies: "This I frankly allow: nay, this I delight to show, *while the bishops of Rome were orthodox*, they were pillars of orthodoxy." But, he continues: "When a Bishop of Rome became a heretic, it was no advantage to any one to be in communion with him." He then goes on to state that we are bound to exclaim in pious horror that such a thing is impossible, viz., that a Pope could be a heretic, and then attempts to prove by a quotation from "Bossuet, the greatest of all modern bishops," that such is the fact. Needless to say that the words of Bossuet prove nothing of the sort, and although we believe that no Bishop of Rome ever became a heretic, we are not *bound* to believe that *such a thing cannot be*. We are bound to believe that no Bishop of Rome ever taught, or could teach, *ex cathedra*, in his official capacity of teacher of the Universal Church anything heretical, false, or immoral. Here is a distinction which some people do not see, or care to make, and no wonder that infallibility in this sense, *personal* infallibility, or that Catholics were bound to believe the Pope *in himself* to be infallible, was declared to be a *Protestant invention*. It is then a baseless fabrication, an "Old Catholic," invention, that we have made a God of the Pope, or believe him to be impeccable, and hence how vain and hopeless the task of combating Papal infallibility by charges of corruption, vice and wickedness made against certain Popes.

The terms of the Vatican definition are too plain to be misconstrued in this way, and precisely to obviate this difficulty, to anticipate this objection, and preclude the possibility of this wrong interpretation, the title of the fourth chapter, which originally read: "On the Infallibility of the Sovereign Pontiff," was changed to that of, "The infallible *teaching authority* of the Sovereign Pontiff." And is it not a very significant fact—a fact which may be said even to constitute a *prima facie* evidence in favor of the doctrine of the Pope's infallibility—that, although in every age from the beginning of Christianity, disputes and controversies concerning points of belief, doctrinal questions most grave, complicated and vital to the unity and integrity of the faith of Christ were referred to the Holy See from every quarter of the Christian world, were answered and decided by the Sovereign Pontiffs, not a single one of the long, unbroken line of Supreme

Pastors, from Peter down to Leo XIII., now gloriously reigning, can be convicted of teaching *ex cathedra*—in his official capacity—erroneous doctrine or erring in his Pontifical decision of what was to be held as of faith by the Universal Church. When again we reflect that in the mass of official acts of Popes, Pontifical constitutions, bulls, decrees and encyclicals accumulating during nineteen centuries, ransacked, sifted, keenly scrutinized, carefully and searchingly examined in the discussion of a question now happily closed, nothing positive could be discovered in conflict with the infallible prerogative of the chair of Peter, is not the conviction forced upon us that the "finger of God is here," that this astounding fact can be reasonably and satisfactorily accounted for only by the special assistance of the Holy Ghost, promised to His Church by Christ our Lord. With all this before us, what difficulty can we find in believing and professing that the same divine help, the same supernatural guidance, the same assistance of the Holy Spirit will ever be vouchsafed to the visible Head of the Church in the discharge of the sacred and sublime duties of his Apostolical office of vicar of Christ and teacher of the Universal Church, especially in view of the promises made to Peter by our Lord, and of the absolute need that the truth of faith should be thus divinely guarded through the divinely appointed Supreme Pastor and shepherd of the whole flock of Christ: "Feed my lambs, feed my sheep." (*John xxi*, 16, 17.)

IX.

POPES LIBERIUS AND HONORIUS.

NOW, we said above, that since the days of Peter, for whom our Lord prayed that his faith might not fail: "I have prayed for thee, that thy faith fail not," (*Luke xxii.*, 32) nearly nineteen hundred years ago, nothing has been discovered in the official acts of his successors in the See of Rome in conflict with the decree of the Vatican Council concerning the infallible teaching authority of the Sovereign Pontiff. In fact, of only two in that long line of Pontiffs has the orthodoxy been questioned, and even these two, Liberius, whose Pontificate extended from the year 352 to 366, and Honorius, who reigned from 625 to 638, rigid historical research has fully vindicated from the charge of teaching error. As these charges are again repeated in the pamphlet before me, and with so much confidence, I must beg my readers' pardon for detaining them by a brief refutation. A cursory review of these points of Church history may not prove uninteresting or uninstructive. Liberius was the immediate successor of Julius, who asserted the jurisdiction of his See over the whole Church, East and West, and severely rebuked the Eastern heretical bishops for daring to take decisive action in the case of Athanasius without his authority, and the immediate predecessor of Damasus, of whom

St. Jerome says: "Following no leader but Christ, I am associated in communion with thy Holiness, that is, with the chair of Peter; upon this rock I know that the Church has been built." Honorius was appealed to in the question of jurisdiction and precedence between the sees of Canterbury and York, and although some people will say that England was never subject to Rome, or acknowledged the supremacy of the Roman Pontiff, this same Honorius gave the pallium to Honorius and Paulinus, archbishops of Canterbury and York, granting them the faculty, that whichever of them should survive might ordain the successor of the deceased. But now to the charges: "Liberius turned Arian," "Athanasius is condemned by the Bishop of Rome for adhering to orthodoxy," "The holy and orthodox bishop of Poictiers says: 'Anathema to thee, Liberius, to thee, and to those who are with thee. I repeat—anathema! Again, a third time, anathema to thee, thou prevaricator, Liberius.'"

Now, it is certain Liberius never became an Arian, and never condemned St. Athanasius. The most that is said of him by his enemies is, that worn out by the sufferings of exile into which he had been sent by the Arian emperor, Constantius, on account of his unconquerable firmness in sustaining the orthodox Catholic faith, he at length weakened and signed one of the specious and deceptive professions of faith, cunningly devised by the wily Arian tricksters, and thus purchased his release from banishment and return to Rome. It is doubtful that St. Hilarius ever wrote the words here ascribed to him; many regard them, and with good reason, as an interpolation; again, though there were three different formulas or professions of faith framed in three different Arian conferences or gatherings at Sirmium, one of which Liberius is said to have subscribed, yet no one can determine which of them; and lastly, if he did sign the most objectionable of them, it militates not in the least against the doctrine of Papal infallibility, in as much as when under compulsion and in exile, in a moment of weakness he subscribed a profession of faith which, though capable of an orthodox interpretation, might be construed as favoring Arianism and condemning St. Athanasius, the great champion of orthodoxy, he was not teaching the Church, was not, *ex cathedra*, deciding what should be held by the Universal Church. But with the great mass of authorities, we do not believe that he ever subscribed any such doubtful formula, and it cannot be proved that he ever did. We do not believe that St. Hilarius ever pronounced the anathemas above mentioned, and even if he did, it is no ways conclusive against the orthodoxy of Liberius, for we can easily suppose him deceived by the lies of the Arians seeking to support their errors by the authority of the Bishop of Rome, or giving vent to overwrought feelings of indignation and holy zeal at what he conceived to be siding with the enemies of the faith.

In concluding this question of Liberius, I can not do better than quote from a great and learned historian, who after noting the different authorities making these charges against the Pontiff, and among them the fragments of Hilarius, says: " But considering the silence of Socrates, Theodoret, Cassiodorus and Sulpicius Severus, there is a strong suspicion that this passage was interpolated by the Arians, whose restless spirit stopped at nothing that might further their cause.

The passage has, moreover, no connection in the context either with what precedes or follows. This we find in a note on page 542, Alzog's "Church History," vol. i. (*Pabisch and Byrne*), and in the text the same author says: "Constantius yielding to the prayers of the most estimable ladies of Rome, granted permission to Pope Liberius to return to his *See;* but it is thought that the menacing conduct of the Roman people, who openly protested against the imperial decree authorizing a rival bishop, and cried out in the circus, that as there was but one God and one Christ, there should be but one bishop, contributed more than anything else to extort from the emperor this act of clemency." What becomes now of the *anathema* to Liberius? How unlikely that he ever *turned Arian*, or *condemned St. Athanasius!* But how evident, and demonstrably certain, that he never in any official document, or by any *ex cathedra* pronouncement, taught error, or promulgated anything unorthodox, which would be necessary to constitute a valid objection to the doctrine of Papal infallibility. What additional strength does all this acquire when we find St. Jerome, who was not wont to fawn on or flatter either bishops or Popes, in the very next Pontificate, when he certainly could not have been ignorant of anything that occurred under the previous Pope, declaring communion with the See of Rome the test of orthodoxy: ": Whoever is not in communion with the Church of Rome is outside the Church, and therefore was one of the twelve set over all the others as the recognized Head, that all occasion of schism might be removed ;" and Pope Hormisdas, some time afterwards, in the beginning of the 6th century, declared : ."The faith of the Apostolic See has always been inviolate; it has preserved the Christian religion in its integrity and purity." Enough, then, about Liberius, whom we think we have fully vindicated from the charges brought against him. Can we do as much for Honorius?

HONORIUS VINDICATED.

THE vindication of Honorius is equally easy, at least as far as the charge of officially teaching heresy goes, for all we pretend or care to do, is to show that the prerogative of Papal infallibility as defined in the Vatican Council has been in no wise impaired or obscured by the *ex cathedra* teaching of these two much maligned Pontiffs. Here, then, are the charges against him quoted from Bossuet's "Defence of the Declaration of the Gallican Clergy": "Honorius being duly interrogated concerning the faith by three Patriarchs, gave most wicked answers. He was condemned by the Sixth General Council under anathema. Previous to this anathema, he was sustained by the Roman Pontiffs, his successors; but since the *supreme judgment of the council*, the Pontiffs have condemned him under the same anathema." We are then asked by our "Old Catholic" friend, "where infallibility was in those days, when one Bishop of Rome taught heresy from his throne, and of his successors some upheld him and others anathematized him as a heretic?" But as Bossuet, "the greatest of all modern bishops, who have lived and died in communion with the Pope, and who had no mind to be a mere worshipper of Popes," is cited against us, it is only fair to that illustrious bishop to tell our readers

that in the opinion of such men as de Maistre, the
" Defence of the Gallican Declaration" should not be
taken as the expression of the true and permanent
sentiments of Bossuet ; that it was a work wrung from
one who, though a bishop, and, if you please, the
" greatest of modern bishops," for we wish not to dim
his glory or extenuate his fame, was forced to act the
courtier to a royal despot who not only claimed to be
the incarnation of all political or state power, "*l'état
c'est moi*," but would have all ecclesiastical and spiritual
authority subject to his beck. It was a posthumous
work, which he never wished to publish, for although
he lived twenty-two years after the famous declaration
of 1682, he never would publish its " Defence," and it
is an insult to the memory of the immortal prelate to
have published it under a title of which he seemed to
be ashamed. The work itself, undertaken in obedience
to a royal master, he altered and revised, and changed
so often and so much that his historian declares that
" no one can doubt, that it was his design to change his
whole work, as he had actually changed the first three
chapters." The work which we have under the title
of the " Defence of the Declaration of the Gallican
Clergy," does not then express Bossuet's real mind, and
is deprived of all authority, as his purpose was to
change it entirely, and his manuscripts show that he had
nearly completed his design when death overtook him.
With Count de Maistre we may say of Bossuet, that :
" In the same man there seemed to be two different
characters, the Roman Catholic bishop and the French
courtier: the bishop, who speaking the language of
the Patriarchs, the Prophets, the Apostles and the
Fathers belonged from the very bottom of his soul

to the Roman Church: the courtier, who to please his master, extends one hand to the centuriators of Magdeburg, and the other to Voltaire, the better to falsify history, to the prejudice of the Popes and the profit of kings."—(*Quoted by Rohrbacher, T. xxvi., p.* 359, *Paris,* 1852.)

But how grandly and how eloquently does this "greatest of modern bishops, who is no worshipper of the Popes," when writing in his true character of a Catholic bishop, untrammelled by court influences or royal favors, speak of the See of Peter, the prerogatives of the Roman Church, and the authority conferred on, and the obedience due to the successors of him to whom the keys of the kingdom of heaven were entrusted. We cannot forbear a short extract from the "Discourse on Universal History," revealing the lofty genius and true Catholic mind of the illustrious bishop of Meaux: " What consolation for the children of God, what conviction of truth! when they see that from Innocent XI., who now (1681) fills so worthily the first See of the Church, we go back without break even to Peter, established by Jesus Christ Prince of the Apostles: and there taking up the Pontiffs who served under the law, we go back even to Aaron and to Moses; and thence to the Patriarchs and the origin of the world. What a succession, what a tradition, what a marvellous connecting chain. If our mind, naturally uncertain, and by its incertitude become the sport of its own reasoning, has need, in questions where salvation is at stake, to be steadied and determined by some certain authority, what greater authority can there be than that of the Catholic Church, which combines in itself all the authority of past ages, all the ancient traditions of the human race up to its origin.

Thus the society which Jesus Christ in fine, after ages of expectancy, founded on the rock, and over which Peter and his successors should preside by His orders, is justified by its own continuity, and bears in its eternal duration the impress of the hand of God. It is this succession, which no heresy, no sect, no other society but the Church of God can claim. The founders of new sects among Christians, and the sects established by them, will be found to have been detached from this great body, from this ancient Church which Jesus Christ founded, and in which Peter and his successors held the first place."—(*Ibid. p.* 354.) To this let us add what this "greatest of modern bishops, and no worshipper of Popes" says in the first part of his "Discourse on the Unity of the Church:" " What is intended to sustain an everlasting Church, can itself have no end. Peter will live in his successors ; Peter will always speak in his chair; this the Fathers assert; this six hundred and thirty bishops in the council of Chalcedon confirmed. * * * This is the Roman Church, which taught by St. Peter and his successors, knows no heresy. * * * Thus the Roman Church is always a virgin Church, the Roman faith is always the faith of the Church ; what has been believed, is believed still ; the same voice is heard everywhere ; and Peter remains in his successors, the corner-stone of the faithful. Jesus Christ Himself has said it, and heaven and earth shall pass away sooner than his word. But let us see the consequences of that word. Jesus Christ pursues His design and after having said to Peter, the eternal preacher of the faith :

Thou art Peter, and on this rock I will build my Church,' He adds : 'I will give to thee the keys of the kingdom of heaven.' Thou, who hast the prerogative of preaching the faith, thou shalt have also the keys, which designate the authority of government; 'whatsoever thou shalt bind on earth, shall be bound in heaven, and whatsoever thou shalt loose on earth, shall be loosed in heaven.' All are subjected to these keys; all, my brethren, kings and people, pastors and flocks; we publish it with joy, for we love unity, and glory in our obedience. Peter was commanded first 'to love more than all the other Apostles,' and then 'to feed' and govern all, 'both the lambs and the sheep,' the little ones and their mothers, and the shepherds themselves; shepherds towards the people, but sheep in regard to Peter."—(*Ibid. pp.* 356-7.)

Thus does Bossuet, following the Patriarchs, the Prophets, and Apostles, proclaim aloud the infallible promises of God to his Church and her head. In justice to the great Bossuet, we deemed it a duty to say this much. We now return to Honorius, whose case, in our opinion, is correctly stated by Archbishop F. P. Kenrick in the brief notice of the Sovereign Pontiffs appended to the fourth volume of his "Dogmatic Theology," in these few words: "That he was imposed on by Sergius of Constantinople and inopportunely commanded silence in relation to one or two wills in Christ, most authors admit; but that he was guilty of heresy is devoid of every semblance of truth." But the gist of the charges against him, and his vindication may be at once discovered from words already quoted from the closing lines of cap. xxvii., Lib. vii., "Defensio Declarationis cleri Gallicani."

"Honorius being duly interrogated concerning the faith by three Patriarchs, gave most wicked answers." In the first place, we would ask, why was the Bishop of

Rome interrogated by these three Eastern Patriarchs? Is not this very fact an additional and undeniable evidence that in the East as in the West, by Patriarchs, as well as by bishops, and even by heretics the primacy of the Roman See and the supreme jurisdiction of the Roman Pontiff were acknowledged? The three Patriarchs referred to are, Sergius of Constantinople and Cyrus of Alexandria, both tainted with the Monothelite heresy, and Sophronius, of Jerusalem, an able and learned champion of the Catholic faith. To these Honorius is said to have given *wicked answers*, and all the charges of heresy alleged against him are to be found in his letters to them, and particularly in his letters to Sergius. Is not this of itself sufficient to show that the case of Honorius offers no difficulty in regard to the doctrine of Papal infallibility, as we have already explained it, and as it has been defined in the famous Vatican decree of 1870? Where does he teach, or pretend to teach the Universal Church? where does he define or pretend to define what must be held by the whole Church as of Catholic faith? Suppose that in these letters some expressions are found not entirely consistent with orthodox Catholic faith, and grant that he was deceived and fell into the trap sprung upon him by the wily Sergius and wrote to suppress all discussion about one or two wills in Christ, can any one reasonably say that he *taught heresy from his throne?* or made a dogmatic, *ex cathedra* definition in regard to faith or morals? But more than that. With the letters of Honorius before us, and after a careful study of the subject as presented by the clear, keen, argumentative mind of Bossuet himself, Honorius cannot, in our opinion, be convicted of heresy, he wrote nothing but what is capable of a Catholic meaning. He repeatedly proclaimed Christ to be perfect God and perfect man, thus condemning the errors of Nestorius and Eutyches, showing that though he expressed himself inaccurately, he *thought correctly* on the two operations in Christ.

No wonder, then, that John IV., his second successor, declared, as we read in Alzog's "Church History," "that Honorius mistook the question at issue to be, whether or not there were two *conflicting human* wills in Christ, the one of the spirit, and the other of the flesh, which, if such were the case, would necessarily imply the opposition of the human to the Divine will—an error of which Honorius wished to disabuse Sergius." In speaking of one will and one *theandric* operation, he meant nothing more than the moral unity of the Divine and human wills. "Not having seized the real drift of the controversy, it was but natural that he should express himself obscurely, and with a lack of precision in his reply to the craftily worded letter of Sergius."—(*Alzog's* "*Church History*," *vol.* I., *p.* 635.) From the same source we learn that not only did his *successors sustain him*, but the Abbot Maximus, the most acute theologian of his age, and foremost champion of the Catholic cause against the Monothelites, especially after the death of Sophronius, asserts emphatically in two different places that Honorius was an *opponent of the Monothelites.*—(*Ibid. p.* 636—*Pabisch & Byrne, Cin.*, 1874.) The heretics, however, used the hasty and ill-considered letter of Honorius in support of their error, and his secretary, the Abbot John, in vindication of his first (cursory) letter asserted openly that it had been falsified (falsely interpreted) by the Greeks. Whereupon the Abbot Maximus exclaims: "Who then, is a more reliable interpreter of that letter—the enlightened abbot, who is still alive, who wrote it in the name of Honorius, or they of Constantinople, who say what they please?"—(*Ibid. note, p.* 637.) So much, then, in vindication of the orthodoxy of Honorius, but what now about his condemnation by the Sixth General Council? "He was condemned by the Sixth General Council under anathema. Previous to this anathema, he was sustained by the Roman Pontiffs, his successors, but since *the supreme judgment of the council*, the Pontiffs have condemned him under the same anathema."—("*Defense,*" *etc.*) This sixth œcumenical council, called also the *First Trullan Synod*, was opened at Constantinople Nov. 7, 680, and presided over by three legates of Pope Agatho. The Pope's dogmatical epistle was read as the basis of the council's deliberations, which defined the controverted point of faith regarding the two wills in Christ corresponding to the two natures so clearly and succinctly, that the assembled fathers cried out with one voice: "Peter hath spoken by the mouth of Agatho." In the fourth session of the council another letter of the same Pope, who was recognized as the very mouth-piece of blessed Peter, was read and received without opposition, in which he thrice solemnly declares: "Through the grace of the omnipotent God, this Apostolical Roman Church will be proved to have *never* erred from the path of Apostolical tradition, nor has it succumbed to heretical novelties, but as from the beginning of the Christian faith it received from its founders, the Princes of the Apostles, so it remains untainted even to the end, according to the divine promise of our Lord and Saviour, spoken to the Prince of the disciples in the holy Gospel."—(*Luke xxii.*, 32.—*Ibid. note, p.* 642.)

This much premised, we answer the objections in the words of Cardinal Hergenröther: "A Pope is not infallible in proceedings such as those of Honorius, who contributed unintentionally to the increase of heresy by not issuing decisions against it. His letters contain no decision, neither do they contain any false doctrine. No decision of his ever was, or ever could be condemned as false, otherwise the sixth council would have contradicted itself, for it recognized that the Holy See had in all time the privilege of teaching only the truth. He was condemned for having rendered himself morally responsible for the spread of heresy, by having neglected to publish decisions against it, and in this sense alone was his condemnation confirmed by Leo II."—("*Catholic Church and Christian State,*" *Hergenröther, vol. i., p.* 83.) In this sense, then, and in this sense only, did the council condemn Honorius, and succeeding Pontiffs re-echo the condemnation, that by his negligence he *allowed* the unspotted faith to be defiled. Not as a heretic, then, but as one who had actually by his culpable indecision become an abettor of heresy and heretics, and he was justly blamed and severely taken to task for doing precisely what so many wished Pius IX. to do, viz., to put off and leave undecided a grave doctrinal question that was agitating and disturbing the Christian Church and severely testing its unity and peace. Pope Leo II., who succeeded Agatho before the close of the council, confirmed its decrees and its condemnation of Honorius, because the heretics, distorting the meaning of his words, made use of his name and his authority to propagate their errors, and as he wrote to the Spanish bishops, " because he did not at once extinguish the flame of heretical error, but *by his negligence contributed fuel to the fire."—Alzog, p.* 642.) We have dwelt, perhaps unnecessarily long in vindication of these two much abused Popes, but we thought it well to clear up a matter, out of which the enemies of the Papacy make so much capital, and it is not always easy for everybody to have access to the historical documents or the authorities on which the solution of these questions rests.

XI.

ST. GREGORY THE GREAT CLAIMING AND EXERCISING PAPAL SUPREMACY.

IN the pamphlet before us we are told that: "by usurpation Boniface III. began, and Nicholas I. completed a Papacy;" and that: "St. Gregory was the last Bishop of Rome who obeyed the canons of the Church in this respect," that is, as far as we can gather the meaning of the words from the context, the last who held that all bishops were "the equals of their brother in the See of Rome," and denied "any supremacy of one over the others, such as is claimed by the Popes." Now we propose to show, from his own words and official acts, that St. Gregory claimed this Supremacy of spiritual jurisdiction over his brethren in the episcopate throughout the whole Church, just as fully, and as uncompromisingly as Boniface III., or Nicholas I., or as Pius IX., or Leo XIII. Of course we can show that in every age, from the Apostles down to Gregory, the same supreme authority was recognized in and by the successors of St. Peter in the See of Rome, yet we are pleased to have here a starting point and a deliberate acknowledgment that St. Gregory was a bishop who obeyed the canons, and is a reliable witness of the "doctrine of Catholic antiquity." I will not now stop to discuss a *"primacy* or *presidency* consistent with the co-equality of all bishops which the Church itself has instituted or regulated by canons, but forbidding any supremacy of one over the other," as " St. Gregory, who obeyed the canons of the Church, in this respect," recognizing a primacy regulated indeed by canons, but instituted by Christ, and resting, as all the laws of the Church, rest, on the divine law, claims, and as we shall presently see, exercises a supremacy of spiritual jurisdiction or authority over bishops, archbishops and Patriarchs, but as St. Gregory is a recognized, legitimate, and orthodox Bishop of Rome, " who obeys the canons of the Church," we cannot be much deceived in holding to the primacy of the See of Peter, and Papal supremacy, as he understood it. Neither will I stop to point out the childlike naïveté of the following passage : " Christ gave a primacy among the Apostles to St. Peter; but he limited it by rebuking the inquiry, 'who should be the greatest,' and by commanding them to call no man master, they being all brethren, with one Father in Heaven. St. Peter himself was rebuked as a 'Satan' the moment he departed from the words of Jesus."

It were surely labor lost to argue with a man who can assert that our Lord's instructions to His disciples regarding personal humility and warnings against personal ambition, His intimation that our Father in Heaven is incomparably more to be regarded than any father upon earth, and that no master is to be followed, who would lead us away from Christ ; His paternal chiding of Peter, calling him "Satan" on account of his indiscreet zeal and his ardent but unenlightened and too human love for his Divine Master, were intended to limit, or rather destroy—in the opinion of those who deny any primacy, or at least any of divine institution—a primacy which our Blessed Saviour deemed necessary for the government of His Church, and which, though previously promised in strong and solemn words (*Matt. xvi.*, 18, 19), was actually conferred only after Peter had fully atoned for his shameful three denials, by his triple profession of greater love on the shore of the sea of Tiberias.—(*John xxi.*, 15, *et seq.*) But now, to return to St. Gregory, who is introduced to us as the model Christian Bishop of Rome, in contradistinction to the "despotic Pontiff of the modern Roman Church," in these terms "And here is the place to quote St. Gregory, the last Bishop of Rome who obeyed the canons of the Church in this respect. When a bishop flattered him with the pompous title of universal jurisdiction, Gregory rebuked the brother kindly but sharply, in the following weighty words: (*Epis. v.* 20, *et seq.*) "None of my predecessors would use *this impious word* (Universal Bishop), because in reality if a Patriarch be called *universal*, this takes from all others the title of Patriarch. Far, very far from every Christian soul be the wish to usurp anything that might diminish, *however little*, the honor of his brethren. * * * Give not *to any one* the title of *universal*, lest you deprive yourself of your own due, by offering what you do not owe to him."

Surely our "Old Catholic" brother never read these letters of St. Gregory, from which he pretends to quote, and to which he gives references. He surely would not knowingly and deliberately impose on the public. If he ever read these letters he would know that these words of Gregory are not addressed to a brother "bishop, who flattered him with a pompous.

title of universal jurisdiction." He would know that this very fact in the history of St. Gregory's pontificate affords the strongest possible proof that he claimed universal jurisdiction, and this sharp rebuke is administered in the exercise of his unquestioned right to reprove, correct and condemn not simple bishops only, but Patriarchs as well, and even the Patriarch of Constantinople. Now what is the fact in the case? The Patriarch John of Constantinople, called the Faster, sending to Rome an account of the sentence passed against a priest accused of heresy, styles himself repeatedly, œcumenical or universal Patriarch, and Pope St. Gregory, in his undoubted right as head of the Universal Church and guardian of the rights of other bishops and other patriarchs, reproves this as an arrogant, ambitious usurpation of a pompous title, and observing the order of fraternal correction, twice admonished him privately by his nuncio in Constantinople, and when this failed to bring him to a sense of his fault, he wrote in sharp but fatherly reproof to himself, to the Emperor Mauritius, to the Empress Constantina Augusta, and to other eastern bishops, and in particular a joint letter to St. Eulogius, Patriarch of Alexandria, and St. Anastasius, Patriarch of Antioch. It is from this letter to those patriarchs, the xliii., not the xx., that the language above quoted is taken, though words to the same effect and in the same sense are found in all of them.

To make the matter clearer, I will give a short extract from some of these noble productions, worthy the pen of Gregory the Great; and first from Epist. xx. L. 5, written to the Emperor Mauritius, and given as authority for the utterly false assertion that the great Pope was only rejecting a pompous title offered to him by a flattering brother: "It is evident," writes the pope to the emperor, "to all acquainted with the Gospel, that by our Lord's words, the care of the whole Church was committed to St. Peter, Apostle, and Prince of all the Apostles. For to him is said: *Peter, lovest thou me? Feed my sheep.*—(*John xxi.*, 17.) To him is said: *Behold Satan hath sought to sift you as wheat and I have prayed for thee, Peter, that thy faith fail not, and thou at length converted, confirm thy brethren.*—(*Luke xxii.*, 31.) To him is said: *Thou art Peter, and on this rock I will build my Church, and the gates of hell shall not prevail against it. And I will give to thee the keys of the kingdom of heaven, and whatsoever thou shalt bind on earth it shall be bound also in heaven, and whatsoever thou shalt loose upon earth it shall be loosed also in heaven.*—(*Matt. xxi.*, 19.) Behold he receives the keys of the kingdom of heaven, the power of binding and loosing is given to him, the care and the princedom of the whole Church are committed to him,"—verily St. George does not agree with our friend about the limitation of the primacy of Peter—" and still he is not called the universal Apostle, and the most holy man, John our fellow priest, affects to be called the universal bishop. I am compelled to exclaim and to say: *O tempora! O mores!*"

He concludes his letter to the emperor thus: "In obedience to our Master's orders I have written to our aforesaid fellow-priest kindly, and I have humbly admonished him to correct this desire of vain-glory. If he is pleased to listen to me, he will have a devoted brother. If he persist in his pride, I see what will follow: he will have *Him* his enemy of whom it is said;

God resisteth the proud, but giveth his grace to the humble."—(James iv., 6.) In the same strain he writes (*Epist. xxi.*) to the empress, asking her to use her influence to bring John to a sense of duty, and then turning to another matter that concerned him as head of the Church and Supreme Universal Pastor, exercising the power of the keys committed to Peter, he writes: "The bishop of the city of Salon, Maximus, has been consecrated without my knowledge, or consent, and thus has been done what was never done under previous princes. Which as soon as I heard, I wrote to the prevaricator that he should not presume to celebrate the solemnities of Mass, until I should learn that this was done by orders of our most serene Lords, and this I commanded him under pain of excommunication." But we will find instances enough in Gregory's pontificate of this claim of authority, and enforcement of obedience, or in other words that Gregory, *who obeyed the canons* and was *the* model Bishop of the Christian Church of antiquity, claimed and exercised all the privileges and powers, all the authority and jurisdiction over all the bishops of the Universal Church, which the Pope of to-day claims. To John himself, the Patriarch of Constantinople, St. Gregory writes: (*Epist. xviii., L.* 5.) "Your fraternity remembers how great was the peace and concord of churches when you were promoted to the sacerdotal dignity. But with what hardihood and strange swelling pride, have you sought to usurp to yourself a new title, from which the hearts of all your brethren might receive scandal." He then reminds him how Pope Pelagius, his predecessor, had written to him and ordered the archdeacon not to hold commuuion with him until he laid aside his pretensions, and that abominable name of Universal Bishop, so derogatory to the honor, not only of the Holy See, but of all bishops, and continues: "Certainly Peter, the first of the Apostles, was a member of the Holy and Universal Church. Paul, Andrew, John, what else were they but heads of their respective people, and still they were all members under one head. To embrace all in a brief speech, the saints before the law, the saints under the law, the saints under the dispensation of grace, all perfecting the body of the Lord, are constituted members of the Church and not one even wished to have himself called *Universal.* See and own, then, what an arrogance it is to ambition a name which none of the saints presumed to bear. Were not the bishops of this Apostolic See, to which, God so disposing, I have been raised, called as a title of honor, Universal Bishops by the venerable council of Chalcedon? And nevertheless no one ever wished to have that title, no one used that rash name, lest in taking to themselves in that rank of Pontiffs a special or singular glory they might seem to deny the same to all their brethren."

This same he repeats again and again in several of his epistles, showing how unseemly it was in the Patriarch of Constantinople to arrogate to himself a title, which was conceded to the Roman Pontiffs, but which they never would use, and which, even when exacting obedience to their supreme authority, and exercising, as in this very instance, the powers of a Supreme Pastor over the whole flock of Christ, they would not employ, but rather would in their humility be called "the servant of the servants of God," and addressed the bishops, archbishops, and patriarchs as do the Popes of our own day as *brothers*. St. Gregory then protested against the title of œcumenical or universal Pope or patriarch, in the sense just explained, and called it blasphemous in the mouth of the Byzantine Patriarch, who unrighteously arrogated to himself a name which the Roman Pontiffs were unwilling to accept even when offered by general councils. Many other beautiful and pointed things I might cite from these fervent and eloquent letters of the great Pope, and in particular, I may mention those written to his friend Eulogius, in which, as the historian Rohrbacher tells us, the holy Pope sums up and teaches, " what are the principle, the model, the means and the end of the Catholic Church and its unity. Its principle is one God and three persons ; the model of its unity, the union of the three divine persons in the same essence ; the mediator, who unites it to heaven, and in heaven to the one undivided Trinity, is Jesus Christ, giving to Peter the keys of the kingdom of heaven ; the means of this unity among men, is the union of the three Patriarchs and the other bishops with the same Peter, from whom their authority proceeds ; the final end, is the consummation of this unity in the three divine persons. The pretensions of the bishops of Constantinople were directly at variance with this divine *ensemble*. They grounded their claims, not on God, nor on Jesus Christ, nor on Peter, but on the residence of the emperors in their city. Therefore they would be called *Universal Bishop*. And the Greeks argued later that this title of universal belongs not to the Roman Pontiff from the time the empire passed from Rome to Byzantium, which implies that the authority and hierarchy of the Church came not from Jesus

Christ but from Cæsar. And thus this frivolous title, which appeared to Mauritius but an unmeaning word, concealed the whole system of Anti-christ, and its full significance the Pope alone realized."—(*Rohr.*, *T. ix., L. xlvii., p.* 456.) As in the Eastern Church, so also in the West, was the authority of St. Gregory recognized. His untiring vigilance, and inflexible firmness and burning zeal for the integrity of the faith and the observance of ecclesiastical discipline are seen in his numerous writings, but what we wanted to show was that St. Gregory the Great, who is acknowledged to be a true and model Bishop of Rome, living up to the canons of the ancient ChristianChurch, was as much a Pope by the universal jurisdiction which he claimed, and the supreme pastoral authority which he exercised over the Church and the bishops of his day as the Popes of our own times.

This is seen abundantly in this affair regarding the title of œcumenical or universal bishop, and the Patriarch, John the Faster, afterwards publicly acknowledged Gregory's authority and referred ecclesiastical causes, even those regarding simple priests, to him for final and definitive judgment. A few more examples of the exercise of supreme appellative jurisdiction by St. Gregory may not be out of place. Honoratus, arch-deacon of Salon in Dalmatia, accused his bishop, Natalis, of unjust treatment, and appealed to St. Gregory to be reinstated in the office from which Natalis had deposed him. The saint wrote to Natalis to restore Honoratus, and if there still remained any subject of strife, "let the arch-deacon come hither, and send some competent person to plead your cause, that thus with the help of the Lord we may be able, without regard to persons, to decide in favor of jus-

tice."—(*L. i., Epist. xix*). The bishop not heeding this command, Gregory wrote to him again in March, 592. " Reinstate Honoratus immediately on the receipt of this our letter. If you defer longer, know that you are deprived of the use of the pallium, which has been granted you by this See. Should you continue in your obstinacy, you will be deprived of the participation in the body and blood of our Lord, after which we will examine juridically whether you shall continue in the episcopacy. As to the one whom you have ordained arch-deacon to the prejudice of Honoratus, we depose him from that dignity, and if he continue to exercise its functions, he will be deprived of Holy Communion."
—(*L. ii., Epist. xviii.*) The bishop submitted, and after his death, which occurred shortly afterwards, Honoratus, with the approval of the Pope, was elected by the clergy to the vacant see. The bishops, however, of the province did not concur in his election, and preferred another, called Maximus, whereupon the Pope wrote to the bishops of Dalmatia, forbidding them by the authority of St. Peter to consecrate a bishop of Salon without his consent, under pain of being deprived of the participation in the body and blood of the Lord, and of the nullity of the election.—(*L. iv., Epist. x.*) It is of this Maximus that St. Gregory spoke in his letter to the empress. If we now turn to Gaul, we will see his authority everywhere acknowledged. He made, as we have already remarked, Virgilius of Arles, his own vicar, sending him the pallium, and giving him metropolitical jurisdiction over other bishops. In England, whither he had sent St. Augustine, he regulated all the ecclesiastical affairs, gave authority to Augustine to consecrate other bishops, and expressly declares

that, " Besides the bishops ordained by yourself and the bishop of York, we wish also all the bishops of Britain to be subject to you." (L. xi., Epist. lxv.) In a memorial replying to St. Augustine, he even goes into details of Church government, and among other things allows St. Augustine, whilst the only English bishop, to consecrate without the assistance of other bishops, thus forestalling by centuries, objections of the violation of canonical rule made against some of our consecrations, and showing that a Bishop of Rome even as observant of the canons as St. Gregory is acknowledged to be, could dispense with canons of discipline when there existed sufficient cause.

Thus is St. Gregory shown to have acted the Pope much more than poor Boniface III., his second successor, who is blamed for having initiated the usurpations of the Papacy, though he only reigned from February 19th, 607, to November 10th of the same year. The honor of beginning the Papacy within so brief a pontificate is doubtless accorded to him, because he is said to have obtained from the Emperor Phocas, who had succeeded Mauritius, an acknowledgment that the Apostolical See of St. Peter, that is, the Roman Church, was the first and chief of all the churches. Whether the emperor actually subscribed to such a document or not is of little consequence, as what we have seen of St. Gregory, how emphatically this claim was made, and positively enforced by him, shows the existence of a full-fledged Papacy before either Boniface or Phocas. Not to become entirely too prolix, we beg to refer our readers to Dr. Hergenröther's, admirable little work on the " Catholic Church and Christian State," (*vol.* 1, *Essay* 11, *p.* 93) for clear and convincing testimony that not only was the Papacy in existence, but that Papal infallibility was believed and taught in the first six centuries. I ought, perhaps, for such as wish to verify my statements, say that I have quoted the epistles of St. Gregory from the *Abbé Migne's Patrologiæ cursus completus, tom.* 77. Paris, 1849.

XII.

CATHOLIC BISHOPS NOT SIMPLE PRESBYTERS OR MERE VICARS OF THE POPE.

THE next gross misstatement of Catholic doctrine growing out of this controversy, which I feel myself called upon to correct, is that Catholic bishops are now "reduced to the rank of presbyters;" that, "The modern theology of Rome has abolished the episcopal *order*, and maintains nothing but an episcopal *office*, which is held at the nod of the Pontiff by a class of men in the order of presbyters who are mere vicars of the Pope in their several dioceses, but have no power at all as true bishops." This same idea is frequently repeated under various forms of expression, all more or less discourteous, and sometimes actually insulting, and in proof of all this, references are given to the Catechism of the Council of Trent, and St. Liguori's Theology; references which, as we shall presently see, prove nothing of the kind. To prove that the *modern Roman Church* does not *reduce its bishops to the rank of mere presbyters;* that the *modern theology of Rome* has not *abolished the episcopal order,* and that *as true bishops,* the bishops of the Catholic Church have all the power both of order and jurisdiction ever possessed or exercised by bishops in the *primitive Roman Church in its Catholic purity,* we acknowledge, and, if necessary, can demonstrate that in the first, second, third and fourth centuries of the Church, bishops were held to be a distinct order from *mere presbyters*, and by divine institution, superior to them in rank, dignity and power, and we will give a simple brief statement of the authoritative teaching of the Catholic Church of to-day from the Council of Trent and St. Liguori, the two authorities quoted against us. We beg, moreover, to refer any one wishing either to satisfy himself that this is in harmony with the *modern theology of Rome*, or to see the question more fully discussed, to a compendium of dogmatic theology, a copy of which last year I had the honor of receiving from the hands of its venerable and learned author, H. Hurter, S.J., S.Th., et Ph.D. (*tom. iii.*, *Œniponte*, 1879), a professor in the University of Innsbruck, and a son, by the way, of the illustrious Hurter, who so nobly vindicated the character of Innocent III. "If any one say that there is not, in the Catholic Church, a sacred hierarchy by divine ordinance instituted, which consists of bishops, priests and ministers, let him be anathema,"says the Council of Trent.—(*Sess.* 23, *Can.* 6.) As presbyters or priests outrank deacons, so bishops outrank presbyters, and that this body of sacred ministers in the Church, thus graduated, co-related and subordinated, is of divine institution, is the express teaching of modern Rome.

Not mere presbyters, then, are bishops, but by divine institution they are distinct. But not only are they distinct from, but they are, by the teaching of the same council, superior to simple presbyters: "If any one say, that bishops are not superior to priests, or that they have not the power of confirming and ordaining, or that that power is common to them and priests, let him be anathema." (*Sess.* 23, *Can.* 7.) How then can it be said that bishops are simple presbyters when the highest authority of the Church thus distinctly and explicitly states the contrary, and all *modern* theologians teach with the Church that there are powers attached to the episcopal order which simple priests cannot exercise. The simple priest, through the sacred laver of regeneration, begets children to the Church, but only bishops can by the imposition of hands beget fathers and masters. That this power attaches to the episcopal order by divine right and not by any ecclesiastical law, may be shown from the fact that although in case of necessity laics may validly confer baptism, and priests by special delegation may be empowered to confirm, never has the Church held valid an ordination of priest or bishop unless when administered by a validly consecrated bishop. And never has the Church attempted to withdraw this power from the bishop. She simply declared such ordinations illicit and sacreligious, but still valid, even when performed by an excommunicated, deposed, or heretical bishop, from whom she has withdrawn all jurisdiction, and thereby disqualified him from transmitting lawful succession.

Not only does the modern theology of Rome then establish the superiority of bishops over simple presbyters but the Roman Pontifical, in the ordination service of the priest, plainly distinguishes between the high priests (*pontifices summos*), placed over the people to rule them, and the men of a lower order and second dignity (*sequentis ordinis viros, et secundæ dignitatis*), chosen to co-operate with and aid the higher order, as the seventy prudent men aided Moses.

in the desert, and as our Lord associated with the Apostles other disciples and teachers of faith. The learned Hurter, in the work already mentioned (p. 428), lays down this thesis: "The rite by which bishops are consecrated is a true order, distinct from the other orders and a true sacrament," in which he combats the teaching of the ancient scholastics that the episcopacy was only an extension of the priesthood, and maintains that it is now the common opinion, and the one by all means to be held, that the episcopate is an order distinct not merely in grade or rank (*gradu*), but also in species (*specie*) from the priesthood. We may with the same author sum up the teaching of the Church regarding the hierarchy in these three points: (1) The hierarchy is divided into three degrees; (2) The origin of this division is divine; (3) As priests are superior to deacons, so bishops are superior to presbyters. This surely were more than sufficient to vindicate the teaching of modern Roman theology on the point in question, and to show how ungrounded and false the assertion that we had *abolished the episcopal order*, and *reduced bishops to the rank of mere presbyters*.

We need then take no further notice of such glaringly false charges as these: " Popes had taught them that bishops were only presbyters, in order to magnify themselves as the only and universal bishops." " Such was the common teaching of school divines before the Reformation:" " It is the Roman doctrine now." Yet as our good friend insists that these are *dogmas* of our own Church, *established by infallible authority*, and in proof hereof quotes in a foot-note " Liguori, who says some think the episcopate, *probably*, an order, tom. vi., p. 10," we beg our readers to bear with us a little longer, while we show what St. Liguori really does say, for although we do not regard him as in any respect an "infallible authority," we respect him as a saint and doctor of the Church, and certainly of higher authority on points of Christian doctrine and Catholic theology than the man who pretending to give tome and very page, misquotes and travesties his statements. Leaving some one else to hunt up and verify the reference, tom. vi., p. 10; in the edition (*Mechliniæ MDCCCXLV.*) of the works of St. Liguori now before me, we find (*tom. 7., Lib. 6, Tract. 5, de ordine, p.* 220) as follows : " The episcopate is an order, by which special power is conferred of confirming the faithful, and ordaining ministers of the sacraments, and of consecrating things appertaining to the divine worship." And in the same treatise : (*p.* 223) " It is asked—is the episcopate an order distinct from the priesthood? St. Thomas, St. Bonaventure, and others deny, saying that it is an extension of the order of the priesthood. But more commonly *theologians* affirm that it is an order distinct from the priesthood, because in it a distinct character is communicated, and a special power regarding the Eucharist is given, namely, that of consecrating ministers of this sacrament ; also, because the order of the episcopate is conferred by the laying on of hands and the form, *receive ye the Holy Ghost*, etc." To this let me add a short extract from a work by Rev. Aloysius Togni, entitled, " Instructio pro Sacris Ecclesiæ Ministris," which, we are told, is of the highest authority in Rome, being commonly used in the Roman seminaries. This we copy from note viii., in Appendix to " The Anglican Ministry," by Arthur W. Hutton, M.A. :

"What is the difference between a priest and a bishop? A bishop by divine right is superior to a priest, both in power of order and jurisdiction. In the power of order, for he administers the sacraments of Orders and Confirmation, in regard to which, the Council of Trent says, others of an inferior order, and therefore priests, (presbyters) 'have no power:' in jurisdiction, also, because the bishop has proper and ordinary jurisdiction through the whole diocese; but the priest has either only vicarious and delegated jurisdiction or ordinary jurisdiction in a certain part of the diocese. Whence the bishop is the summit (*apex*) and complement of the priesthood (*sacerdotii*) holding the first place in the ecclesiastical hierarchy."

Clearly then modern Roman theology has not abolished the episcopal order or confounded bishops with presbyters, and it only remains for me to remark, that those Catholic theologians, such as St. Thomas and St. Bonaventure, whose names stamp value and weight on whatever opinions they may defend, or whatever side of a controversy they espouse, in denying that the episcopate was an order distinct from the priesthood, never dreamt of saying that *bishops were simple presbyters* or *mere vicars of the Pope in their several dioceses*, as "Old Catholic" does. They taught that there were seven orders, four minor and three major or sacred orders; that the priesthood (*sacerdotium*) was the highest order in the Church; that this *sacerdotium* or priesthood was two-fold, embracing the presbyterate, or inferior priesthood, and the episcopate, or superior priesthood, that *sacerdotium* was therefore a generic term, of which the episcopate was the extension, the plenitude and the crown; and that though in rank the bishop was even by divine institution distinct from, and superior to, the priest, yet the episcopate was not, properly speaking, a distinct order and sacrament. This differs, *toto cælo*, from the misstatments we are combating, and it shows how easily persons may be deceived, who take things at trust, or at second-hand, or who know of Catholic theology only what they glean from a superficial reading of some elementary hand-book of Christian doctrine.

XIII.

TEACHINGS OF ANCIENT FATHERS VINDICATED.

WE can hardly excuse a man making pretensions to theological knowledge and patristic lore, quoting the ancient fathers and their writings, and yet putting forth garbled, falsified, and interpolated citations, thus misleading simple, unsophisticated minds, to the prejudice of Catholic truth and the doctrines of the Catholic Church. With a theologian's knowledge of the question in dispute between Catholic doctors regarding the Sacrament of Holy Orders, and the decisions of the Council of Trent on the same subject, no sincere seeker after truth could quote the catechism of the Council of Trent, Chapter vii., Questions xii., xxii., xxv., in proof of assertions which we have proved above to be so false and so contradictory to the decrees and canons of the council. Again, " St. Cyprian (A D. 250) on ' The Unity of the Church,' lays down certain maxims, which in his days were universally accepted, thus." Here follow four propositions, all more or less garbled, and evidently intended to convey the idea that St. Cyprian, who occupied the See of Carthage from 248 to September 14th, 258, held principles and taught maxims in opposition to the primacy of the Holy See, yet perhaps not one of the early Fathers more strenuously defends the prerogatives of the chair of Peter, which he styles the *ruling* chair, or who more frequently appeals to the authority of Peter's successors, as the centre and source of unity in the Church. Certainly no one who ever read his admirable treatise, "On the Unity of the Church," could have the face to mention either it or its author in assailing the claim of Papal supremacy, and universal jurisdiction of the See of Peter. We would ardently desire to have the whole treatise in a good English dress introduced to the English-speaking community. No better testimony could be adduced, that the maxims and principles of St. Cyprian, and *universally accepted* in his time, regarding the Papacy, are identical with those held by the Catholic Church to-day Pardon us then, dear readers, a short extract to supplement the mutilated excerpts of our "Old Catholic" controversialist. "The proof of faith is easy and compendious, because true. The Lord speaks to Peter: 'I say to thee,' He says, 'that thou art Peter, and on this rock I will build my Church, and the gates of hell shall not prevail against it. And to thee I will give the keys of the kingdom of heaven, and whatsoever thou shalt bind on earth, shall be bound also in heaven; and whatsoever thou shalt loose on earth, shall be loosed also in heaven.' And again he says to him, after His resurrection. 'Feed my sheep.' *Upon that one individual He builds His Church, and to him He commits His sheep to be fed.* And although after the resurrection He gives to all His Apostles equal power, and says: 'As the Father hath sent me, I also send you ; Receive ye the Holy Ghost; whose sins you shall forgive, they shall be forgiven them ; whose sins you shall retain, they shall be retained ;' yet, to manifest unity, He disposed by His authority the origin of the same unity, which begins from One. Even the other Apostles were certainly what Peter was, being endowed with equal participation of honor and power, but the beginning proceeds from unity, *and the primacy is given to Peter, that the Church of Christ may be shown to be one, and the chair one.*"

In other places St. Cyprian calls the Church of Rome, *the root and matrix* of the Catholic Church, the *ruling Church whence sacerdotal unity has arisen.* So that, as the learned Dr. Kenrick, in his "Primacy of the Apostolic See," tells us, the violent opponent of the Pope's supremacy, Barrow, admits that, "St. Cyprian considered St. Peter to have received from Christ a primacy of order," and Bishop Hopkins of Vermont was forced to sigh over the fact that so *early did the Bishops of Rome endeavor to secure dominion and supremacy,* and that it must be granted that *in the year 220, the doctrine was partially admitted that the unity of the Church took its rise in the See or diocese of Peter.* And Hallam ("*Middle Ages,*" *Chap. vii.*) confirms this, saying: "Irenæus rather vaguely, and Cyprian more positively, admit, or rather assert, the primacy of the Church of Rome, which the latter seems to have regarded as a kind of centre of Catholic unity." (*Primacy of H. See, c. vii. p.* 100, *Philad.,* 1845.) The appeal, then, to the early Fathers furnishes little comfort to the enemies of the Holy See, and a study of those early lights of the Christian Church must convince any earnest, candid inquirer that the Papacy, its powers and prerogatives, are of divine origin, and hence neither Tertullian, nor St. Vincent of Lerins, teach anything but what we teach to-day in the quotations urged against us. And I would here close this reference to the Fathers did not our reviewer summon the illustrious doctor of the Western Church, St. Jerome, to testify in behalf of "Old Catholicism." I cannot allow that great man, stern of feature and blunt of speech, whose classic Latinity, and rigid asceticism made him worthy to be the secretary of the learned Pope Damasus, and spiritual guide of a Paula and Eustochium, whose biblical knowledge qualified him to undertake and faithfully execute the task of translating the Bible from the original text; I cannot, I say, allow *him* to be put on record in the 19th century against the Papacy whose sturdy and fearless champion he was in the 4th and 5th centuries. Thus then, St. Jerome is made to speak: "If one is looking for authority, the world is greater than one city. Wherever a bishop may be placed, whether at Rome or Eugubium; whether at Constantinople or Rhegium; whether at Alexandria or at Tanis, he has the same authority, the same worth, the same priesthood. The power of wealth, the lowliness of poverty, render a bishop neither higher nor lower. All are successors of the Apostles."

Now, please to remark that the only words in this extract from the letter of St. Jerome having any semblance of force or point against Catholic doctrine are those "*the same authority*," and these words St. Jerome never wrote; they are a pure interpolation. Now, I do not charge that our Buffalo "Old Catholic" committed this fraud, or falsified St. Jerome's letter; he simply did here, what he has been doing all along; he has taken these things at second-hand, has accepted a falsified, interpolated version as the genuine text, without ever examining the original. I am the more inclined to put this construction on the matter, because I think if he had read this letter, to which he accurately refers in a foot-note as Epist. cxlvi., he would never have cited it as authority, for in this letter St. Jerome seems to do what modern Roman theology is charged with doing, he seems to reduce bishops to the level of priests, and says that bishops and priests are all the same. We will let our Episcopal friend settle the matter with St. Jerome and Presbyterians, who often quote this very epistle of St. Jerome, in support of Presbyterianism. For ourselves, we know what the Church teaches on this point, and we know that St. Jerome himself elsewhere acknowledges the superiority of bishops, and we know that this letter was written to correct an abuse, by which deacons pretended an equality with priests, and grounded their claims on certain Roman customs and privileges.

XIV.

CANONS OF NICE AND EPHESUS.

JUST here I may call attention to another very misleading statement, professedly inferred from the canons of the Councils of Nicea and Ephesus. In a lecture delivered in St. Joseph's Cathedral, 1874, I referred to the letter which Pope Julius I. wrote to the Eastern bishops, A. D. 342, sustaining the appeal made by St. Athanasius, in proof that, at this early period there was a Pope claiming and exercising jurisdiction over the whole Church, East and West, as fully and emphatically as the Popes in our own times; to which our "Old Catholic" reviewer replies: "Had Julius addressed the bishops of Britain, A. D. 342, even in terms of *patriarchal* authority, they would have reminded him that his limit was Lower Italy." A few sentences before he averred that, "Western Europe had but one such (Apostolic) See, and in the nature of things that gave Rome a canonical primacy;" and still a few lines above, he asserts that in the letter to which I referred, written to the bishops of the East, in answer to an appeal to the Pope: "Julius was claiming his *patriarchal primacy* under the canons." So that although Julius' "patriarchal authority was limited to Lower Italy," "Rome had a canonical primacy over Western Europe," and "a patriarchal authority, under the canons" over Alexandria and the Eastern Church. But it is not to these contradictions that I wish to call special attention, but to this following statement: "After Ephesus, they (the bishops of Britain) would have said, that England, with Cyprus and other islands, was canonically exempt from all such jurisdictions; which was and is the fact." But even stranger than the statement itself is the bold attempt to sustain it by reference in a foot-note to: "Canon vi., of Nicea, afterwards Canon vii., of Ephesus."

Now, although we cannot be expected here to discuss these canons, we affirm positively and categorically, that these canons do *not* exempt England, Cyprus or any other islands from the jurisdiction of the Holy See, and that there was no question of such exemption in either the Council of Nicea or Ephesus. The question before the Fathers of the Nicene Council was in regard to the jurisdiction of the See of Alexandria, honored and privileged from earliest days because it was the See of St. Mark the Evangelist and disciple of St. Peter. The Meletian schism gave rise to this controversy, for after Meletius was condemned by St. Peter of Alexandria, and deposed from his see, he rebelled against the authority of the Apostolic See of Alexandria, and this it was that caused the synod to define the rights and jurisdiction of that see over the provinces of Egypt, Libya and Pentapolis, which it does in these words: "Let the ancient custom throughout Egypt, Libya and Pentapolis be strictly adhered to, so that the bishop of Alexandria shall have jurisdiction over all these; since this is also the custom of the Bishop of Rome." Now, there has been some difference of opinion about this last clause, or about the true meaning and correct translation of the original Greek text, some, with Bellarmine, maintaining the true meaning of the canon to be: " Let the bishop of Alexandria govern these provinces, because such was the custom of the Bishop of Rome; that is, because the Roman Pontiff, prior to any definitions by councils, was used to permit the Alexandrian bishop to govern, or have jurisdiction, over these provinces," which would be a clear acknowledgment by the first general council of the primacy of Rome. Others say, with Phillips, that, " This canon does not demonstrate the primacy of the Pope, as the Council of Nicea did not speak of this primacy, simply because it had no need to be established or confirmed by it," and hence, with Heféle, they translate the clause: " There is a similar custom for the Roman Bishop," that is, jurisdiction over different provinces, a patriarchate is recognized in regard to Rome, and the same should hold for Alexandria. Now, we will not discuss this disputed point, though from the text the first is plainly the true meaning.—(*See a scholarly article in* "*Amer. Cath. Quarterly Review*," April, 1880, *by Rev. Jas. F. Loughlin, D.D.*) It is in any case undeniable that the Council of Nicea never dreamed of curtailing the jurisdiction of the Pope or exempting England, Cyprus, or other islands from his jurisdiction. So much then for Canon vi. of the Council of Nicea. What about Canon vii. of Ephesus? In the first place, with most authors who have written the history of this council, we hold that that council formulated but six canons. " If in some *codex*," says Heféle, ("*History of the Councils*," tom. *II.*, *p.* 389, *French Ed.* 1869), " eight canons are found, it is because the resolution passed by the council on the motion of Charisius, is regarded as Canon vii., and the decree concerning the bishops of Egypt is put down as Canon viii." This decree, then, passed in the council at its seventh session, is referred to by our learned divine as Canon vii. of the Council of Ephesus. Those wishing to obtain full information regarding the nature and meaning of the decree of the council, I must refer to Hefélé's History above cited, or to the authorities which he quotes. (*ibid. pp.* 386, 387.) Let me, however, briefly as possible, state the question proposed to, and acted on, by the council, in order to show that it has no connection at all with the jurisdiction or primacy of the Roman Pontiff, although, with an unaccountable assurance, evidencing either bad faith, or inexcusable reliance on second-hand, untrustworthy information, we are told that: "After Ephesus, England, with Cyprus and other islands, was canonically exempt from such jurisdiction."

The Apostolic See of Antioch, which the Apostle St. Peter himself founded, like that of Alexandria, claimed special privileges and an extensive jurisdiction, which the sixth canon of the Council of Nicea seemed to recognize and confirm, in thèse terms: " In like manner, regarding Antioch and the other provinces, let the churches retain their special privileges." The bishop of Antioch claimed superior metropolitan or patriarchal rights over Cyprus, in particular the right of consecrating its bishops. As the metropolitan of Constantia died about the time of the convocation of the council, the proconsul of Antioch, at the suggestion of the Patriarch, forbade a new election to be held until this disturbing question of jurisdiction should be finally adjudicated. In defiance of the prohibition, Rheginus was elected to the see of Constantia, and with two of his suffragans, Zeno and Evagrius, he appealed to the council against the pretensions of Antioch, and the question was warmly and lengthily discussed in the seventh session, and it was decreed, that: "The churches of Cyprus should continue to enjoy their independence and the right of consecrating their own bishops (and of electing them), and that the synod renew in general all the liberties of the ecclesiastical provinces, and forbid encroachments on foreign provinces." Thus a contest between local churches regarding ecclesiastical privileges, and disciplinary canons regulating the mutual relations of these churches, has been strangely twisted into a canonical exemption from the jurisdiction of the Bishop of Rome, and it is more than insinuated that such, forsooth, was the purpose and scope of these canons. Such contests and rivalries and disputes regarding jurisdiction have been not unfrequent in the Church, since the Apostolic ages; such existed between Canterbury and York in England, between Arles and Vienne in Gaul, and such, in very possible contingencies, may yet exist between the metropolitan sees of Baltimore and New York.

Voluminous are the canonical enactments adjudicating such rival claims, deciding such controversies, and regulating and defending the limits and extent of diocesan, metropolitical, primatial and patriarchal jurisdiction, yet what student of church history would assert that by such ecclesiastical legislation a blow was aimed at the supremacy of the Holy See, or the universal jurisdiction of the Pope? It is even still more astonishing that any one denying the primacy of the Pope, or claiming independence of his supreme pastoral authority, should make any reference to the Council of

Ephesus, held in the year 431 composed of two hundred bishops, mostly of the East. Cyril, of Jerusalem, opened the first session, on the the 22d of June, and presided, as the acts of the council state, in the name of the Pope. It proceeded to condemn Nestorius, who refused to the Blessed Virgin the title of *Theotokos* or Mother of God. "Forced," says the council, "by the canons and by the letter of our most holy Father, and co-laborer, Celestine, Bishop of Rome;" it vindicated the divine maternity of Mary, and originated the prayer so dear to Catholics, adding to the Angel's greeting the words: "Holy Mary, mother of God, pray for us sinners, now, and at the hour of our death."

In the second session, held on the 10th of July of the same year, Cyril is again expressly designated in the minutes or *procès verbal* of the session, as the representative of the Bishop of Rome. In time to assist at this session came three legates of the Pope, Arcadius and Projectus, bishops, and Philip, a priest, bringing a dogmatical letter from Celestine, which was read before the synod, first in the original Latin, and then in a Greek version, which was received with loud applause. The letter of the Pope declares that : " He sent three legates to assist at the deliberations of the synod, and to attend to the execution of what the Pope had previously concluded ; and he doubted not, but that the assembled bishops would be in accord with these his decisions." The third session was held the following day, the 11th of July. The legates of the Pope declared that they had read, in the interval, the acts of the first session, (at which they had not assisted) and had found the sentence against Nestorius entirely canonical and according to the discipline of the Church, but that, according to the orders of the Pope, they should require the acts of the first session to be read in their presence, which was immediately done. (*Hefélé, tom. ii., p.* 379.) This, surely, does not look much like snubbing the Pope, or repudiating his jurisdiction. Does Ephesus limit the Pope's jurisdiction to Lower Italy? What gives Celestine, Bishop of Rome, the right to preside by his representatives at the General Council of Ephesus and to impose his authority and his doctrinal decisions on the assembled bishops? Can it be his dignity as Patriarch of the West? How came Rome to have a "*canonical* primacy?" Where are the canons to be found conferring, formulating, or promulgating this primacy? Is it not plain and undeniable that this primacy had its origin in a higher source, existed, and was acknowedged prior to councils and canons? and that these, as Boniface I. writes to the bishops of Thessaly, "did not dare pass laws regarding the Bishops of Rome, knowing that no act of man could confer additional power on one, who had received all power from the words of our Lord Himself." With the history of the Council of Ephesus before us, its acts and its canons, how difficult it is to be patient on reading repeated assertions of this kind: "By the ancient canons (A.D. 431) it was impossible for him (the Pope) to assert even a *patriarchal* authority, in England, which enjoyed the insular privilege of entire self-dependence," giving as authority " Third General Council, Ephesus," when there is nothing of the kind to be found in the Council of Ephesus, nothing more than what we have already mentioned, that the churches of the island of Cyprus are not subject to the see of Antioch, but should continue to enjoy their independence in the election and consecration of their bishops.

XV.

THE CATHOLIC DOCTRINE REGARDING ECCLESIASTICAL JURISDICTION.

OUR opponents seem to have no idea of the power of jurisdiction as distinct from the power of order conferred in priestly and episcopal ordination, and hence much of their confusion, bewilderment, and erroneous inferences. We have already said that the power of order may exist without the power of jurisdiction, as in the case of a priest regularly ordained by any lawfully consecrated bishop, but who has not yet received faculties or a mission from his own ordinary; or in the case of a bishop consecrated merely to perform certain special acts, such as confirming, ordaining, etc., and these on this account are called in German, *weihbischof,* and they perform acts which none but bishops, none but those having the episcopal character and order can do. So, too, jurisdiction may be exercised without orders, as when a simple cleric is appointed to a benefice, or when a priest has received from the Pope his appointment to a see, but has not yet been consecrated. This premised, we say we hold, with St. Jerome, that a bishop in Buffalo is the equal of a bishop in Rome as far as his episcopal order, and the power attached to and inherent in his order, are concerned, for the episcopate is one, the episcopal order is one and the same in all bishops, wherever they may be placed, *whether at Rome* or *Eugubium;* at Buffalo, or New York, though there are various grades or degrees of jurisdiction, as is clearly explained in the Catechism of the Council of Trent, Chap. VII., Question xxv., to which reference has already been made. Take an illustration. Our present revered metropolitan, lately, to the joy of Catholic and non-Catholic America, made by our late loved and saintly Holy Father, first American cardinal, before his promotion to the archbishopric of New York, was the bishop of Albany, and then he and the bishop of Buffalo were on a perfect equality, each governing his respective diocese, and discharging the duties of his episcopal office with the same powers both of order and jurisdiction. Elevated to the archiepiscopal dignity, and installed in the archiepiscopal see, and invested by the Sovereign Pontiff with the pallium, things are somewhat changed. His episcopal order has undergone no change, no new character has been impressed on him, no new consecration conferred, but besides the ordinary jurisdiction which he has now over the diocese of New York, as he had before over the diocese of Albany, and as the bishop of Buffalo has over his own diocese, he now has an enlarged or extended jurisdiction according to the canons and laws of the Church over a whole Province, embracing seven dioceses. Another illustration. Our present illustrious Pontiff, Leo XIII., was consecrated bishop in Rome on the 19th of February, 1843, with the title of archbishop of Damietta *in partibus infidelium.*

He then received the full powers of the episcopal order, with only a nominal jurisdiction. He was sent as nuncio to Brussels; and for three years in the capital of Belgium, as bishop, was on a footing of equality with the bishops of that kingdom, though, except by special delegation, he could exercise in any of their dioceses no act of an Ordinary, no episcopal jurisdiction. His health somewhat impaired, he travelled, we are told, through Belgium and parts of Germany, visited England, and on his way back to Italy, passed through Paris, Lyons, Marseilles as a simple bishop, as the equal of the bishops whom he met, everywhere esteemed and admired for his learning, ability and virtue. We find him then a simple bishop again in Rome, and as such the bishop of Buffalo, had there been one at the time, would have been the equal of a bishop in Rome, nay, in some respect superior to him, for he would have jurisdiction as Ordinary over a diocese, and Bishop Pecci in Rome had not. But in 1846 Monsigneur Pecci was appointed to the see of Perugia ; on the 26th of the same year the new bishop took solemn possession of his see, and without any new consecration or any addition to the power of the episcopal order, by the appointment of the Sovereign Pontiff, he was invested with the additional power of jurisdiction as ordinary of the see of Perugia and metropolitan of the Province of Umbria. On the 20th of February, 1878, Monsigneur Pecci, who on December 19th, 1853, had been made cardinal, and on the 21st of September, 1877, camerlengo, was elected, and on the 3d of March solemnly crowned Pope, under the name and title of Leo XIII. He is now, not a bishop in Rome, but *the* Bishop of Rome, successor of St. Peter and vicar of Christ. Though there has been no addition to, or extension of his power as a bishop, or more properly of his episcopal order, yet, on his legitimate and canonical elevation to the See of Rome, the chair of Peter, he has acquired by divine right, by the institution of Christ and the Divine constitution of the Christian Church, supreme and universal jurisdiction over the Church, is made Supreme Pastor of the whole flock, and thus, as among the Apostles, who were all equal, "one was selected," as St. Jerome says, "that by the appointment of a Head, the occasion of schism may be taken away," so among bishops, though there is a solidarity, "the episcopate is one and indivisible," according to St. Cyprian, and "each bishop can hold a part without division of the whole," yet "Christ gave the keys to Peter as a token of unity," and for the preservation of that unity, He made the Roman Church, the chair of Peter, the *radix* and *matrix* of the Catholic Church, so that, though she "pours abroad her bountiful streams, yet there is one source, one Head, one Mother, abundant in the results of her fruitfulness."—(*St. Cyprian, De Unitate Ecclesiæ.*)

Is not this just what we should expect in a Church founded by the Word and Wisdom of God, into which all were to be gathered that were to be saved and come to the knowledge of the truth, that thus, as He himself declared, there might be, "one sheep-fold under one shepherd." Thus then, with St. Jerome and "old Catholic" we agree that a bishop in Buffalo is, as to his episcopal order and the power of order, not only the equal of a bishop at Rome, but the equal of the Bishop of Rome, and Pope Leo XIII., in this respect possesses no higher or greater power, is no more a bishop in the sense explained than was simple Monsigneur Pecci after his consecration on the Viminal hill, in Rome, in the year

1843, though as to jurisdiction we now own him as Bishop of bishops, holding a primacy of honor and jurisdiction over the whole Church, and we hesitate not to repeat in regard to Leo XIII., what, when spoken in 1874 of Pius IX., of saintly memory, so much riled certain parties here: "As one man, we all, bishops, priests and people, lay at the feet of his Holiness all the devotion, love, reverence and submission due to the Supreme Head of the Church and vicar of Christ." This is probably more than enough to explain the twofold power of order and jurisdiction, and our relations as bishops governing our respective dioceses in communion with, and subordination to, the Holy See. Are Catholic bishops then simply *vicars of the Pope*, holding their office and their powers '*at his nod?*' The episcopacy is of divine institution; it belongs to the organic constitution of the Church as founded by Christ. The titular bishop is the Ordinary of his diocese, governing it not by vicarious or delegated powers, but "placed there by the Holy Ghost, to rule the Church of God." (*Acts xx*. 28). His power both of order and jurisdiction over his flock, is from God, therefore, he is styled Ordinary, exercises ordinary jurisdiction, which he delegates to others. Here we see the necessity of the distinction, which we have already brought out at some length, between the power of order and jurisdiction, and between the divine institution of the episcopate and the appointment of individual bishops. Bishops are successors of the Apostles, but each individual bishop is not the successor of some one Apostle, as the Bishop of Rome is the successor of St. Peter. The mission of the Apostles was "to teach all nations," "to preach the gospel to every creature." No bounds were assigned to them for the exercise of their jurisdiction; the jurisdiction of a bishop is limited by the diocese to which he is appointed.

The power of order in all bishops is, as we have seen, equal; so is it essential, inamissible, indestructible. In spite of Popes and councils, in spite of canonical prohibitions, excommunication, and even deposition, a true bishop can validly perform all the acts proper to his episcopal order, because, not from the Church, not from the Pope, not from canons or councils, but directly and immediately from God, is his power of order, and it is conferred by consecration. Not so the power of jurisdiction; it is conferred by his appointment, and before consecration is possessed in all its fulness and extent. It is not equal in all bishops, for then there could not be metropolitans, primates, patriarchs, any more than Popes, and yet these have existed in the Christian Church from the earliest ages, and are interwoven into the texture of her constituent laws. Nothing is more clear in the history of the Church, and of the Church of England in particular, than that the jurisdiction of bishops has been modified, changed, enlarged or curtailed by canonical enactments and the actions of Popes. The history of the Pontificate of Gregory the Great, and the sees of Canterbury and York, affords ample proof of this, whilst it is superfluous to say that the Holy See has erected new sees, divided and subdivided dioceses and provinces, and even, though rarely, abolished sees. Witness the Church of France after the French revolution, the establishment of the American Church, the re-establishment of the English and Scotch hierarchy. The power of jurisdiction, then, in the episcopacy is divine and from God, but indirectly, and through the Pope, Christ our Lord so organizing and constituting His Church, giving to Peter the full power of the keys and the feeding and government of the whole flock, lambs and sheep.—(*Matt. xvi.*, 19. *John xxi.*, 15, 16, 17.) " The episcopal power of jurisdiction is therefore not derived *immediately* from Christ, in so far as it exists in individuals: it has been *established* by Christ, but is not conferred immediately by Him upon *individual bishops;* it is imparted to them by the Head of the Church, or bishops whom he has authorized. Thus the unity of the episcopate, so much insisted on by the Fathers, is fully upheld ; the Holy See is head, root, spring, origin of the spiritual authority." (*Hergenröther,* " *Church and State,*" *vol.* I., *p.* 177.)

This is sufficient explanation of the formula used in the appointment of bishops, " In virtue of the power of God, of the prince of the Apostles, and of the Ruling Pope:" and also of that used by bishops themselves, "By the grace of God and of the Holy See," for even those who maintain with Thomassin that bishops obtain their jurisdiction immediately from Christ, ackowledge that : " They have not received immediately from him their particular territory or peculiar diocese, since this partition has been made in the course of ages by the Church, nor could it be made or perpetuated unless with the consent of the Head, in whom is the pivot and centre of the ecclesiastical unity." (*Thomassin,* cited *by Hergenröther, as above.*) More clearly and correctly does the learned Gerdile, quoted in the same place by the same author, express the Catholic doctrine on this point, thus : " For jurisdiction, the assignment of a people as subjects is requisite, and this is done by human, not divine right. Though the form and manner of this assignment may vary in different places and times according to the diversity of discipline, yet none could be lawful unless approved by the Holy See, from whose consent it receives force and strength, according to the plenitude of power shed over the universal Church." That is, by the positive act of the Holy See assigning a diocese, and determining its limits, the subjects of a bishop are determined and actual jurisdiction over the same is conferred, which jurisdiction is from God, though not immediately, but through the vicar of Christ, it is ordinary, not delegated or vicarious, and hence he can delegate the same to others, which he could not do, were it a delegated power. And though the manner of making appointments to episcopal sees has varied at different times, no appointment could ever have been lawful, if the Holy See rejected it, or if the Sovereign Pontiff did not expressly or tacitly consent to it.

This a Bishop of Rome who was faithful and exact in the observance of the canons, St. Gregory the Great, explicitly declares; writing to the empress of Constantinople, he says in regard to the consecration of Maximus, elevated to the episcopate against his wish: "A thing was done which never happened under previous princes." (*L.* 5, *Epist. xxi.*) And to Maximus himself, he writes: "An unheard of wickedness is added, that after our interdict, excommunicating yourself and those ordaining you, you are said," etc. (*L.* 4, *Epist. xx.*) Rightly then do we "object to any ordination not proceeding under warrant from Rome." Nor does this "overthrow the orders of St. Chrysostom, St. Augustine and St. Ambrose," as any student of history knows that these illustrious saints and doctors of the Church acknowledged the supremacy of the See of Rome and were in turn acknowleged by the Sovereign Pontiff. How false, then, and misleading the assertion, that because the Papacy is the source and centre of all ecclesiastical jurisdiction, in the Catholic sense now explained, Catholic bishops are "not true bishops, have no power at all." I almost deem it beneath me, especially after all we have already said, to notice the insulting remark : " They are not permitted to bear any corporate witness whatever ; and when summoned to meet the Pope in council, it is only to tremble around his throne, accept his oracles, and renounce their own convictions at his command, or submit to be stripped of their dignities, such as they are." Catholic bishops are, by divine right, witnesses and judges of the faith, and they can neither abdicate their rights, nor be despoiled of them by any earthly power.

It is precisely when assembled in council under the presidency of the Pope, that they represent, and are successors of the College of the Apostles, and in their corporate capacity speak with the full, supreme and infallible authority, vested by Christ our Lord in His holy Church. Are judges in our courts not true judges, void of all power and authority, because there are judges of higher courts to whom appeal may be taken, who have a wider jurisdiction, and who are empowered to review, confirm or reverse their decisions? Have bishops no power, because by our Lord's divine ordinances their power in the Church is subordinated to that of him whom He appointed as Supreme Judge in faith and morals, and Supreme Ruler and Pastor of his whole flock? Does not the Council of the Vatican clearly and emphatically state that its decrees do not curtail, weaken, or in any way belittle episcopal authority; that the universal and supreme jurisdiction of the Sovereign Pontiff does not conflict with that of the bishop in his own diocese? " But so far is this power of the Supreme Pontiff from being any prejudice to the *ordinary* and *immediate* power of episcopal jurisdiction, by which bishops who have been sent by the Holy Ghost to succeed and hold the place of the Apostles, (*Coun. of Trent, Sess. xxiii., chap. iv.*) feed and govern, each his own flock, as true pastors, that this their episcopal authority is really asserted, strengthened and vindicated by the Supreme and Universal Pastor."—(*Dogmatic Constitution of the Church of Christ, chap. iii.*)

Thus, while thanking our friends for the great interest they take in the maintenance of our rights as bishops, as against the so-called overshadowing and all-absorbing power of the Pope of Rome, we see how jealously the Church guards the original divine constitution given to her by her divine Founder. The Church is to-day as the Redeemer of the world constituted and organized her, holding all her powers from Him, and wonderfully, divinely equipped to do His work, and to do His work unfailingly to the end of ages. To her keeping the fruits of redemption, the merits of the passion and death of a God-man, were to be committed, through her to be dispensed to the souls of men. She was to guard the deposit of faith, and teach it to all nations, and He himself was to be with her all days, to the end of time, and the Holy Ghost was to abide with her forever to teach her all truth. Her ministers to-day can say with St. Paul, " Let a man so look upon us as ministers of Christ and stewards of the mysteries of God," (*I Cor., iv.* 1.) and because sent by Him, delegated and empowered by Him, He says: "He that hears you hears me."—(*Luke x.* 16.) But they have no arbitrary powers, they can exercise no usurped authority, and nothing is plainer in Holy Writ, than that our Lord chose his own ministers: " I have chosen you, not you me ;" (*John xv.* 16.) and appointed them to do His own work, and " I have appointed you that you should go and bring forth fruit and that your fruit should remain."—(*Ibid.*)

The Church is God's own work. He founded it, and "other foundation no man can lay but that which is laid."—(*I Cor. iii.* 2.) " Built upon the foundation of the Apostles and Prophets, Jesus Christ Himself being the chief corner-stone."—(*Eph. ii.* 20) His own mystical body, moulded into perfect shape and form by His own hands, living a divine life breathed into it on the day of Pentecost, it is destined to gather into one fold, under one shepherd, all mankind, for, as St. Cyprian teaches, there is "one God, one Christ, one Church," and St. Paul, "one Lord, one faith, one baptism," and does this not imply one Head, one Supreme Authority, one Universal Pastor? Can the smallest meeting be organized without a chairman ? Can any society exist without a presiding officer? Can any city successfully conduct its municipal affairs without a mayor? Would any rational man dream of a state without a governor, or a nation without a ruler? How long would our union hold together without a president, and does not the setting up of rival presidents involve the disintegration of the nation? Could any of our parishes or congregations ever remain one, united and prosperous without a spiritual guide and pastor, having authority to teach and to govern? How preserve in agreement of discipline and faith the priests and people of a diocese without a bishop invested with superior jurisdiction, recognized higher pastoral authority, and how maintain "one faith," "one Church," "one fold," embracing all the world, all the bishops, all the priests, and all the faithful people of Christendom, without one Supreme Head, one sovereign authority, one divinely constituted, Universal and Infallible Pastor? Did not our Lord provide for this in selecting one among all His Apostles, giving him the name of Peter, establishing him as the rock on which His Church was to be built, pledging His infallible word that the gates of hell should never prevail against it, praying with a prayer of divine efficacy that his faith fail not, for he was to confirm his brethren, and finally, actually giving him the full charge of feeding and governing his whole flock, lambs and sheep, pastors and people? The episcopate and the priesthood are necessary constituent elements in the Church, and can never be absorbed or abolished, but they are, by the very nature and constitution of the Church, subordinated to the Supreme Pastor, the Sovereign Pontiff.

Nor does it follow, because a sovereign ruler, or executive of a nation, may appoint, and, for cause, remove inferior officers, or veto the acts of a co-ordinate branch of the government, that therefore he may abolish such offices, branches, or departments of government, or usurp rights, privileges, and powers, equally valid with his own, and derived from the same source; even though by the law of the land, and the constitution of the state, subordinate to his. In like manner in the Church, by her divine constitution, a master-piece, by the way, of divine wisdom, there is, and it is of faith that there is, besides the Papacy, with its primacy of honor and jurisdiction over the Universal Church, a sacred hierarchy consisting of bishops, priests and ministers; with rights, privileges and powers, as valid as those of the Papacy, reposing on the same foundation, secured by the same charter, a hierarchy therefore that never can be abolished by Papal power, absorbed or confounded in the prerogatives of the Holy See, but without jangle or clashing of any kind, bishops, priests and ministers are ordained of Christ to co-exist and effectually co-operate even to the end of ages, with the supreme power with which He has been pleased to invest the successor of St. Peter, the Prince of the Apostles and first Bishop of Rome. I must now finish what I have perhaps drawn out with, it may be, unnecessary prolixity, but I was anxious to elucidate this point of Catholic faith, which has been so much obscured and misrepresented, in the hope that those large numbers of our esteemed and most worthy fellow-Christians who admire the beauty, and strength, and indestructibility of what they call the Catholic system or Papal polity, may at length see that all this beauty, unconquerable strength, and indestructible vitality are derived from her Divine Founder. Of them, or at least of many of them, whom we sincerely believe to be unconsciously and innocently, outside the true Church, our loving Saviour says: "Other sheep I have, that are not of this fold; them also I must bring, and they shall hear my voice and there shall be one sheep-fold and one Shepherd." (*John x.* 16). Fiat! Fiat!

THE END.

VALUED WORDS FROM FRIENDLY SOURCES.

The following are a few of the many kind letters of congratulation and thanks received by the Rt. Rev. author, showing the appreciation in which the work is held by the American hierarchy:

Many thanks for the handsome volume which you have kindly sent me containing your replies to Dr. Coxe, with important and valuable additions. I am glad you have taken the trouble to embody them in their present more complete and permanent form. You have done good service to the cause of truth, by the publication of this valuable work, which I hope will be widely circulated and produce much good.

✠JOHN CARD. McCLOSKEY, Archbp. of N. York.

Allow me to offer you my sincere congratulations on your recent work in which you so triumphantly refute the claims of the Episcopal Church to Apostolical succession. Dr. Coxe has reason to regret the day when he threw down the gauntlet to you, and the thanks of the Catholic community and of the lovers of truth are due to those friends who persuaded you to publish in book-form your admirable lectures and essays, which would be soon destined to perish if they appeared only in a pamphlet or newspaper. I trust that many earnest inquirers will be induced to study your valuable contributions to polemical literature.

✠JAMES GIBBONS, Archbp. of Baltimore.

Thanking you very much for the beautiful and able work—Protestant Claims Disproved—which you have given us, and which will be most useful in the hands of Catholics to enlighten Protestants, I remain,

✠J. S. ALEMANY, A.S.F.

Your valued present *extinguishing* soi-disant *Episcopal* (?) Bishops is received. What a delusion and a snare! God grant that we may be able to say of *all*, as we do of *some*: ' Laqueus contritus est, et nos liberati sumus."
✠JAMES F. WOOD, Archbp. of Philad.

Please to accept my very sincere thanks for your excellent work on the invalidity of Anglican and American ordinations to the ministry. . . . The second part is equally interesting and instructive. What a pity there is not more distributing of Catholic doctrine, and vindications in tracts and small books.
✠JOHN JOSEPH LYNCH, Archbp. of Toronto.

I take the first free moment to express the great pleasure and profit derived from reading your reply to Dr. Coxe. You have treated him with gentleness—far more than he deserves, and no one can read your book, without feeling convinced that the words come from earnest, well-grounded and most reasonable convictions. And you completely crush the pseudo-Prelate. The gentle sarcasm must be particularly galling to him.
✠M. A. CORRIGAN, Bp. of Newark.

I know not whether I am indebted to you or to your publisher for the copy of your "Protestant Episcopal Claims to Apostolical Succession," but I am indebted to *you alone* for the pleasure I have derived from the reading of the work. I have always taken deep interest in the subject; and I never was better pleased by any author. You have done a noble work for the Church, and have said enough to silence "Old Catholic" forever. Thanks.
✠P. T. O'REILLY, Bp. of Springfield.

Please accept my very sincere thanks for your work on the invalidity of Anglican orders. The work I am confident will, with the divine blessing, produce much fruit amongst a people so fond of reading and investigating as are the Americans.
✠JOHN WALSH, Bp. of London.

Please accept my sincere thanks for the copy you have kindly forwarded of your triumphant refutation of Anglican pretensions. Dr. Coxe, so far as the truth is concerned, has not preached in vain, when this book is the result. I had already read your lecture and most of your articles on the same subject, and I am glad they have been thrown into their present form, and thereby invested with a character of permanence. The pill must be a bitter one for your restless and arrogant neighbor.

✠T. Mullen, Bp. of Erie.

This is the first opportunity that I could avail myself of, to thank you for your admirable book. These claims of the Prot. E. Church have been vainly made by members of that church for some time past. I hope your answer to them will have the desired effect.

✠E. P. Wadhams, Bp. of Ogdensburg.

I read over your work carefully to make a notice of it in the *Quarterly*. But I have read it since over again, and like it even better than before. And any book that improves on a second reading must unquestionably be a good book and of real intrinsic value.

James A. Corcoran.
St. Charles' Seminary, Overbrook, Pa.

I have read your book and I think it most excellent and timely. If the first edition is exhausted I would continue to issue new ones as long as there is a sale. I hope your book may circulate extensively among Episcopalians and do good.
Aug. F. Hewit, C.S.P.

The following letter from a good layman, a convert, we believe, to our holy faith, is appended to the above from ecclesiastical sources:

Rt. Rev. Monsignor,—I am not quite sure that I am not presuming too much upon the slight acquaintance I had with you in Rome some two years ago, in venturing to write to you now. I have, however, derived so much pleasure and instruction from the perusal of your recently published book, on the claims of a Protestant Bishop to Succession and Valid Orders, that I cannot forbear thanking you for it. While living in Europe I had quite a number of Ritualistic Anglican friends, and had occasion to study the

question of difference between them and us, carefully.
I have never met with any argument on this subject,
which seemed to me more concise, and at the same time
more convincing, than is contained in your book. A part
of it is entirely new to me, that founded on the insufficiency of the Ordinal, and this seems to me in reality to
outweigh all other argument. I was very much amused at
the charge of intrusion made by your opponent: It surely
does not come with good grace from men who send their
own bishops to Rome to conduct confirmations. I remember hearing that Pio Nono expressed his surprise and
amusement at finding that Rome lay within the diocese
of Gibraltar! Thanking you again for the valuable instruction I have derived from your work, believe me,.
etc., etc. JOHN DEAN.
Waltham, Mass.

BISHOP RYAN'S BOOK.

From the Catholic Union.

"Claims of a Protestant Episcopal Bishop to Apostolical Succession and Valid Orders Disproved:" With Various Misstatements of Catholic Faith and Numerous Charges Against the Church and Holy See, Corrected and Refuted. By S. V. Ryan, Bishop of Buffalo. In Two Parts. Buffalo: Catholic Publication Company. 1880.

The above is the title page of a work just from the press,. to which we have before called attention in these columns. As noted above, the book is in two parts, and we simply present here the contents of each :

CONTENTS—PART I.

I.—Origin of Our Little Treatise.
II.—Apostolical Succession Essential to the Christian Church—It is not found either in the Anglican Church as by Law Established, or the Protestant Episcopal Church of America.
III.—Communion with the See of Peter the Test of Legitimate Succession.

IV.—Protestant Episcopal and Anglican Succession Repudiated.
V.—Was Matthew Parker Consecrated?
VI.—The Lambeth Register.
VII.—Was Barlow ever Consecrated Bishop?
VIII.—Futile Attempts to bolster up or supply for Barlow's deficient or doubtful Consecration.
IX.—The Edwardine Ordinal not the same as the Roman Pontifical—Invalidity of form of Consecration Devised by Edward VI.
X.—The Insufficiency of the Edwardine Ordinal, Continued.
XI.—Discrepancies between the Roman Pontifical and the Ordinal of Edward, Continued.
XII.—Conclusion.

CONTENTS—PART II.

I.—Introductory.
II.—The Ephesine Succession.
III.—Henry VIII.—To whom he belongs.
IV.—The new Liturgy—Book of Common Prayer.
V.—New Anglican Ordinal.
VI.—Clement's Dispensation to Henry.
VII.—Equivocation—Authority of Saints and Doctors of the Church.
VIII.—Papal Infallibility.
IX.—Popes Liberius and Honorius.
X.—Honorius Vindicated.
XI.—St. Gregory the Great claiming and exercising Papal Supremacy.
XII.—Catholic Bishops not Simple Presbyters or mere Vicars of the Pope.
XIII.—Teachings of the Ancient Fathers Vindicated.
XIV.—Canons of Nice and Ephesus.
XV.—The Catholic Doctrine regarding Ecclesiastical Jurisdiction.

To the ecclesiastical student and intelligent layman, we believe the above headings will convey an idea of the value of this volume, more than any elaborate review of it which we could give. Besides, as a member of the Right Reverend Author's household, and Editor of his recognized organ, we much prefer to leave to our respected contemporaries the criticism of this book. We shall only add that the work is now ready at this office, where all orders will be promptly attended to. Price, cloth, $1.25 ; full gilt, $1.75. Cash.

BISHOP RYAN'S BOOK.

From the Catholic World.

"Claims of a Protestant Episcopal Bishop to Apostolical Succession and Valid Orders Disproved," etc., etc. By S. V. Ryan, Bishop of Buffalo. Buffalo : Catholic Publication Co. 1880.

Bishop Ryan's moderately sized polemical volume, like the priesthood, is "bi-partite," and contains less than three hundred pages, but is thoroughly well charged. Seldom is so much compressed into a small compass without being crowded. It is the result of a controversy of six years standing with Dr. Arthur C. Coxe, who resides in Buffalo, where he has a handsome cathedral church not far from the beautiful cathedral of Bishop Ryan, and disputes with him his claim to be the Catholic bishop of that region, professing to be himself the only true and lawful bishop, and to preside over an " Old Catholc" church, Bishop Ryan and his flock being, in common with all the Presbyterians and other " non-Old Catholics," mere schismatics, in fact the the worst schismatics of all. Dr. Coxe is a man possessing many fine natural gifts. He is a poet, an orator, a fearless champion of his own cause, and possessing a great deal of general culture, though not remarkable for either logic, sound judgment, candor, or courtesy, at least toward Catholics who are not " Old."

It is surprising to see what a quantity of absurdities, idle fables, and phrases after the manner of Henry VIII. and Martin Luther, he has contrived to heap up and make into ecclesiastical shrapnel while he has been waging war with his two neighboring episcopal antagonists, the bishops of Buffalo and Rochester. But then, he is in a hard position. He is the Bishop of Western New York. A bishop has intruded into his see, with quite an army of priests, and is obeyed by a much greater number of subjects than he can induce to pay due allegiance to himself. Besides, this bishop is sustained by the great host of bishops in all parts of the world whom mankind in general, a few "Old" Catholics only excepted, will persist in calling the bishops of the Catholic Church. The Eastern Christians who are so dear to Dr. Coxe will not recognize his episcopal character, all those Protestants who are not "Protestant Episcopalians" hold it in light esteem, and in general, the prospects of "Old Catholicism" are far from being such as to cheer the mind of our member of that ancient society. *Causa facit Martyrem*, in a new sense.

Bishop Ryan is a true son and disciple of St. Vincent of Paul, whose name he bears. He is quiet and gentle, but he is solidly learned, and cogent in reasoning, always carrying on controversy *fortiter in re*, and generally *suaviter in modo*. Betimes, he administers some severe castigation to his opponent, but not near so much as he has deserved and provoked. Those who are interested in the controversy between the Catholic Church and the portion of the Episcopalian denomination who are called the High Church, will find in the First Part of this book a brief, but clear and thorough exposition of the questions of Anglican jurisdiction and orders. The Second Part contains supplementary matter on the same subject, and some other short chapters in which are treated such topics as Papal Infallibility, the cases of Liberius and Honorius, etc., in such a way as to correct some common misstatements and refute certain false accusations. We recommend this volume specially to the members of the "Old Catholic Church" in the diocese of Western New York, and elsewhere, not doubting that they will have a great curiosity to read it. They will find in the controversy which it sums up some real curiosities of literature. In fact, the controversy with the High Church and Ritualists, which was long ago finished as a serious work, has become something like a pastime, and on their side has degenerated into the irrelevant, the reckless, the ludicrous, and as Lowell humorously travesties the word, the *grand-delinquent* style. It is a great bore to have to keep up this controversy. Mr. Lowell, in *Among my Books*, quotes a passage from an old letter of Henry Jacie to John Winthrop, which we find apropos : "The last news we heard was that the Bores in Bavaria slew about 300 of the Swedish forces and took about 200 prisoners, of which they put out the eyes of some, & cut out the tongues of others,

& so sent them to the King of Sweden, which caused him to lament bitterly for an hour. Then he sent an army & *destroyed those Bores*, about 200 or 300 of their towns. Thus we hear." Every serious and honest Episcopalian, and all such we respect sincerely, must join with us in the wish, that controversy should be carried on for the purpose of clearing up the question, What is the True Church of Christ ? and be rid of all the rubbish which has been thrown upon the real point of importance for him, whether as an Episcopalian he can be sure that he is in the communion of the Catholic church. There is one Bore, which shows a reckless and suicidal folly, the casting of slurs and suspicions upon our orders, and retailing such an absurd fable as that Archbishop Bedini was sent here to rectify a flaw in them. We are credibly informed that this idle tale was invented and set afloat by its author merely as a joke, without any expectation that any credence would be given to it. We charitably suppose that most of those who have given circulation to this very poor and unseemly jest are no worse than dupes of their own credulity ; but this excuse will not avail Dr. Coxe.

Another Bore is the assertion that Catholic bishops are intruders on the lawful domain of Protestant bishops in the United States. Bishop Ryan disposes of this ineptitude quite sufficiently. We may add another *argumentum ad hominem*. What are the Protestant bishops who invaded the domain of the Catholic bishops in Canada, Louisiana and other French and Spanish possessions which were afterwards annexed to England or the United States ?

Again, there is the attempt to trace a succession to Mark Antony de Dominis, an apostate archbishop who assisted at some consecrations in England. This is a *pis aller*, intended to show, that, failing a direct succession through Barlow and three assistants, there was an indirect rehabilitation through which the grace of order might have slid into the Anglican priesthood *per accidens*. Besides the usual refutation of such an absurdity, it may be added, that no consecration by a true bishop could produce any effect upon men who *were not priests*, and were therefore incapable subjects.

To condense the whole matter of Anglican succession and priesthood into a small compass, which may help some persons to read Bishop Ryan's excellent book more understandingly,

I. If the Protestant-Episcopalians had really true bishops and priests this would not make them members of the Catholic Church. For, their schism and many heresies suffice to cut them off from the church.

II. They have no bishops, and no priests except a few apostates from the Catholic priesthood, because 1. The fact of Parker's alleged consecration by Barlow is doubtful. 2. It is doubtful whether Barlow ever had true consecration, certain that Scorey and Coverdale had not, doubtful whether Hodgkin really assisted in the ceremony, and certain that the form of consecration alleged to have been used by Barlow in consecrating Parker was invalid. Therefore, conceding that there is some probability that the Lambeth consecration really took place, that possibly Barlow may have been a bishop, and that Hodgkin, the only one of the four who was certainly a bishop, may have imposed hands and pronounced the prescribed form over Parker, that such an act of an assisting bishop may be of itself sufficient for a valid consecration in the defect of powers in the other prelates who participate, there is only a slender probability and no certainty whatever, that some external rite was accomplished in the case of Parker by a real bishop before he was made by the queen the head of the English Protestant hierarchy. Yet, though Anglicans may satisfy themselves with this dubious sort of succession, according to the doctrine of Catholic canonists, there was, in any case, no valid consecration, through a defect in the necessary form and intention. The Holy See, which is the supreme judge in all such matters, has practically determined the case, by setting aside altogether Anglican Orders as null and invalid. The only wise and safe course for all Anglicans is to study the subject of the pope's supremacy, and thus cut the perplexed knot of interminable controversies. The Protestant-Episcopal Church is simply one among the Protestant denominations, with an episcopal polity for the sake of order, certain decorous liturgical forms for the sake of propriety, and a very flexible doctrine for the sake of comfort. The attempt to make it into a small fac-simile of the Greek Church and rechristen it "Old Catholic" is simply ridiculous. As Dr. Storrs has facetiously and with evident relish put the case of our sentiment on the subject : " The occasional attempts of High-Churchmen to emulate that which the blending genius of many centuries and lands has produced, are to him simply ludicrous ; like building another equal St. Peter's of scantling and board, or reproducing Warwick Castle in cake and sugar." [Ev. All., 1873, p. 457]

BISHOP RYAN'S BOOK.

WHAT FOREIGN PAPERS SAY OF IT.

From the Toronto (Ont.) Tribune.

The Bishop of Buffalo, Dr. Ryan, has published a very learned work on the pretended Anglican ordinations. It sums up all that can be said for or against their validity ; and proves to the satisfaction of any fair mind that the church by English law established in Great Britain, and her offspring in America, has no honest claim to Apostolical succession either of order or jurisdiction.

In the violent break with the Catholic Church and its Head in Rome, brought about by the tyranny of a lecherous monarch, a valid consecration of a true bishop could hardly take place.

1st. The belief in Holy Orders as a sacrament was set aside, and the nomination of the king substituted for it, with a farce of a consecration by unbelieving and corrupt men.

2nd. The ordinal of the Catholic Church was overhauled and an invalid form of consecration substituted, for that formerly in use, by men of Calvinistic views, who did not believe in the Episcopacy as a divine order. It was by this ordinal the first Anglican bishops were "*ordered.*"

3rd. No proof can be brought forward that would satisfy an honest searcher of titles, to prove that the first consecrating king-nominated bishops were themselves consecrated, and according to the axiom accepted in the matter, "No one can give what he has not, ' an " unordered" or unconsecrated bishop cannot give consecration or orders which he himself has not received. Just as Charles Wesley said to his brother John: "You cannot consecrate a bishop inasmuch as you are only a simple presbyter."

So our friends the Anglicans, of the high church at least, ought to wake up to the consequences of these facts. Having no valid bishops, they have no validly ordained ministers, consequently, no sacrament of the altar, and the whole super-structure of their faith and religious practices crumbles with that article of their belief.

The worthy prelate has conferred a benefit on both Catholics and Protestants by his able work. To Catholics is shown the necessity of adherence to the line of Apostolic succession, and that we have the happiness to possess that privilege; to fair-minded Protestants is given another proof of the inconsistency of their assumed position and claims

From the London (Eng.) Tablet.

Protestant Episcopal Claims.—The lectures containe in this volume were delivered in the State of New York by Bishop Ryan, in reply to a sermon by Dr. A. Cleveland Coxe, Protestant Bishop of Western New York. They examine the claims of a "Protestant Episcopal Bishop" to apostolic succession and valid orders, and also correct and refute Dr. Coxe's numerous charges against the Church and Holy See. They prove that the Apostolic Succession is necessary, but not shared by Anglican or American Protestants; that its true test is communion with the See of St. Peter; that Matthew Parker was not duly consecrated, nor Barlow, and that the Ordinal of King Edward VI. was corrupt and inadequate. In the second part of this series of Lectures, the subject of the Papal Infallibility is treated with admirable perspicuity, and the cases of Pope Liberius and Honorius are fully considered. It is shown in the most satisfactory manner that nothing can be proved against these Pontiffs which compromises the doctrine of the Church as to the inerrancy of the Holy See when delivering its judgments on point of faith and morals *ex cathedra.*

BISHOP RYAN'S BOOK.

From the Ave Maria.

"Claims of a Protestant Episcopal Bishop to Apostolical Succession and Valid Orders Disproved." With Various Misstatements of Catholic Faith, and Numerous Charges Against the Church and Holy See, Corrected and Refuted. By S. V. Ryan, Bishop of Buffalo. In Two Parts. Buffalo: Catholic Publication Company. 1880

This book contains a fund of useful information. It will prove, we think, a valuable contribution to the discussion of a question which our Anglican friends can never bring themselves to look upon as settled. The arguments are not new—in fact the Right Rev. author disclaims all pretensions to originality in this respect—but they are presented in a manner both forcible and conclusive. The line of reasoning is substantially as follows: Apostolical succession presupposes not only valid orders but a lawful mission, and in both these points the claims of the Anglicans are hopelessly weak. Even if it be granted that the Anglican orders are valid, the line of Apostolical succession has been broken between the Primitive Church and the Anglican and Protestant Episcopal Churches, and every attempt to bridge the chasm separating the Catholic England of the Middle Ages from the Anglican establishment of to-day has been vain. Not only are the Anglicans wanting in this first test of legitimate succession but their orders are hopelessly invalid. There are grave doubts as to whether Barlow, the consecrator of Matthew Parker, was ever a regularly consecrated bishop, and still graver doubts exist as to the authenticity of the Lambeth Register, on which Anglicans rest their whole proof of Parker's consecration. Besides he was consecrated according to the form of the Edwardine Ordinal, which was intrinsically insufficient to confer valid consecration; Parker therefore, was never a bishop, and consequently he never could validly consecrate others, and so the whole fabric of Anglican orders falls to the ground.

The second part of the work is a refutation of numerous charges brought against the Church and Holy See. Too great credit cannot be given the Right Rev. author for the able manner in which he has brought into view "matters of profound interest and serious controversy, scattered over the wide range of Church History." Throughout the work the treatment of the historical questions evinces deep learning and extensive research, and the book deserves the careful attention of students if for no other reason than that it makes accessible to them "authorities which are in many cases either out of print or very rare."

BISHOP RYAN'S BOOK.

From the American Catholic Quarterly Review.

"Claims of a Protestant Episcopal Bishop to Apostolical Succession and Valid Orders Disproved." With Various Misstatements of Catholic Faith and Numerous Charges Against the Church and Holy See Corrected and Refuted. By S. V. Ryan, Bishop of Buffalo. In Two Parts. Buffalo: Catholic Publication Company. 1880.

Bishop Coxe, of the Protestant Episcopal Church, against whom this masterly work was written, does not appear to much advantage as a controversial divine when compared with his deceased Presbyterian father. The latter had his strong religious and politico-reilgious crotchets, some of them very offensive to the sober-minded portion of the American public; but for him we must charitably suppose they were leading principles, and he stuck to them with a consistency for which even enemies might praise him. His Episcopal son, on the contrary, has no principles whatever, or rather two grand contradictory principles which he uses in turn, as occasion may require. In other words, he tries to be both Catholic and Protestant. With his fellow-Protestants, including even the majority of those of his own Episcopal communion, for whom he cannot disguise his contempt, he takes high Catholic ground, or rather puts on ultra-Catholic airs. To believe him, he is a Protestant, but a "Catholic" bishop of the 'Anglo-American branch," whatever that means theologically or historically; for no rational explanation of such terms has ever been or can ever be given. Ecclesiastically, the Catholic Anglo-American branch is not only a nonentity but an illegal figment, seeing that the name of "Catholic" was solemnly adjured by the

American Episcopal Church in council assembled some thirty-six years ago, when an effort was made by Dr. Jarvis and a few other enthusiasts of his stamp to coax her into the assumption of this hateful name. The habitual attempts of Dr. Coxe to fasten upon her a name that she has rejected with scornful solemnity can scarcely be regarded as fair and honest; or else they argue on his part a deep-seated conviction that, instead of being taught by his Church, he has received a commission to be her teacher, since he understands her doctrine and constitution better than she does herself. For him, as a "Catholic" bishop, all American Protestants are mere dissenters and separatists, the bulk of his own church-people stupid Erastians and heretics at heart, though outwardly united to what, deny and despise it as they will, he will persist in calling their "Catholic" communion. He is highly indignant that a handful of scholars, Anglican, Presbyterian, Liberal Christian, and the like, have lately banded together for the purpose of reforming the Protestant English Bible, without first obtaining the leave and goodwill of himself and his invisible fraction of the American Catholic Episcopalian Church. And this feeling of indignation he expresses through the newspapers, to the great amusement of the Protestant public.

Such is the "Catholicity" of Bishop Coxe when dealing with his Protestant brethren, with those of his own household. But when he comes face to face with real Catholicity, when he has to take up arms and assume the defence of his petty sect against the true Catholic Church, then he all of a sudden, as if by magic, changes his principles and he appears in his true light. He is an ultra Protestant, and there is among the whole band no foul-mouthed Thersites,

Loquacious, loud, and turbulent of tongue,

who can excel him in evil speech and wanton vituperation. Confronted with the true Church, he flings candor, honesty, and truth to the winds, and willingly takes his place in the foremost ranks of those dissenters whom at other times he affects to despise. All his assumed airs of Catholicity are thrown aside, and he sinks to the level of Maria Monks and Gavazzis in the service of their common cause.

Such is the Janus Bifrons, the adversary of double face and shifting principles, whom Bishop Ryan has had to encounter. And he has dealt with him most effectually, scattering into the air all his idle claims and pretensions, and triumphantly repelling all his assaults upon the Catholic Church and her visible head. The good bishop has done that not only with a vigorous logic that must convince every reader, but with a meekness that is edifying and truly wonderful, considering the character of his opponent, whose reckless slanders and persistent disingenuousness would sorely try the temper even of a saint.

The right reverend author has, however, done something far more important than merely stripping Dr. Coxe of his borrowed Catholic plumage. He has laid before his readers, in an easy and popular, yet clear and forcible way, the whole intricate question of Anglican ordinations. He has proved conclusively that in the Anglican Church there is no shadow of Apostolical succession, no valid priestly orders. Besides, many of the current calumnies against our holy religion are examined and satisfactorily refuted. The work, we are confident, will not only be relished by all candid readers, but will accomplish a great deal of good, and will be classed hereafter among our standard books of controversy.

PROTESTANT EPISCOPAL CLAIMS TO APOSTOLIC SUCCESSION.

From the Catholic Times.

To those who believe in the divine institution of the episcopal order and in the necessity of Apostolic succession in the ministry of the Church of Christ, the validity of what are known as Anglican orders will always be a matter of interest. To the Church of England and to the Protestant Episcopal Church in the United States it is a question of life or death. If Episcopalians have the succession, they have real bishops and real priests of some sort ; if in any way they have lost the succession, the link, the heritance, they have no bishops, no priests, no orders.

According to the doctrine of Christ and His Apostles, there is no church without a pastor, no pastor without a mission or commission, no mission but by way of succession, no succession but by way of ordination. On this indissoluble chain is established the perpetuity and identity of the Church of Christ. Our Divine Lord in establishing this Church, gave to the Apostles the powers of orders and jurisdiction. The power of order, which is inherent in the episcopal character, is perpetuated without interruption by ordination, the rite of which was determined by Christ. The Apostles ordained the first bishops, these ordained others to succeed them, so that the validly ordained bishops of our day have received the same character, the same power of order which the immediate successors of the Apostles received. He who has not been ordained cannot participate in the apostolic ministry.

The power of jurisdiction is that by virtue of which the power of orders is exercised and the Church governed.

The transmission of these powers of orders and jurisdiction which the first bishops received from the Apostles and handed down to their successors is what is understood by apostolical succession.

The Episcopalians believe the transmission and reception of these powers are necessary to the Christian ministry; hence the importance of the question to them. If they can establish an unbroken chain of orders and jurisdiction from the Apostles, no one can question their status in the Church of Christ; but if they fail to do this, if it be shown, on the contrary, that the line of succession has been broken —that their ministers never received valid ordination and jurisdiction, it follows that those ministers are mere laymen, respectable, it is true, polite and generally learned, but mere laymen nevertheless, having no authority to preach or teach in the Church of Christ or to administer the sacraments instituted by Him.

The question of Anglican orders began to be discussed shortly after Matthew Parker assumed the title of Archbishop of Canterbury, in the time of Elizabeth (1559). Both the fact and the validity of his consecration were denied, not only by Catholics, but also by the Presbyterians and non-conformists. From that time up to the present the controversy has continued, the leading writers pro and con seeming to have by common consent looked upon this issue as vital and ultimate.

In England interest in the question has of late years somewhat subsided, but in this country a new impulse has been given to it by the extraordinary and surprising assumptions of that offspring of Anglicanism, the Protestant Episcopal Church of the United States. This denomination, by a well known law of social dynamics, is gradually separating itself from its former Protestant associates, and is tending back to the old landmarks from which it drifted in the early years of the Reformation. But instead of coming back in sorrow and repentance, like the prodigal son, it returns full of fussy assumption and arrogant conceit. After three hundred years of bad company keeping, it wants, with all its sins of unfaithfulness upon it, to be received as the oracle of God, and demands the birthright which it sold for a mess of pottage. It assumes to be the heir by uninterrupted succession to the Church founded by Christ and promulgated by the Apostles. When a sect presents such extraordinary claims it is necessary that those claims should be carefully examined and scrutinized. It is this unwarranted assumption on the part of Episcopalians that makes a renewed examination of the validity of their orders necessary.

The Catholic Church is the most conservative in the social world; the Protestant Episcopal Church is the most conservative of the sects. It is more conservative than any other of the sects because it has retained more of the doctrines and principles of the Catholic Church than they. Because it is more conservative than they it is destined to outlast them. Inasmuch as it is destined to outlast the other Protestant sects, it is worthy of the respect and attention of the Catholic polemic. No Catholic writer at the present day thinks seriously of attacking Calvinism, Presbyterianism, Lutheranism, or Methodism; he knows that these sects have only to be left to the process of dry rot or spontaneous combustion, knowing that they nourish within themselves the principle of their own destruction, and that their members will drift eventually into the Catholic Church or into infidelity and atheism. The suicidal principle is equally in the Episcopal Church, but owing to some Catholic and conservative principles which it possesses, the development of decay will in its case be delayed. Thus in the future the Catholic Church in the United States will have three enemies to combat: Episcopalianism as an adverse claimant in the religion of Christ, Free Masonry as an adverse claimant in religion in general, and infidelity as adverse to all religion.

America is a new country ; we are a new peopbe ; battles that have been fought out in the old world must be fought out here anew—to the generation that is coming into activity old questions are new, and they must be reviewed and represented and re-examined. New combinations, social and intellectual, give old thoughts and facts new force and direction, and it is the duty of men of thought to recognize these changed conditions and apply old principles and ideas to them.

The claims of the Protestant Episcopal church in the United States, its bold assumption of Apostolic succession, its wanton attack through Bishop Coxe on the Catholic Church, made it necessary for some one to call attention to the *bar-sinister* on its escutcheon, and to bring out in bold relief the historical facts and theological principles which prove that the golden link of succession was broken and that the claims of such arrogant laymen as Bishop Coxe are utterly groundless. This Bishop Ryan has done in an able and thorough manner, in his book entitled : " Protestant Episcopal Claims to Apostolic Succession Refuted." This book is timely and opportune, and leaves nothing to be desired. While it deals with every question that has any bearing on the subject, its author has succeeded in presenting the case in a form so explicit and succinct, as to enable the most casual reader to acquire with little labor a clear and comprehensive knowledge of the facts and principles involved. It is in this that the merit of Bishop Ryan's book consists. The researches and studies of the best writers have been so successfully epitomized by the author that his name will be inseparably associated with the discussion of the subject in future.

There is one characteristic about Bishop Ryan's book which detracts somewhat from it, which yet adds piquancy to it, and makes it exceedingly interesting reading. It is, if we may coin an expression, its *ad hominisity*. The reader can never lose sight of the fact that the Catholic Bishop of Buffalo is always talking at the Protestant Bishop Coxe. It is more than probable that the author intended that the reader should never lost sight of this fact—it is in truth evident he did not. The book is a reply to Coxe—an *argumentum ad Coxem.* Its polemic and *ad hominem* character is apparent on every page, and while a spirit of Christian charity pervades the whole, the author, here and there, gives way to his justly aroused indignation, and when he does so he lashes unmercifully and strikes the vulnerable parts of his opponent with the precision of fate. Next to Newman's cold-blooded murder of Kingsley in the "Apologia," comes this manslaughter of Coxe. If we were on the jury we would feel bound in conscience, notwithstanding St. Alphonsus Liguori's casuistry, to find the Catholic Bishop guilty of murder in the first degree, with extenuating circumstances.

Aside from the preliminary chapters, Bishop Ryan deals with the following questions:

1st. Was Parker consecrated? Answer. No, or extremely doubtful.

2. Is the Lambeth register genuine and authentic, or was it a fraud? Answer. Most probably a fraud. All evidence tending in that direction.

3d. Was Barlow, who is supposed to have consecrated Parker, ever consecrated a bishop himself? Answer—No.

4th. Granted that Barlow was a bishop, and granting that he tried his best to consecrate Parker, did he succeed in doing so? No. Because the form used on the supposed occasion was invalid.

5th. Granting the naked fact of consecration, and granting its validity, who gave commission to Parker? Barlow, a simple bishop, could not give a commission to an archbishop. Beyond Barlow, Parker never pretended that he received any authority or commission save that granted him by Queen Elizabeth, which at that time was deemed all sufficient.

We commend Bishop Ryan's book to those who desire to get a comprehensive knowledge of the whole question in a very limited space.

BISHOP RYAN'S BOOK.

From the New York Tablet.

PROTESTANT-EPISCOPAL CLAIMS TO APOSTOLIC SUCCESSION DISPROVED. By Bishop Ryan, of Buffalo. Buffalo Catholic Publication Co.

THIS work is in two parts, and handsomely bound together. It gives satisfactory proofs that Episcopalians have no claims to apostolic succession. The right reverend author points out numerous charges against the Church, and shows how the different sects have made very many misstatements concerning our faith and the Holy See Further, these misstatements are all fully refuted by the most convincing logic. It is first shown how apostolic succession is essential to the Church, and quotations from eminent authorities are brought in to prove the point. Next it is explained to demonstration that such apostolic succession does not exist either in the Anglican Church, as by law established, or the Protestant-Episcopal Church of America. The following extract from the work will give a pretty fair idea of the balance. The author takes the objections of his adversaries and refutes them in simple yet most forcible language. For example, we quote: "As to the value to be attached to assertions like these, 'the succession in the Church of England is more demonstrably canonical and regular in all particulars than any other succession in Christendom,' or 'it may be shown that nobody competent to form an opinion, and who has taken the pains to investigate the matter, has ever professed a doubt concerning Anglican succession': our readers will be able to judge presently. Apostolic succession requires, as those making the above assertions admit, something more than valid ordination. We may admit not only the fact but also the validity of a bishop's consecration, and yet deny him, even though validly consecrated, any participation in the divine commission given by Christ to his apostles, any claim to apostolic succession. Valid ordination is essential to, but insufficient for, legitimate succession. In the whole history of the Christian Church there is nothing more evident than this, that when a bishop or priest, or bishops and priests, revolted against ecclesiastical authority, or contumaciously erred against faith, they were silenced, suspended, deprived of their faculties, deposed from their sees. The Church which had commissioned them and given them authority, jurisdiction, a right to teach, and assigned them a mission in which to exercise their ministry, simply revoked their commission, recalled her grant of powers, and annulled all license to act for her in her name or by her authority. Thus she acted towards the validly-ordained and rightly consecrated heretical Donatist, Eutychian, and Arian bishops, and who among our orthodox Anglicans or Episcopalians will recognize such excommunicated, deposed, and deprived heretical bishops as successors of the apostles?" In this way the author clinches the matter.

The style of the book is easy and unpretentious, not a big word in it from beginning to end, but a thoughtful vein of common sense and plain reasoning running through every page. He points out among other things that communion with the See of Peter is the test of apostolic succession, and proves it in various ways. For any one wishing to become a Catholic this volume is an excellent one ; for those within the fold it is equally good, as furnishing matter whereby they can "prove the faith that is in them"; but it is especially valuable for priests and students.

www.ingramcontent.com/pod-product-compliance
Lightning Source LLC
Chambersburg PA
CBHW022019240426
43667CB00042B/949